"Goodman presents us with a multidimensional portrait of the age. The canvas is huge but the detail is drawn with intricate, bold strokes.... In this marvelous collection, Goodman emerges as loving testimony to the best the '80s has to offer. Her faith in human potential resounds throughout."
Los Angeles Times

"Goodman is master of the felicitous phrase as well as of the penetrating thought.... *Keeping in Touch* is a splendid collection of punchy lessons about everything from sperm banks and smoking to abortion and the peace movement."
Washington Journalism Review

"TIMELY AND TO THE POINT...READING ELLEN GOODMAN CAN BE HABIT-FORMING."
Library Journal

"Ellen Goodman has a knack for looking at things from a different angle, so that you can see the real issue."
Northwest Herald

KEEPING IN TOUCH

Ellen Goodman

FAWCETT CREST • NEW YORK

ACKNOWLEDGMENTS

Writing a newspaper column is both solitary and social, a lone pursuit and a collegial one. I write by myself stringing green letters across a computer screen, but I don't work alone. Not at all.

I have spent the last eighteen years at the *Boston Globe*. That's a lot of time and I am lucky to have spent it in such a congenial and supportive environment. I have chosen to dedicate this book to the man who literally shaped that environment, Tom Winship. Tom was editor of the *Globe* until last January. It was Tom who hired me, Tom who gave me a piece of the paper to call my own, Tom who encouraged me dozens of times. Without him, this book, these columns, wouldn't have existed.

In my top desk drawer I still save the notes he scribbled, notes that littered and fertilized the whole paper. "Great stuff!" "A corker!" "That's a beaut." In a day when women talk about mentors, Tom has been something more, a friend.

I also want to thank Bill Taylor, the paper's publisher. If the *Globe* is a paper of integrity, the Taylors have been the keepers of that integrity.

At the office, my assistant everything, Celia Lees-Low, makes it all possible. She takes on all the details—the mystery caller, the obscure fact that needs to be checked, the plane that needs to be reserved—with intelligence, good sense, and spirit. She is the center that holds it all together.

My column travels—by the mysterious inner workings of a computer—to the Washington Post Writers Group. There for the past nine years, Bill Dickinson has been my colleague and the most benign of overseers. He and Anna Karavangelos deserve respective medal halos for valor under deadline pressure, humor under stress, and dealing with my private punctuation. They have even convinced me that "no one" should be written as two words.

I also live and work in a web of friendships which nurture me. My friend, my sanity check, and "first reader" for nearly all of these columns is Otile McManus. Otile and I share everything from tea bags to ideas to family cares—the real stuff of life. My friend Pat O'Brien is an anchor in my life whether she's on the other end of a phone line or the other side of a table. My life would not be the same if it weren't shared with them.

As for my family, this enlarged renovated family, I have all the gratitude of midlife, when nothing can be taken for granted. I am grateful to Bob Levey for becoming my husband while remaining my best friend. I am grateful to my daughter Katie, for her company, her insight, and her sensitivity. She and my two stepchildren, Greg and Jenny Levey, are part of this book as they are part of our life.

CONTENTS

Part 3 THE REAGAN YEARS

Part 4 OF WOMEN AND MEN IN TRANSITION

Part 5 SCIENCE AND NON-SENSE

Part 6 A SENSE OF PLACE

Part 7 OF GENDER AND OTHER GAPS

Part 8 TAKING LIBERTY

Part 9 A FAMILY ALBUM

Part 10 ELLEN GOODMAN: IN TOUCH

INTRODUCTION

It's been four years since I last collected my columns between the hard covers of a book. As we measure years in political time, that's one presidential term. In newspapers, it's nearly 1500 daily editions.

During this term as a columnist, I have witnessed some curious and controversial landmarks of change. The woman in the Maidenform bra ads became a doctor. An entrepreneur began marketing the first burial in space. Americans transplanted a baboon heart into a human baby, injected the sperm of Nobel Prize winners into fertile women, and installed pay phones in airplanes.

If you asked what has surprised me the most in the past four years, I would have trouble choosing. Geraldine Ferraro? Star Wars? Yuppies? The campaign to adopt your very own Nicaraguan contra? I could not have predicted many of the stories that fill these years and these pages.

The Reagan imprint on this time has been strong. In his first term, the president proclaimed the end of self-doubt and we witnessed a rise in self-righteousness. His government talked less about the rich and the poor, and more about winners and losers. Today, the public world has more potholes and a few private gardens are better tended.

Arguments which many of us thought had been settled were reopened. Evolution went back on trial and censors went back after books. Abortion clinics were bombed in the name of life and the death penalty was inflicted again in the name of deterrence. There were some who welcomed herpes as a punishment for sex and AIDS as a scourge for homosexuality.

At the same time, the social evolution we call the women's movement proceeded at its uneven, lopsided, disorderly pace. The Equal Rights Amendment may have failed, but the first woman was nominated to a national ticket. Sally Ride put on an astronaut uniform, but pregnant women were taught to dress for success in three-piece maternity suits.

We talk less now about roles—male roles and female roles—and more about values—the values of caretaking and the values of worldly achievement. There is, in the air and in these columns, a good deal of debate about the definition of "women's values," and about the direction of change. It seems to be much easier for women to get equal access to the values of success and competition, than to get equal time for the values of nurturing.

The gap between family and work is still wider than the gender gap. The workaholics of both sexes may share the room at the top.

There has also been a flow of energy from the women's rights movement to the peace movement. Women have been a primary force pushing through layers of national denial about nuclear war. The same women who began talking in peace slogans are now learning the language of defense.

It seems to me that the more Americans are overwhelmed with information—daily news, bulletins—the more we need to wrest some sense of meaning out of the current of events. It is my job and my predilection to try and put the scattered items from the daily newspaper scrapbook into context. This is one of the challenges of newspaper column writing—to write with some perspective from the middle, always the middle, of a story.

I occupy a listening post as well, and what I hear in my

travels and own circle of friends and family keeps me in touch with the range of American concerns, private and public conflicts. We are, after all, people who worry about our weight on Monday and nuclear winter on Tuesday. We leave our suburbs empty every day in order to pay for homes in the suburbs. This collection reflects many of these confusions and ironies.

In the last few years, I have been in more than forty of the fifty states. I've talked with people in North Dakota who live with missiles on their farmland. I've talked with college students in Ohio and Arizona who seem less sure about the global future and more anxious to control their personal future. I've talked with young couples who are trying to plan their parenthood with a perfect sense of timing.

I've spent many plane rides home, filling notebooks with what I learned in Flint, Michigan, or Sioux Falls, South Dakota, or Riverside, California. These people are sometimes the text of a column; they are always the subtext.

I try to chronicle the ambivalence I hear, the mixed feelings and values. That isn't easy in an era of thirty-second bites and bumper sticker politics, an era of images. It isn't always easy in 750 words either. But I think it is important to counter the centrifugal force that spins us toward opposite poles. In an argument between true believers, I often side with ambivalence. I'm drawn to the ambidextrous Americans who argue with both hands.

If this book says a good deal about the last four years in American life, it also says much about my own life. As a fellow traveler, my life has changed in ways that are personal but not unique. I have remarried and remerged families in this time. I write this introduction in the home my husband and I share, in a family that has extended horizontally in enriching ways. My own daughter is nearly a woman; it takes only four years for a thirteen-year-old to become seventeen. Our house is filled now with young people, their concerns and conversations.

I am not just an observer of the pressures of daily life in the 1980s; my days are also lists and I write about them as I know them. Like others, I commute between the demands and rewards of work and home. The pieces on our Maine retreat resonate with questions about the sanity of busyness, dailiness, and the other, urban, work life.

I have called this book *Keeping in Touch*, because in the end that is what these columns are about. Keeping in touch with these times and my times, with public life and private lives. It is about as good a job description and as good a life as I can imagine.

Part 1

AMERICAN FOLLIES

A WORKING COMMUNITY

BOSTON—I have a friend who is a member of the medical community. It does not say that, of course, on the stationery that bears her home address. This membership comes from her hospital work.

I have another friend who is a member of the computer community. This is a fairly new subdivision of our economy, and yet he finds his sense of place in it.

Other friends and acquaintances of mine are members of the academic community, or the business community, or the journalistic community. Though you cannot find these on any map, we know where we belong.

None of us, mind you, was born into these communities. Nor did we move into them, U-Hauling our possessions along with us. None has papers to prove we are card-carrying members of one such group or another. Yet it seems that more and more of us are identified by work these days, rather than by street.

In the past, most Americans lived in neighborhoods. We were members of precincts or parishes or school districts. My dictionary still defines community first of all in geographic terms, as "a body of people who live in one place."

But today fewer of us do our living in that one place; more of us just use it for sleeping. Now we call our towns "bedroom suburbs," and many of us, without small children

3

as icebreakers, would have trouble naming all the people on our street.

It's not that we are more isolated today. It's that many of us have transferred a chunk of our friendships, a major portion of our everyday social lives, from home to office. As more of our neighbors work away from home, the workplace becomes our neighborhood.

The kaffeeklatsch of the fifties is the coffee break of the eighties. The water cooler, the hall, the elevator, and the parking lot are back fences of these neighborhoods. The people we have lunch with day after day are those who know the running saga of our mother's operations, our child's math grades, our frozen pipes, and our faulty transmissions.

We may be strangers at the supermarket that replaced the corner grocer, but we are known at the coffee shop in the lobby. We share with each other a cast of characters from the boss in the corner office, to the crazy lady in Shipping, to the lovers in Marketing. It's not surprising that when researchers ask Americans what they like best about work, they say it is "the schmoose [chatter] factor." When they ask young mothers at home what they miss most about work, it is the people.

Not all the neighborhoods are empty, nor is every workplace a friendly playground. Most of us have had mixed experiences in these environments. Yet as one woman told me recently, she knows more about the people she passed on the way to her desk than on her way around the block.

Our new sense of community hasn't just moved from house to office building. The labels that we wear connect us with members from distant companies, cities, and states. We assume that we have something "in common" with other teachers, nurses, city planners.

It's not unlike the experience of our immigrant grandparents. Many who came to this country still identified themselves as members of the Italian community, the Irish community, the Polish community. They sought out and assumed connections with people from the old country. Many of us have updated that experience. We have replaced ethnic identity with professional identity, the way we replaced neighborhoods with the workplace.

This whole realignment of community is surely most obvious among the mobile professions. People who move from city to city seem to put roots down into their professions. In an age of specialists, they may have to search harder to find people who speak the same language.

I don't think that there is anything massively disruptive about this shifting sense of community. The continuing search for connection and shared enterprise is very human. But I do feel uncomfortable with our shifting identity. The balance has tipped and we seem increasingly dependent on work for our sense of self.

If our offices are our new neighborhoods, if our professional titles are our new ethnic tags, then how do we separate our selves from our jobs? Self-worth isn't just something to measure in the marketplace. But in these new communities, it becomes harder and harder to tell who we are without saying what we do.

FEBRUARY 1984

JUST CALL ME FAMOUS

BOSTON—Now maybe you still haven't heard about C. Vernon Ayers. Maybe Kingston, Georgia, isn't on your map yet.

But Ayers and Kingston are famous now and I can prove it. I can show you the segment on the network news. I can show you the stories on the news wire. I can show you the pictures in the paper.

This is the mayor and this is the town that have pursued a dream which is deliciously, quintessentially American. This is the mayor and this is the town that have gained fame in the fame biz.

The whole success story began inauspiciously two years ago when Ayers was looking for some Name to come to town. Kingston already had 729 people of its own. These people had names, but no Names.

The town also had twelve historic markers, eighteen buildings in the National Register of Historic Places, and an official historic district encompassing the entire two-block business section. It even had an annual Historical Festival.

The problem was that they had a festival without a "celebrity" and a historical event without a modern "personality." As anybody who's been to a shopping-center opening in the past ten years can attest, you don't have an important event without a Famous Person.

So for two years, Mayor Ayers tried to import a genuine, bona fide Famous Person. He invited Jimmy Carter. He invited Ted Kennedy. He invited both Georgia senators, one Georgia governor, and a bunch of stars, including Burt Reynolds.

His rejection record was unblemished by a single acceptance. It seemed that Nobody who was Anybody wanted to pay his own way to Kingston in order to celebrate the recapture of a train by the Confederate Army during the Civil War.

Then last year, Ayers did something different. He issued a sort of open call for "any famous person." His desperate plea made the network and the wires and pretty soon lots of people wanted to come to Kingston.

Now, I know that Goethe once wrote, "To seek, to hunt after fame is a vain endeavor." But Goethe never lived in our century or our country.

In late twentieth-century America, the town of Kingston, Georgia, sought after the famous and got fame to boot.

If all goes according to plan, the two-day historic celebration will be a convention of beauty queens, Santa Clauses, radio broadcasters, and clowns, plus a cookie maker, Ronald McDonald, and a genuine TV actor. No one will leave without a signed certificate proving that he or she is famous.

If all goes according to plan, Kingston will also end up wearing a laurel wreath of Americana: It'll be a two-day media event.

I don't know about the rest of you, but the story of Kingston strikes me as a Walt Disney musical-comedy portrait of the whole weird process of fame in America.

The characters are from some odd central casting. A small town that wants a big Name. Why? Who knows. A bunch of small names who want to become Big Names. Why? Who knows. This odd couple, with only their ambition in common, get together.

Then we have the media. In the process of describing an unknown place and its unknown uncelebrities, the media makes the biggest change in a Georgia town since Plains. The town becomes famous and makes the mayor a genuine celebrity.

This real-life plot is thickening quite nicely. As I write this, the citizens of Kingston are getting ready to distribute their cache of T-shirts and buttons labeled I'M FAMOUS and I'M NOT FAMOUS to distinguish the out-of-town guests from the citizens. By the end of the weekend, they're going to have to switch shirts.

Only in America.

APRIL 1982

THE PALEOLITHIC DIET

BOSTON—Just when you thought there was nothing new in the diet world, just when you had lowered your cholesterol, complicated your carbohydrates, and sworn off sodium, along comes a stunning leap forward into the distant past. We are about to reintroduce an ancient cuisine to the modern world. Ladies and Gentlemen, let us welcome The Paleolithic Diet.

This down-home, or down-cave, cuisine was recently touted in an article in the *New England Journal of Medicine*. Two Atlanta health researchers reported on their exhaustive anthropological studies of prehistoric menus.

8

They began with the theory that some of our modern diseases—stroke, heart diseases, and some forms of cancer—have spread because we are eating today's specialties with yesterday's genes. The food on our platters may be fresh, but we were created out of 40,000-year-old genetic stock. We are essentially Cro-Magnons at the ice-cream counter.

These researchers came to the conclusion that the real way to be healthy in the A.D. 1980s may be to eat more like they did in 40,000 B.C. We are to eat the high-protein, low-fat produce of a hunter-gatherer world, in which even the red meat was not fat, happy, and domestic, but lean, mean, and wild. As the researchers put it: "The diet of our remote ancestors may be a reference standard for modern human nutrition and a model for defense against certain 'diseases of civilization.'"

Well, pass me the fried mastodon. This research may make scientific sense, but I have a strong suspicion it is part of a trend. We are being led, like spelunkers, down into the ancestral caves in search of eternal health and well-being.

Earlier, another researcher from Minnesota suggested that the potassium in the primitive diet might ward off the diseases of civilization. Sociobiologists are continually rooting about for mental-health tips in prehistory. Soon, we may all be told to wrap our happiness in skins.

After all, there are so many other health secrets locked into the life-style of our genetic ancestors just waiting for an enterprising researcher with a fertile if backward turn of mind. Consider how much the twentieth-century American could benefit from following our forebears' method of acquiring their food. These were people who truly ran out to get a bite.

The primitive folk remained lean by chasing and then devouring animals who remained lean by running away. Any number of domesticated Americans already follow that model, except they run off what they have already eaten.

The Paleolithic people had another advantage on us, another built-in form of exercise that would make a splash in the magazines. As Mel Brooks explained in his routine on the Two-Thousand-Year-Old Man, the basic method of transportation in the old days was "Fear." If modern Americans can get in shape merely because we want to eat, imagine what we could do to avoid being eaten. A Cro-Magnon Marathon would do wonders for the heart.

Then, of course, we could literally follow the Paleolithic Diet for health and happiness. One of the staples of the period, a delicacy inscribed on the entire chain of cave restaurants, was "mammoth." What a boon it would be to the average overweight modern gourmet to follow the latest in food, the all-mammoth diet. Fat would become, like the critter, extinct.

The life-style itself, or what we know of it, has further advantages which researchers might boost for a prehistoric health kick. For example, the interior lighting of that period was not what it might have been. If we followed their decor, the midnight junk-food attack might disappear along with the refrigerator light. If all goes well, perhaps we can set up a series of health spas in caves all across the West where, for a mere $950 a week, we can learn to dig roots.

Do I sound suspicious of this back-to-primeval-basics movement? The truth is that I fully accept my genetic ancestors as health mentors. Some of them did develop medical problems—lion bite, for instance—that we rarely see in the civilized world. But I am convinced that the average Paleolithic person was the very role model of good health when he died at the ripe old age of thirty-two.

FEBRUARY 1985

A GENETIC LOTTERY GAME

BOSTON—It's been more than two years since the story about a California sperm bank for Nobel Prize winners first inseminated the news wires.

I, for one, foolishly dismissed The Repository for Germinal Choice as just another phallic symbol . . . without the symbolism.

The stated purpose of the sperm bank was to cast the seed of assorted geniuses upon the ova of the land. This was their "means of breeding higher intelligence."

But there was apparently a market for this sort of matchmaking. The first genius to report for duty was William Shockley, a seventy-year-old Nobel Prize-winning inventor of the transistor. He's a man who believes that the disadvantaged slid to the bottom of the heap on their genes.

When he announced that he was willing to donate his sperm for the improvement of the human race, I began to fervently pray that egotism was not transmitted along the DNA.

Lo these years, the repository has been collecting and disseminating sperm from an underground chamber in the backyard of a ten-acre estate near Escondido, California. Finally, after this lengthy gestation, it gave birth in April to its first baby, a healthy nine-pound girl, offspring (or off-sperm if you prefer) of an "eminent mathematician" in his thirties with an IQ of over 200.

All this is fine and dandy. Right now, we should all be breathlessly waiting for Victoria to start learning her Sesame Street numbers at three months.

But the latest news from the genetic front lines about the creation of the new Master Race, or Mistress Race, is a bit startling. It turns out that Victoria's mum (or egg donor if you prefer), thirty-nine-year-old Joyce Kowalski, has two previous children by an earlier marriage. These children were removed from the custody of Joyce and her second husband Jack after allegations of child abuse.

If that weren't enough, it also turns out that Joyce and Jack are ex-cons. They did time in federal prison in 1978 on fraud charges. Their scam was a simple one. They sent away for birth certificates of people who had died in infancy, and then assumed their identity to get loans and credit cards.

It now appears that the friendly neighborhood repository was more picky about the sperm than the egg, let alone the environment of its heirs.

Nobody knows what the "eminent mathematician" with an IQ of over 200 feels about all this. But we can guess. After all, true believer Shockley told *Playboy* magazine that his own children represent a very significant regression because "my first wife—their mother—had not as high an academic achievement standing as I had."

Now I won't leap to the conclusion that Victoria's mother was inferior. She was never given an IQ test, but she does have a literary streak. She wrote about the birth for the *National Enquirer*: "'God, thank you, thank you,' I cried. Tears streaked down my eyes as the nurse lifted my newborn baby girl into my arms—a baby who could be the first of a new breed of genius children. . . . 'These are the greatest minds of all time and one of them might be the father of my child,' I gasped." There you are, a Nobel Prize for Literature.

Still, the whole thing sounds like all of those wonderful

12

stories about mad scientists whose experiments go awry. Instead of producing the cure for cancer, they produce The Cell That Ate New York. Instead of producing the Master Race, they produce the Master Criminal Race.

Imagine, after all, how useful Victoria's mathematical mind could have been in the former Kowalski endeavor. Instead of a mere birth-certificate scam, she could have devised a computer scam.

In a famous incident of the nineteenth century, a famous actress suggested that she mate with George Bernard Shaw. She envisioned a child with his mind and her looks. Shaw recoiled out of the terror: What if they produced a child with his looks and her mind? In this genetic lottery, what if little Vicky has her daddy's math IQ and her mommy's ethics?

The saga of Victoria should be enough to abort the entire sperm-bank genius project, but don't count on it. You know how geniuses are. In the words of the one in charge of this repository, "A high IQ doesn't guarantee emotional stability."

JULY 1982

SHAME, SMOKING, AND THE SPITTOON

BOSTON—The man seated at the table on my right is smoking. Actually, he is just holding. The cigarette is smoking. Nevertheless, due to my own charm and magnetic appeal, the smoke has chosen to drift directly from his left hand to my right eye.

With a gesture born of years of experience, I subtly wave my menu at the offending current. The man doesn't notice. I then lean over, tap him on the shoulder, and ask if he would mind redirecting the smoke. The man apologizes sheepishly and shifts the cigarette from one hand to the other.

The smoke now begins to drift into the eyes of another diner. This man tips his chair back, touches the smoker on the arm, and asks if he would please rechannel the flow. The smoker sighs and with a gesture of defeat, squashes the glowing offender into the glass ashtray.

At the moment his cigarette meets its premature end, the same vignette is being repeated a thousand times a day in a thousand restaurants, offices, airports, and shopping lines.

The smokers who once owned the air are being pushed back into special zones and corners and closets. They can be seen searching desperately for ashtrays, stepping out for smokes, and holding their cigarettes over their heads, directly under an exhaust fan.

It's all a bit like watching the Virginia Slims reel go into reverse. Smoking in public is again becoming bad manners. The private label "impolite" may ultimately have more effect on people's behavior than the surgeon general's label "unhealthy."

If so, it won't be the first time that social pressure has made social history. This is precisely what happened to an ancient and honorable habit known as spitting. In Norbert Elias' book, *The History of Manners*, he describes a host of changing attitudes and habits from medieval times to ours. He even gives a brief chronology of how spitting became a victim of "civilization."

Medieval etiquette authors started with the basics: "Do not clean your teeth with your knife. Do not spit on or over the table." Spitting under the table in those days was allowed even among the best company.

Sometime during the sixteenth century, our genteel ancestors were being advised to refrain from spitting during mealtime. By the seventeenth century, they were admonished not to spit on the ground.

The spit repression went on for centuries. In 1859, when spittoons had become a proper substitute for the ground or the napkin, one arbiter of good taste was advising: "Spitting is at all times a disgusting habit. I need say nothing more than—never indulge in it." Fifty years later, by 1910, even the spittoon had vanished like some relic of a coarser age.

By now, public spitting itself has virtually disappeared except among the crude, the coughing, and the baseball players. Even writing about it feels vaguely improper. We now consider spitting "uncivilized" and this whole change in social behavior is called "progress."

As Elias describes the evolution of manners: "The decisive role [was] played in this civilizing process by a very specific change in the feelings of shame and delicacy."

Admittedly, during the past half-century smoking flourished. There was little support in this era for the virtues of "shame and delicacy." People worried more about repression than rudeness. I suspect that smoking was an example of pseudofreedom.

But now, with the help of medical researchers, civilization is creeping up again on the tobacco barbarians. You can see it in clear signs—SMOKING NOT PERMITTED—and dirty looks. The balance of embarrassment has shifted from nonsmokers to smokers. The balance of rudeness has shifted from the critics of smoke to the purveyors of smoke.

Will smoking go the way of spitting, from rude to extinct? Remember what happened to the spittoon. If you have any stock in ashtrays, sell.

OCTOBER 1982

CRIME AND PUNISHMENT, SEX AND HERPES

BOSTON—I never expected to see Phyllis Schlafly get into the sex-education racket. I thought she disapproved of that sort of thing. Didn't the hawk of the Eagle Forum always have her eye on other creatures preying on schoolchildren?

But here she is beginning to distribute 100,000 pamphlets to junior- and senior-high school students about, gulp, sex.

Well, not to worry. Phyllis hasn't lost her balance. The scourge of the ERA has taken on a new target—herpes—and she is still trying to scare people straight.

The brochure that she has published features a cover picture of the herpes simplex virus and goes on, in a fit of misinformation, to blame the epidemic of genital herpes on the four Ps: *Playboy, Penthouse*, and *Planned Parenthood*. Schlafly's pamphlet then lectures the young about the dangers of this disease in a style reminiscent of Army sergeants in World War II: "There is only one way to be sure you never get herpes: Avoid sexual relations. Remain a virgin until you marry, marry a virgin and remain faithful to each other."

Frankly, I don't know a soul who is in favor of herpes, a disease which has been on more magazine covers lately than Jacqueline Onassis. There are now estimated to be some twenty million Americans who have recurrent breakouts of herpes sores. There is even a list of macabre jokes about it. ("What is the difference between love and herpes? Herpes is forever.")

But I have an uneasy feeling that the Schlaflys of the world regard this virus as a godsend. At last, a modern punishment for sex, a warning from the heavens above that human beings must mend their ways or suffer the sores of sex.

As Schlafly said about her pamphlet: "One of our aims is to provide a deterrent to promiscuity." If herpes didn't exist she would have invented it.

The lady from Alton, Illinois, isn't alone in portraying herpes in the bright light of sin. *Time* magazine recently called it "Today's Scarlet Letter" and wrote the word herpes across its cover in bright red. *Mother Jones*, in a fine cover for its November issue, calls this media coverage the "sex-as-sin/disease-as-punishment thinking. . . ." The author also suggests that sexual guilt is "perhaps the most pervasive of all herpes symptoms."

There are others, outside the Eagle Forum, who regard this as good news. As the *Time* magazine piece concluded: "But perhaps not so unhappily, it [herpes] may be a prime mover in helping to bring to a close an era of mindless promiscuity."

This week a *Washington Post*-ABC News poll suggests that fear of herpes is indeed changing sexual behavior. A full 22 percent of the unmarried people ages eighteen to thirty-seven agreed with the statement, "I have changed my behavior to avoid the risk of contracting herpes."

The people interviewed offered comments like, "People are thinking twice" and "I don't just hop into bed with anybody."

The whole herpes social syndrome is fascinating. Not long ago, extramarital sex in any form was weighed down with fears of brimstone, not to mention pregnancy. Many people continue to need some sort of deterrent, some external reason to abstain, some fear of punishment, to deal sanely with their sexuality. We have gone from hell to herpes in three generations.

Imagine, needing a fear of herpes to make you "think twice" about a one-night stand, about a stranger in your bed, about having sex with someone whose toothbrush you wouldn't share.

We went through a period when sex was portrayed as a need to be fulfilled rather than a relationship to be explored. There was a time gap between the sexual revolution and the emotional revolution. Many people still find it difficult to sort out their own standards of caring and exploitation. Surely some of the singles who cite "herpes" as their reason for "thinking twice" were looking for a reason.

Still, I refuse to applaud the epidemic of herpes as the heavenly harbinger of a renewed right and sexual wrong. I'd rather have a cure than a deterrent. I'd rather people made decisions about their sexual lives carefully than fearfully.

The pamphlet that blisters on my desk this morning makes me realize how disappointed some will be if the new Finnish remedy, something called gossypol, actually works against herpes. What would the Schlaflys do with a cure? Ban it?

OCTOBER 1982

THE STAR OF THE LIZ TAYLOR STORY

BOSTON—Imagine for just a moment that you are Elizabeth Taylor. Go ahead, try it. You are sitting in front of your television set viewing a miniseries, a docudrama dubbed "The Liz Taylor Story."

What you see before you is an actress playing you. The actress looks and sounds exactly like a younger, thinner, violet-eyed you. Then she opens her mouth, and in words you never uttered, declares "your" undying love for Michael Wilding, Eddie Fisher, or Richard Burton.

By the end of the series, this same actress had told the public what "you" said, how "you" felt, what "you" did. The problem is that you didn't necessarily say it, feel it, do it. But you have had no more control over the content—or the profits—from the story of your life than any other television viewer.

The whole idea is enough to make your head spin. Unless of course you really are Elizabeth Taylor. In which case it would be enough to make you sue.

In fact, the actress filed suit last month against ABC and the film company that was to produce a docudrama of her life. She staked out two grounds: (1) She alone owns her life story, and (2) a docudrama with its mixture of fact and fiction would necessarily present her in a false light.

It's hard to think of Liz Taylor's life as private property, and Liz as sole owner. She's lived in public since she was sixteen years old. As First Amendment lawyer Bruce Sanford says rather harshly, "Her sphere of privacy has grown smaller over the years with her deliberate and calculated manipulation of the American media." It is a touch late to turn shy.

But over time, the courts have ruled that celebrities can control the use of their own name and image. In the 1940s, for example, a bunch of baseball players sued a bubble-gum manufacturer who was packaging their pictures without permission, and they won. The law now would prevent anyone from sewing the letters L-i-z T-a-y-l-o-r onto the pocket of a pair of blue jeans.

At the same time, the First Amendment protects the media's right to print that name on the jacket of a book or the cover of a magazine or a television news show. If a court ever ruled that Elizabeth Taylor owned the exclusive rights to "her life story," then so might Jimmy Carter or Herschel Walker. The only biographies of a living person we would see would all be "authorized."

The second problem that Liz Taylor raised is more complex. It has to do with the whole fuzzy business known as docudramas. Part fact, part fiction, they purport to tell people the absolute truth while they embellish, edit, and rewrite it.

We have had some form of this activity ever since Shakespeare began putting words in the mouths of kings. We allow a good deal of "literary license" in historical fiction.

We have seen a rash of docudramas about live people: Jacqueline Onassis, Jean Harris, Princess Diana and Prince Charles, and most recently, and dreadfully, Gloria Vanderbilt.

In each instance, the authors didn't quote the principals, they wrote the quotes. The lines were then spoken by actors who had learned to look and sound like the real thing. The stories were neither entirely false nor precisely factual.

If the Liz Taylor story is written, we'll see an actress playing the part of an actress. Harriet Pilpel, an intellectual-property lawyer, describes this critically as "impersonation." Surely a portion of the audience will accept the story as the real McCoy, or the real Liz. Many will even accept the actress as the real Liz.

If the audience is confused, so is the law. Harvard law professor Arthur Miller, a self-described "privacy nut," calls this case "a goulash of rights." In the goulash, he says, is "the public's right to know [about Liz Taylor's life], her own rights to privacy, her property rights and the need to give the creative act some license."

This particular goulash, however, is labeled docudrama. The ingredients are one part documentary, one part drama, one tablespoon fact, one tablespoon fiction. It's not just Liz Taylor who gets indigestion at the notion her life could be presented "imaginatively." Docudrama is more than a goulash of rights; it's a recipe for a four-star media disaster.

NOVEMBER 1982

TOUCH-TONE

BOSTON—My friends live in other places: other neighborhoods, other towns, other states. When we get together, it is often our fingers that do the walking from one home to the other.

For us, the telephone is a meeting hall, a neighborhood, the way we keep our own small community together. We advise and consult each other by dial tone; we console and congratulate by area codes and digits.

By voice, we do the maintenance that keeps friendships alive, and sometimes families. If we have some piece of news to share, it goes out almost always, almost exclusively, by word of mouth.

This is called, in our culture, keeping in touch.

Yet I sometimes wonder whether there isn't a hidden cost to this piece of technology, too. I don't mean the costs of intrusion. It's true that the phone insults our quiet and insists its way into our privacy. But I will trade that for this lifeline.

Nor do I mean the cost that shows up on my bill. I rationalize that easily with friends from other area codes: Long distance is cheaper than planes or therapy . . . or disconnection.

But isn't it possible that this staple of modern life has had some odd consequences for us? Isn't it possible that the instrument has actually been an actor in our culture over a century?

John Staudenmaier, a Jesuit and visiting assistant professor at MIT's Center for Science, Technology and Society, talks about the birth of the phone in 1876 as "the first time in human history that we could split voice from sight, touch, smell and taste."

What does that mean to us? That we no longer have to be in the same room to talk to each other. That we can choose friends across space and keep friends over distance.

But doesn't it also mean that we can ignore the people who live in our hallway? In some ways, the same machine that offers us a handy shortcut through loneliness may also make it more likely for us to live alone.

"The hometown, the street and neighborhood have also

been eroded particularly by the telephone," believes Staudenmaier, "because the real relationships in my life are not the people on my street and not the people in my apartment building. They can be strangers because I have 'real' friends connected by electronic rather than physical bodily connections."

It isn't just the phone that does this, I know. The car, the television set, and manufacturing have also changed us so we live more in the wide world and less on our block.

But I suspect that this odd and utterly routine ability to communicate by sound alone has altered another piece of our human psyche. We are more able now to protect and distance ourselves in human communication.

How many difficult conversations today take place by phone because we won't have to see someone else's tears? How skillfully have we learned to control our voices and hide our emotions? How often do we use the phone so we won't have to, literally, face each other?

I know a woman who bought a portable phone so that she could garden or scrub the sink or unload the dishwasher when her mother called. I know a man who regularly broke up with the women in his life by phone because it was so much easier.

We have all, at one time or another, retreated to a phone to share something personal while we are invisible. We are able to screen our messages, offer less, reveal less, feel less vulnerable. We can even hang up. The telephone is wonderfully efficient, and less intimate.

I am no Luddite, raging against electronics. In my home there are four extension phones, a hundred feet of cord, and one teenager. I work by phone, send my column from one city to another by phone. I maintain—though I never make—friendships by phone.

Yet I think it's crucial to remember the limits, to remember the trade-offs of the technology we live with. The telephone company encourages us to reach out and touch someone. Funny, that's the one thing we can't do by phone.

MARCH 1983

THE CASE OF THE PERIPATETIC GERM

BOSTON—No one knows where the germ had originally germinated, but it is believed to have spent the summer of 1983 hibernating in Houston. By September, however, this particular germ was once again on the move, lodged in the throat of a small boy named Mike who was entering the Houston school system.

On the first day of the school year, Mike fell into the care of a student teacher by the name of Allison, who spent the morning comforting the crying boy on the assumption that he was emotionally upset. Reconstructing the scenario today, we estimate that Allison kept the boy on her lap for a cumulative two hours during that Monday morning. But let me continue.

Between that day and the following Tuesday, when Allison had developed a certain ringing in her ears and a stuffed nose, she had split a pizza with two of her roommates, Sally and Beth, breathed into the ear of her boyfriend Charles, and shared the telephone with at least six other students in her dormitory.

Beth, who was only nineteen and not yet what you would

call independent, soon decided to take her sore throat home. On the plane back to Mom and Dallas, she sat in the non-smoking section next to Jess, a wholesaler for a California health-food outlet, who believed in vitamin C and mind over matter. Jeff gave Beth a sample of ginseng tea, which came in handy a week later when Beth's mother was laid low by a cold of unknown origin.

As for Jeff, he later found himself in a Chicago hotel functionally unable to work. For the first time since he had had moved from Athens, Ohio, to San Diego he was suffering from balloon-headedness and the realization that people will not buy health foods from a sick man. Soon Jeff disguised himself in a business suit and took the germs back to San Diego on an L-1011 with precisely 256 other passengers.

But at home things began to get out of hand. Jeff, running a fever of 102, opened a childproof aspirin bottle the only way it could be opened, with his teeth. The next teeth on that bottle belonged to Jeff's boss, Elizabeth, who at that time suffered only from a modest headache. Elizabeth, whose nickname back East was Biffy, was an air kisser. By now it was almost Christmas, deeply into party season, and soon Elizabeth was kissing air all over southern California.

Among those inadvertently smacked was the caterer, Toshihiro, who did these wonderful things with avocado and sushi and was in great demand all the way north to Los Angeles and San Francisco. It was bad enough that Toshi spread something besides wasabi on the sushi which infected the entire table. Toshi also had dinner with his son, Peter, who worked in Silicon Valley and was having an affair with a computer programmer, Helen.

There was an uncomfortable moment a week or so later, when Peter's wife came into the office to discover that all three of them shared the same symptoms. At that point, since it was almost Valentine's Day, Helen decided that it might be wise to go home to St. Louis for a while, where she poured out her soul and her cold into wads of tissues which she left on the table belonging to her college roommate's husband, Thad.

This man, by general acclamation, was healthy as a horse and always wore his rubbers. But ten days later, that same Thad kissed his wife good-bye, poured some cough medicine down his throat, squeezed some decongestant up his nose, and took off for Washington to give a training session to the Secret Service men about to cover the presidential candidates.

Due to a shortage of equipment, the very sort of thing that Thad railed against in his annual memos, he was forced to lend his ear receiver to an agent named Brian who was soon to be assigned to the Massachusetts primary. Now Brian, mind you, had a reputation for utter closemouthedness. He was a loner, you might say, a human isolation ward, and the entire chain of medical history might have ended there if it weren't for a particularly aggressive TV reporter assigned to Brian's candidate.

In pursuit of a quote on Super Tuesday, Jane tried to press past Brian at the very moment when this man, a model of restraint, did something unprecedented in the history of the service: He sneezed all over her microphone. So it was that precisely one week later, Jane was just beginning to feel a little fullness in the nasal passages as she sat at a friend's table in Boston.

She and her friend laughed. They poured two glasses of wine. They poured two more. One's wineglass got confused with the other's. One's germs leapt to the other. And that, for the medical record, is the shaggy germ story of how I got such a miserable cold.

MARCH 1984

PAC-MAN THE HEARTBREAKER

BOSTON—I met him in the Detroit airport.

I know what you're going to say. I should have known better than to get involved. Any relationship begun in an airport is going to be, at best, transient.

But you know how it is. I was between planes with time on my hands. He was available, enticing. So what if I'd been warned about him. I figured it would be different for me, for us.

Then, before I knew it, I was hooked on the guy.

Pac-Man was his name.

Now there are some men in the world who ought to be forced to wear a warning in public, a scarlet B for Beware. Pac, I tell you, is one of them. He took me for every quarter I owned.

Frankly, I was had by Pac-Man. If I confess this now, it's because he is just one of a species. There are 95,000 others like him spread across the country, getting fed a fat share of the $5 billion in videogame quarters every year.

They've seduced others just like me from coast to coast. Some of the people never go home anymore, others drop out of school. In California, a nineteen-year-old was arrested for allegedly robbing homes just to feed him.

So if I'm willing to put aside my silly pride, it's on the chance that maybe I can save some other victim.

You see, I was once innocent, too. For all I knew, Blinky,

Speedy, Shadow, and Bashful were The Four Dwarfs. I'd never even heard about Pac-Man's self-defeating monsters. But let's be honest: How much does any woman know about the demons chasing the man in her life?

Then I put in my first quarter. I played it my usual way—straight. It was a disaster. I pushed him right into the arms of the nearest monster.

I should have quit right then. But for some strange reason this defeat didn't discourage me. It enticed me down the silvery path. I wanted to try again. I figured I could make it work. I wanted, for gawdsakes, to save him.

Slowly, I upped my investment in our relationship, cash-dollars, throwing good money after bad. Each time, I strung it out a little longer. In fairness, our relationship wasn't all sick. There was something special about Pac-Man. He was, as videogame makers say, "a real quarter sucker."

Maybe it was his cute round shape. His oral fixation. His endless appetite for dots and occasional fruits. His neat little energizers. Maybe it was because he seemed so easy to manipulate.

But basically he had all the fatal charm, the promising allure, of a sadistic lover. He was like all the three-dimensional people you know who lead their lives by micro-chip. They're programmed to get you in the end.

I had fallen into the old trap, the masochist's special. If at first you don't succeed . . . I was seduced by the challenge, the high energy of the chase, the intrigue of the maze. I learned to keep the monsters at bay another second or two. I began to believe that I was playing blackjack or poker. I began to believe there was a chance to win.

But eventually, the old monsters would jump out. All Pac-Man wanted to do was play with my feelings, again and again. I can still see his brazen word on the screen of my defeat: READY.

People have said that Pac-Man is a drug addiction. Out in California, someone labeled him a metaphor for life. It wasn't until I gained some distance, until I was in the air between Cleveland and Rochester, that I could think clearly.

Take it from me. Pac-Man hooks those people who confuse a victory with a slow defeat.

As for me, I escaped. I didn't trade in my ticket or my child for more quarters. But if you see a Man out in Detroit with a bad case of the munchies, do me a favor: Walk on by.

Pac-Man's his name. No-Win is his game.

MAY 1982

"GUARANTEED TO WRINKLE"

BOSTON—My own flat-out, full-tilt admiration of the business of American business began decades ago when I first started noticing perfume ads. I was intrigued by the idea that dozens of manufacturers actually sold a smell to American consumers through their eyes. Never mind the nose, perfume was sold for what you might all its Essence of Vision.

The way I figured it out, a perfume that became successful through magazine ads was like a ventriloquist who won fame for performing on the radio. This, as satirist Tom

Lehrer has noted, was the truly weird part of the legend of Edgar Bergen and Charlie McCarthy.

Today perfumes are also glued onto magazine inserts, which end up smelling more or less the same, like a New Orleans bordello. But that is just a small part of the story.

The other marketing trick I started to admire was their ability to create a new market where none should exist. There are all sorts of examples throughout business history, but my favorite is the successful pitch selling men's underwear to women. The marketeers' ability to get her into his undies has registered some $5 million in sales to the young and heterosexy. Imagine the necessity of fly fronts for females.

Nevertheless, the Marketing Hall of Fame should probably be reserved for those business alchemists who managed to turn a liability into an asset. Here, I tip my hat to the genius who has attached a few little words to the shirts and skirts made out of 100 percent linen: "This Material Guaranteed to Wrinkle."

I can only imagine the creative ferment of the Madison Avenue agent who was given the challenge of turning the problem of linen into the promise. Guaranteeing that linen will wrinkle is like guaranteeing that smoking will give your voice that wonderful throaty quality. It's like selling property on the San Andreas Fault for the shake, rattle, and roll.

The dilemma for the linen people was that American women abhor ironing the way their nature abhors the vacuum cleaner. Today, we are permanently pressed for time. There have been more women liberated by Dacron than by Betty Friedan. We cling to a belief in wash 'n' wear as an article of faith over fashion.

Some years ago, when manufacturers first started reintroducing so-called natural fibers, many of us considered it a plot. We sincerely hoped that picking cotton would be reclassified as an unnatural act. We hoped that employing silkworms would violate ASPCA labor laws, and that flax would get a lot of legal flak. I personally thought of printing a bumper sticker: SAVE THE POLYESTER.

This time, the marketing strategists had to convince consumers that we could have our linen and our laziness too. Worse yet, they had to do this under truth-in-advertising laws. Their only hope was to turn around the image of the poor benighted wrinkle, to convince women that wrinkling itself was no problem—why, it was even kind of hip.

Thus evolved "Guaranteed to Wrinkle," a motto guaranteed to cloud one's mind.

The reason that I have spent so much time and space contemplating this marketing strategy is because I bought it. "It" in this case is a pink linen suit. I bought it with the complete conviction that I could go cold turkey. I could stop ironing linen the way I once stopped wearing a girdle. It was time to cheerfully accept certain imperfections as "natural."

While I was devising this theory, the suit was perfectly ironed. You will note that the stores do not sell these things with the wrinkles.

Now lo these many months, plane trips, car rides, and workdays later, I have no complaints about the guarantee. But despite the best minds of marketing, I continue to regard the woman in the mirror as a woman in dire need of a good solid straightening. I speak to this woman with the immortal words of my grandmother: "You look like an unmade bed."

Perhaps it is a sign of rigidity. Perhaps it is sociobiology. But I suspect that no woman who has ever bought lotion to remove wrinkles from her face can accept them on her clothing. I'm afraid this is one marketing idea with some problems to be ironed out.

JUNE 1984

31

HOW TO SPEAK BROKEN FRENCH

BOSTON—Let us be frank about it. Frankness, after all, seems appropriate in any discussion about the French.

The French are, to put it mildly, sensitive about their language. For some time, they have been the protectionists of the international language trade. They have been perfectly willing to export words to America, but unwilling to import them.

The French generally regard Americanisms as the kudzu of the language world. Once you let them in, these linguistic weeds start creeping all over the place, and before you know it, they strangle out the sturdy French vines. They have therefore hacked away at Anglo-Saxon intruders as if they were Henry V's troops at Agincourt.

The campaign began almost twenty years ago when a French professor named René Etiemble published a book called *Parlez-Vous Franglais*. It warned of the dire consequences to the Republic of France if the people were getting together at "le meeting" or doing "le shopping" at "le supermarket."

The current minister of French culture, Jack Lang, sounded off against America for "this financial and intellectual imperialism that ... grabs consciousness, ways of thinking. ..." Then, a meeting of worldwide "intellectuals" whom Lang called to Paris came to the conclusion that our very own "Dallas" was the greatest threat to Western culture.

Now English has received another blow from The High Commission for the French Language. The High Commission (I told you the French take their words seriously) released an official list of French substitutes for English words that have been infiltrating the vocabulary of French communications people.

They have constructed replacements for words like "drive-in" and "flashback." They have even ordered that "Walkman," a product that was made in Japan, be renamed "Balladeur." Six months from now, anyone caught saying the word "jingle" on the tube may be in for trouble.

I, for one, refuse to simply lie back on my *chaise longue* and take this act of French aggression. Here at last is a true *cause célèbre*, one might even say a *debacle*. What is at stake is nothing less than the linguistic balance of payments.

If they are declaring war on Franglais, I say that it is time for us to declare War on Englench. No matter what Jack Lang thinks, it is not the Americans who are cultural imperialists, or even *imperialistes*. It's the French.

Who, after all, made us wear *lingerie* when our underwear was perfectly decent? Who turned our cooks into *chefs* and our dances into *ballets*? Where was it writ that a bunch of flowers had to become a *bouquet*? Or that toilet water had to be *cologne*, let alone *perfume*. What was the *raison d'être* for turning a decent American tenderloin into a *chateaubriand*?

What the French resent is not our imperialism but our democracy. We gave them McDonalds. They gave us *croissant*. We gave them the ice-cream cone. They gave us *quiche*.

The people who invented the very word elite simply have a gripe against mass culture. They cheerfully export the notion that the only proper clothing is their *couture* and the only proper hairdo is their *coiffure* and the only proper food is their *cuisine*. Then they complain about "le jeans."

Through their own *largesse*, not to say *noblesse oblige*, they prefer to determine what is *haute* and what is not. They want the exclusive worldwide franchise to separate the *chic* from the *gauche*.

If they want to ban Franglais, we will meet them at the beaches with boatloads of their own Englench. If they turn their drive-ins into *cineparcs*, we shall turn our *quiche* into cheese pie. If they no longer attend *le meeting* we will no longer *rendezvous*.

If they make it *de rigueur* to eliminate Americanisms, we shall refuse to eat our apple pie *à la mode* and our soup *du jour*. We shall, in fact, hoist them on their own petulant *petard*.

And if the French decide to give up and return to the old *laissez-faire* linguistics, well, they better not call it *détente*.

MARCH 1983

VIRTUE AND THE LONG-DISTANCE RUNNER

BOSTON—Let me say right off that I think running is a great spectator sport. For this I must publicly thank the Boston Marathon.

Every year, long after the victory celebrations are over, I drive home from work along the darkening twenty-fifth mile. Annually I dodge the last of the valiant 7000 as they drag their numbed and numbered bodies to the finish line.

Just one glance at their faces rekindles my commitment to remain forever on the sidelines.

But now I have another reason not to run. Running may be good for your opinion of yourself, but it's lousy for your opinion of others.

A study, not enclosed in my marathon program booklet, was done on eighty-one fairly sedentary middle-aged men at Stanford University. More than half of them were randomly assigned to a running regiment for a year.

They ended up—here's the good news—less anxious, less depressed, and somewhat less hostile to others. But there was a wrinkle. The better they felt about themselves, the worse they apparently felt about their nonrunning partners.

What does this mean? According to the lean, running, and unwed head of the research program, Lewis K. Graham 2d, "The exercisers lost a fair amount of weight and became more fit, leaner and more attractive . . . one might assume that they became more comfortable with themselves, with the side-effect that they were a little less satisfied with their spouses."

This confirms my own private research that running has become the latest way for one person to outgrow, or outdistance, another. It is a new standard against which partners may judge each other . . . badly.

In the early 1960s, you may recall, it was common for married men to explain in darkened cocktail lounges how they had simply outgrown their wives. The hometown gal who put them through college, graduate school, fatherhood, and three corporate moves just didn't fit as the vice-president's wife. The higher he got, the wider they gapped.

In the late 1960s, it was equally common for married women to outgrow their husbands. He was still Consciousness I, while she was Consciousness Raised.

A few years ago, self-improvement was the primary co-respondent for divorce. The man who embarked on the One True Course—from Berkeley to Nirvana—wanted his wife to follow. The woman who actualized herself wanted her husband to keep up the psychobabble.

Similarly, a man with a mantra spiritually "outgrew" the woman without one, and the woman with an insight began to look upon her mate as myopic. As for the mate who "did" est alone, he often ended up alone.

Today's self-improvement tack is, of course, physical. Like medieval flagellants, we are supposed to whip our muscles into line and beat our cellulite into shape. It is no longer enough to walk in the path of righteousness, we have to run in it.

So this study makes a lot of sense. It isn't (forgive me, Lewis Graham) that runners feel "more comfortable with themselves." It's hard to feel comfortable with shin splints and a stitch in your side.

What they feel is more virtuous.

From long observation, and brief participation, I can tell you that running is dreadful. The psychic rewards don't come from oxygen; they come from overcoming the desire to quit, squelching the urge to stop this infernal nonsense and lie down.

Runners do not actually enjoy doing it, they enjoy the fact that they did it. Like dieters who live on watercress, they learn to savor the heady flavor of their own willpower.

As the research suggests, it becomes harder for martyrs to live with mortals. The more virtuous they feel about running, the more superior they feel to nonrunning. Not to mention nonrunners.

The Stanford researchers have stumbled upon one of the strange and personal truths of the ascetic eighties. Self-discipline looks down on self-indulgence, the lean look down on the lax, and only the couples who keep pace together, stay together.

But they forgot one thing: A spectator never ran out on anyone.

APRIL 1981

BACK TO WORK

BOSTON—The shot opens up in a train. It is very early. The voice, a Perry Mason voice—deep, masculine, author-itative—talks about the very special sort of person who wants to get there first, wants to be number one, top of the heap.

The camera pulls back, pans the empty seats, and we see that our man, the stockbroker, is the only passenger on the milk run. He's jumped the competition, hits the rails to Wall Street before the sun has come up over Westchester.

The second commercial opens up in a home. The man steps out of his darkened bedroom, leaving his wife asleep, and climbs down the stairs past the dog. Making coffee with one hand, he dials London with the other. First off, he wants to know the price of gold.

The same voices end both commercials, intoning: "The winning attitude at Bache. Put it to work for you."

37

* * *

It's all there, wrapped up in a collection of fifty-second television commercials for stockbrokers. The hard-driving man is a hot item again, bankable. Maybe he lost status in the softer seventies, but he's out front now, boasting of his long hours and his competitiveness.

Steve Goldstein, the ad agency supervisor for the Bache man, makes no bones about it. The man they are pushing is "definitely a Type A."

"We try to demonstrate that our brokers are very special people, hardworking. We'd like to develop him into a symbol of the kind of person you would like to have working for you."

The ads are dramatic ones, even melodramatic, and yet they work. They work because they strike a chord of honesty in the middle of a chorus of ambiguity, a choir of confusion.

Watching them, I realize that Goldstein is right. Very few of us may want to be a Type A, but many of us want to be served by Type A's.

The hard-driven, competitive people are seen nationally and emotionally as lousy spouses. Actuarially, they are seen as lousy insurance risks. But they are often the men and women we would like to have working for us.

You can hear the harshness of this truth echoed throughout the business world. The company chairman quoted in the *Wall Street Journal* told a recruiter bluntly, "Find me some one who is as unhappily married as I am, so he'll really devote himself to the task at hand."

You can hear it more benignly in the ad man's analysis. "One of the things we have found," says Goldstein, "is that clients think investing is a very serious matter. . . . They want someone who is going to work hard for their money, put in the extra effort."

Maybe "workaholic" is a nasty word, smacking of disease, of single-minded devotion to labor instead of people. Surely Goldstein reacts against it: "I don't think he's a workaholic. I think he's just a guy who loves his job."

But behind that defensiveness is something very real. For all the talk about stress, for all the talk about leading a full life, there is still a real tension between the life we want for ourselves and the work we want out of others.

Nobody wants to be married to a doctor who works weekends and makes house calls at two o'clock in the morning. But every patient would like to find one.

No one admires a lawyer who spends vacations and weekends with a briefcase, except, of course, the client.

We all agree that a politician should spend private time with his family. And we all want him to speak at our banquet.

Even in the ad business, as Goldstein ruefully notes, "Clients call at eight A.M. and if you're not here they are disappointed."

So, today we admire the well-rounded, and aspire to balance—then hire the single-minded. The competitive hard worker—the lone man—is on the milk run because we keep him there.

There is simply more of a conflict than we admit between the qualities we value in a person and those we value in a worker.

We put each other in a double bind, and then we wonder why we feel so trapped.

MAY 1981

THE ULTIMATE LUXURY: PEOPLE

BOSTON—There is a bank in New York City at Seventy-second Street and Broadway where you are only allowed to deal with a human teller if you have $5000 or more in your account. If you have less money than that, you have to conduct routine business with an electronic machine.

Ever since I read about this new Citibank policy, I have been trying to figure out what it means. I don't think this is just another Manhattan eccentricity, or another symbol of the world's most impersonal city.

The way I see it, the Citibank is onto something big. What we have here is the ultimate two-track, two-class system. To the rich go the human beings. The rest of us get the machines.

An angry customer accused the bank of being "elitist." But you see, that's the point. People have become the ultimate luxury. The government considers them an extravagance. Industry calls them an indulgence. And the middle class can't afford them.

A couple of generations ago, wealth was measured in material goods like indoor plumbing or a matching set of silverware. When I was a kid, it was a television set or a single-family house.

Back then, the rich were different from the rest of us because they had, you know, things. Luxury was the first name of a car. Now if you want to know who's rich, you don't add up their possessions, you calculate their access to what is truly precious: people.

Trend spotters date the people problem from World War II, when household workers began to disappear and the middle class was tracked onto machines. We learn to bring clothes to one and dust to another and call it convenience.

Today few have real live people who take care of their houses. The rest have machines with user-friendly names that just sound human: names like lawn mower, vacuum cleaner, dishwasher.

The same thing has happened in the marketplace. When our grandparents went grocery shopping, people handed them goods, such as tomatoes. (These were real live tomatoes, too—but we won't get into that.)

Now we go to supermarkets and only the fanciest little grocery stores that specialize in out-of-season asparagus stock up on helpers. They are added onto the bill, sort of like truffles. Under the two-track system, the customers who frequent designer salons and elegant restaurants and fancy hotels and make person-to-person calls get to deal with humans, who ask them nearly extinct questions like, "May I help you?"

The rest of us go through life in discount stores and Automats and motels, talking to answering services and automated voices and watching our bills calculated by computer. We are virtually untouched by human hands, except for those that self-serve us.

It's not only middle-class Americans who have been priced out of the market. It's also our institutions. A community college in Maryland has invited a computer to deliver the commencement speech. Soon you may have to go to Harvard to hear a person.

Now, at Citibank, even middle-class money is considered

too chintzy to be handled by such an expensive commodity. As the bank executives (you only meet them if you have millions in your account) point out, a machine can handle 2000 transactions a day and work 168 hours a week. A teller can only handle 200 transactions, work 30 hours a week, and then has the nerve to take coffee breaks.

I don't know where the two-track trend will lead, but I have a suspicion. Remember the economist who recently announced that the cost of raising a middle-class child was now over $200,000? I wonder if they sell booties to fit machines.

MAY 1983

Part 2

PEOPLE

THE GENTLE WORLD OF A. A. MILNE

BOSTON—He was born on January 18, 1882, into that sentimental Victorian world where proper little English boys in proper nurseries wore their hair in long curls and were dressed in Little Lord Fauntleroy suits.

A. A. Milne was young during an age of romantic, even sentimental, childhood. He was the third son of a schoolteacher who adored his boys, playing with them, teaching them, reading Uncle Remus to them in nightly segments.

The father created a world for his children. The son, who grew up into a less safe century, created a fictional world for all of our children.

To this day, on his hundredth birthday, A. A. Milne's Forest is a benign place, where Tiggers and Owls and Pooh Bears, Eeyores and Rabbits, Kangas and Roos coexist in tolerance and friendship.

His own family lived in this Forest. The father whom he worshiped in childhood and criticized in adulthood ("If Father knew everything, he knew most of it wrong") reappears here as the illiterate intellectual, Owl. The mother he knew as a preoccupied woman, "restfully aloof," lives in the Pooh plot as the busy Rabbit.

The elder and more lovable brother, Ken ("If you knew us both, you preferred Ken. . . . 'Poor old Ken' or 'dear old Ken' had his private right of entry into everybody's heart") was the model for the kindly Pooh. A. A.'s son, Christopher Robin, plays the gentle leader.

But in another way, all of us are related to the fussiness of Kanga, the gluttony of the Bear of Very Little Brain, the gloomy sensitivity of Eeyore, the blithe recklessness of Tigger.

All of us have longings for the Forest of childhood.

Milne grew older and went to a school where he was, like Pooh, constantly hungry. He studied mathematics but, instead, became an editor of *Punch*, a playwright, a poet, a novelist. He served through the searching experience of his generation, World War I.

By 1926, when he took on the double role of father and writer, he must have been eager to fantasize a lost garden of prewar innocence for Christopher Robin and, undoubtedly, for himself.

Milne's Forest is a kind of protectorate of childhood, alive with adventures rather than dangers. Its inhabitants are full of childhood egotism and innocence, malapropisms and insights. Its problems are the result of foolishness or bad luck instead of evil. Its adventures end happily. Every Pooh comes out all right from every pot and every hole.

This Forest also shelters that gentler moment in human history between the fierceness of Grimm fairy tales and the unrelenting sophistication of Freud. Reading among its wistful literary trees, adults and children alike can imagine a place of utter ease and spontaneity, a place to indulge in Christopher Robin's favorite pastime:

"What I like doing best is nothing. . . . It's when people call out at you just as you're going off to do it. 'What are you going to do, Christopher Robin' and you say, 'Oh, nothing,' and then you go and do it."

For me, the books have always had an aura about them, even a premonition. Milne understood what all parents know and all children suspect: Sooner or later, the world interferes with childhood, knowledge complicates innocence.

At the very end of *The House at Pooh Corner*, Christopher Robin has begun to learn things. About the letter A, about Factors, about Kings. He has to leave this Forest for school, the business of knowing and growing up.

"Pooh," he calls to his bear. "I'm not going to do Nothing any more."

"Never again?" asks Pooh.

"Well, not so much. They don't let you."

There is a longing in this good-bye that we share, a longing for a lost idyll of childhood, whether it is our own or our sons' and daughters', or the world's.

"But," as Milne wrote consolingly, "of course it isn't really Good-bye, because the Forest will always be there . . . and anybody who is Friendly with Bears can find it."

This is the gift he left us on his birthday.

JANUARY 1982

WHAT KIND OF ENDING IS THAT, DR. SEUSS?

BOSTON—The taste buds of millions of Americans who grew up on a literary diet of "green eggs and ham" must have perked up when the Pulitzer committee awarded a special citation to their favorite chef, Dr. Seuss.

For almost half a century Theodor Seuss Geisel has concocted children's books that are scrumptiously silly and nutritiously sane. At eighty years old, with 100 million books sold, he has served up characters as memorable as Yertle the Turtle, Horton and the Whos, and the Grinch who stole Christmas.

Yet, despite solid credentials as a certified Seuss fan who has devoured the Dr.'s entire menu, I have to say that the most recent Seuss creation is a touch sour for my palate. *The Butter Battle Book*, which reached number 2 on the best-seller list, is a parable about the arms race that sings with Seuss satire. This time, West and East, U.S.A. and USSR, are cast as the Yooks and the Zooks. They are enemies because, you see, the Zooks eat their bread with the down side buttered while the Yooks keep their butter side up.

The trouble begins when a Zook uses a slingshot against the Yooks' best weapon, a Snick-Berry Switch. Soon, the arms race and the rhyme race are off and running. The leaders build bigger and deadlier weapons with names no more improbable than our MX "Peacekeeper": a Triple-Sling Jigger and a Jigger-Rock Snatchem, a Kick-a-Poo Kid and an Eight-Nozzled, Elephant-Toted Boom-Blitz.

Inevitably, they come up with the bomb: the Bitsy Big-Boy Boomeroo. At the end, we have a Yook and a Zook confrontation on the wall separating the two countries. Each is holding a pink, hand-sized bomb that can obliterate the other, while a Yook grandson is watching.

As the last page reads in its entirety:

"Grandpa!" I shouted. "Be careful! Oh, gee!

"Who's going to drop it?"

"Will you . . . or will he? . . ."

"Be patient," said Grandpa. "We'll see. We will see . . ."

I feel strange criticizing Dr. Seuss on the arms race. I love the lilt and language of his parable. I shall never again be able to read about nuclear weapons without thinking of the Bitsy Big-Boy Boomeroo.

Geisel is no pacifist. During World War II he served in

Frank Capra's signal corps unit making patriotic films, including one called *Designed for Death*, a history of the Japanese people. Now he sees that people may fight according to which side their bread is buttered on.

But what disturbs me is that ending. A child is left helplessly watching and waiting to see whether or not the adults blow up the world. I worry about the effect this bleak nonending, this anxiety-ridden nonconclusion, would have on kids.

The portrait, I know, is close to reality. Perhaps the reason why many adults are buying *The Butter Battle Book* for themselves is that we feel as helpless as children in the face of the arms race. Even Dr. Seuss seems dismayed. "I was tempted to give it a happy ending," he said of the book, "but then I would have gotten into dishonesty. That's the situation as it is."

Still, I wonder whether many of us today justify passing on messages of pessimism and anxiety to our children in the name of honesty. Consider what's missing from this "realism"; consider what's missing from the Yook-Zook arms race: dissent. Not once throughout the tale does someone call for a halt. The Yooks don't march for peace, they march into shelters. The adults are either dangerous or passive. There are no freeze messages or disarmament conferences or Dr. Seusses for that matter.

Psychiatrist Eric Chivian, who has filmed children talking about nuclear war from California to Moscow, says: "I think it's really important for kids to be given unambiguous and positive messages that are coupled with a call to action. When kids ask me if there will be a nuclear war, I say I don't think so because so many people are working against it."

Is he a cockeyed optimist? What is the point really of passing pessimism to our children? To prepare them for the Bitsy Big-Boy Boomeroo? We already are dealing with the syndrome of "futurelessness" in our children. The antidote is activism. Theirs and ours.

Dr. Seuss's portrait of the present—two old enemies standing poised on the wall and on extinction—is an accurate one. But what children need from the good doctor, from all adults, is a dose of hope.

APRIL 1984

CAROLYN KEENE: BRINGING UP NANCY DREW

BOSTON—As an author she had a stable of names.

She was Laura Lee Hope and Franklin Dixon and Victor Appleton, but above all others, she was Carolyn Keene. She wrote about the Bobbsey Twins and Hardy boys and Dana Girls. But above all others she cared about Nancy Drew.

As a nine-year-old fan, I never got a clue about the real name of the lady who died recently at eighty-nine years of age. Without a cipher, I would never have deducted that Carolyn Keene was Harriet Stratemeyer Adams.

But I knew her cast of characters: Bess, the slightly overweight blonde; George, the girl who loved her name; Ned Nickerson, college football player and boyfriend. And most of all I knew Nancy, the "titian-haired" detective who figured things out for herself.

I can't remember why I read all the way through the Nancy Drew series in those years. I didn't much like mysteries then and I haven't read one since *The Clue in the Crumbling Wall*. As literature Nancy Drew never made the list of great masterpieces.

But I guess it was Nancy who intrigued me. Harriet Adams' "girl sleuth" led me, as she has led seventy million others over half a century, into one adventure and out the next.

Nancy was different from the other characters who dotted my childhood. In the fairy tales on my shelves, girls waited to be rescued from their sleep or their cinders by princes. On the movie screens of my Saturday afternoons, men in black hats and white hats fought it out while girls stood by helplessly. I didn't have enough sense to realize that the weakness lay in the literature and not in the women.

But Nancy Drew rescued herself. Nancy Drew solved problems. Nancy Drew behaved the way a child of nine wants to believe she will behave at eighteen: sensibly, competently, independently.

She traveled the world in pursuit of puzzles as if it were the most ordinary thing to do. She saved victims from drowning, escaped from car trunks and boats and planes, she was treated as an equal and an expert in a world of police chiefs and lawyers. Above all, she was blissfully self-confident. The way we wanted to be.

"I like to think I brought up Nancy Drew the way I brought up my own children and they brought up theirs," Harriet Adams said once. But the author's own youth was not so straightforward. She was born in 1894 to Edward Stratemeyer, the writer who originated Horatio Alger and a host of other children's series. Stratemeyer didn't approve of women writers or workers. As a Wellesley graduate, his daughter badgered him into letting her edit manuscripts at home. But after her marriage, Stratemeyer wouldn't give her work to do.

It wasn't until her father's death that Harriet, thirty-eight years old and the mother of four, went into the family book-writing business. She inherited Nancy Drew from her father the way she inherited the pseudonyms and ghost writers. Then she remodeled the "girl sleuth" along her own ideals.

She scripted a new improved father, Carson Drew, who offered Nancy a heady mixture of encouragement and security. She scripted an updated man, Ned Nickerson, who could be at once strong and admiring. And she scripted Nancy.

I suspect that Harriet Adams was in the first generation who could have created a Nancy Drew. To Adams' childhood friends, Nancy would have seemed like a fantasy of freedom. To my own generation, she was an alternative to the passive princesses. To my daughter's generation, she must be, in turn, a relief from the emotion and angst of the Judy Blumes.

But the real clue to Nancy's staying power is simpler than this history. It's got to do with character. Nancy has it to the hilt and to the running board of her blue roadster. She's a confident, curious, straight-forward young woman making her way through Harriet Adams' world and ours.

"The only things Nancy Drew has changed in the past fifty years are her clothes and hairstyle," said Adams before her death. "She's as independent as ever and despite the changing values of society, hers are the same. Fifty years ago Nancy Drew was considered independent. Today her fans say she is liberated. I guess they are trying to catch up with her."

It looks like Nancy Drew is still one step ahead on the case.

APRIL 1982

THE GREAT DORIS LESSING HOAX

BOSTON—In the annals of publishing, it will go down as the Doris Lessing Hoax. Not once, but twice, the much-acclaimed, praised, and "bankable" British author wrote novels under a pseudonym.

As Doris Lessing, she had known "success" for decades with twenty-five books to her credit. *The Golden Notebook* alone sold 900,000 copies. But as Jane Somers she was a modest "failure." And that, she said, was the point.

"I wanted to highlight that whole dreadful process in book publishing that 'nothing succeeds like success'," said the author who finally confessed that she dunnit. "If the books had come out in my name, they would have sold a lot of copies and reviewers would have said, 'Oh, Doris Lessing, how wonderful.' As it is, there were almost no reviews, and the books sold about 1,500 copies here [Britain] and 3,000 in the United States."

So we are told that the ruse was devised as a monument to the unknown writer—to salve ten thousand egos bloodied by the paper cuts of rejection slips, to vindicate all the paranoia about the publishing world. After all, Doris Lessing's own British publisher rejected Jane Somers' novel. After all, not one reviewer recognized the real writer. After all, if Doris Lessing couldn't sell unless she were Doris Lessing, well . . .

It was a wonderful scam that produced a rash of embarrassment in the book world. But I suspect that her motives were more complex than that. Here is a woman who has spent her life wrestling with questions of who-am-I. It's unlikely that she would throw her name away for a cause. If she was toying with the book industry, I suspect that she was playing a more intriguing game with her own identity.

Indeed, the Lessing Hoax reminded me of a passage in her novel, *The Summer Before the Dark*, when a forty-five-year-old woman named Kate, freed from her family for the summer, lets go of every role that propped up her female life. In a powerful scene, Kate, inches of gray hair showing at her roots, body covered by a shapeless jacket, crossed a construction site full of workers who paid absolutely no attention to her.

Out of their sight, she took off the jacket to reveal her slim dress, wrapped her hair dramatically with a scarf, altered her body language, and then crossed the same space. This time, she was greeted by "a storm of whistles, calls, invitations." It was a moving costume drama, in which a woman was covered and stripped of her identity. She had a cloak of invisibility. Her identity hung by a scarf.

Now, in real life, Lessing subjected herself to a different experiment in identity. She left her name at the edge of the public square. Her words were anonymously paraded before the publishers and the critics. If Kate Brown was invisible without her "looks," would Doris Lessing be invisible without her "name"?

There is in all this a simple desire to masquerade, an intrigue as old as the prince and the pauper. People born with names such as Kennedy or Rockefeller must sometimes wish they were called Smith. But Lessing is one of those people who "made a name for themselves." She is not the only one to then worry if she is just valued for the name.

We all know, or know of, people like that. People who cannot introduce themselves without sounding as if they are name-dropping. The superstar who wonders whether he is getting work on his talent or his celebrity. The Nobel Prize winner who wonders if it's the title gathering attention.

There is in many successful people the fear that they are frauds protected by fame. Many wonder if they could do it again, remake it on their own. In the preface to these novels now being published under her own name, Doris Lessing says she wanted to know how she would fare "as a new writer without benefit of a name."

There is the more profound motive for this ruse. It's familiar to any successful person who has ever watched the television ads for the American Express card, who ever stared at a shopping-bag lady in the park and wondered what separates one life from another. Who am I without a name? Would those who claim kinship and offer praise still know me?

Lessing says now of her experiment, "It never crossed my mind that people wouldn't guess my identity when my first book came out." She even dropped hints. But when Jane Somers walked into the public square nobody saw Doris Lessing.

This woman is too world-wise to be victimized by vanity. The point of her experiment was, I am convinced, to address in public a theme that haunts her writing: Life is too fragile if your identity is solely defined by others; it is hard, a lifelong task, to go on defining and redefining yourself.

This extraordinary, vulnerable piece of personal risk-taking, this profound hoax, carries the unmistakable by-line of Doris Lessing.

SEPTEMBER 1984

55

A BATTERED LITTLE GIRL NAMED
ELEANOR ROOSEVELT

BOSTON—It was a childhood you wouldn't wish on anyone. The girl was born on October 11, 1884, into a confounding world of privilege and deprivation. She was rejected by a mother who called her "granny." She idolized a father who was at once loving and unstable. Orphaned by the age of ten, she went to live under the roof and rules of a grandmother so rigid that the girl rebelled by adding a bit of warm water to a cold bath.

The creature of this comfortlessness later described herself as "a solemn child, without beauty. I seemed like a little old woman entirely lacking in the spontaneous joy and mirth of youth." As a cousin put it, "It was the grimmest childhood I had ever known."

Yet, out of this, Eleanor Roosevelt became, quite simply, the greatest American woman of the century.

Those of us who paid homage at the centennial of this woman's birth, those of us who admire her, live now in a rampantly psychiatric age. We have the conceit that adult life is predictable to any nursery-school observer. Yet who could have predicted Eleanor, the First Lady of the World?

Today, out baby talk is psychobabble. We hover over our children, filling out psychological checklists, armed with books that presume to tell us how to carefully nurture children to be achievers. We are afraid they'll be bruised. We forget that, finally, each person creates his or her own life.

Surely the battered girl named Eleanor did.

This same psychiatric age, puffed up with the insights of hindsight, has chosen now to analyze Eleanor Roosevelt's public life as "compensation" for private disappointments. It is only part of the truth. Her role as a mother was surely undermined by the dominating mother-in-law who told Eleanor's children, "Your mother only bore you." Her marriage never fully recovered from her husband's affair with Lucy Mercer, or from the gradual drift of two such different personalities. It made sense to search for meaning outside of her family circle.

But Eleanor Roosevelt's greatness didn't come from finding herself. It came from transcending herself. She didn't have a well-adjusted personality. She had character. Her work was not just thwarted love projected onto the world. It was a life lived on principle.

The woman who did not begin her work outside the home until she was nearly forty, and who never held a formal title until she was a widow, was a professional goad, a citizen busybody. Her own enormous energy, inherited from her uncle Teddy, meshed with the moment of tremendous national need, a depression followed by a world war. In the early days of the New Deal, she transformed the job of First Lady into one of advocate, taking up the cause of one beleaguered group after another.

She had two tools for her work. The first was access to a president-husband about whom she once wrote, "He might have been happier with a wife who had been completely uncritical. . . . Nevertheless I think that I sometimes acted as a spur."

The second was the power of her own conscience. It was her sense of duty that sent Eleanor Roosevelt to the mining communities and pockets of Depression poverty. It was her sense of righteousness that forced Eleanor Roosevelt to place her seat between the black and white aisles of a segregated southern conference in 1939. It was her sense of justice that pushed a Declaration of Human Rights through the contentious United Nations in 1948. She couldn't see a problem without asking: "Can't something be done?"

As the most public woman of her era, Eleanor Roosevelt was mercilessly reviled and admired for breaking female traditions. The woman who once opposed suffrage became the most visible model of what women could do in public life.

A hundred years after her birth, we tend to privatize public lives, to see every social critic in terms of his or her personal pain. We turn politics into psychobiography. Our psychiatric scalpel can cut people down below size. Instead of increasing our understanding, we may inhibit it.

"The influence you exert is through your own life and what you've become yourself," wrote this self-made woman. There are times when we forget the weight of will and principle in the midst of our infatuation with "urges" and "motives."

At her memorial service Adlai Stevenson said, "What other single human being has touched and transformed the existence of so many? She walked in the slums . . . of the world, not on a tour of inspection . . . but as one who could not feel contentment when others were hungry." This is a moment to remember not the disappointments, not the sadness, but the power of an idealist.

OCTOBER 1984

THE NEW NANCY REAGAN

DALLAS—Never before in the annals of American history had so many infant vegetables been sacrificed to a political cause. More than 2000 newborn artichokes, zucchini, and asparagus nestled on radicchio leaves beside chicken breasts at the National Federation of Republican Women's lunch.

But when the plates with the baby everythings were cleared, when Joan Rivers had finished her routine, when the prominent Republican women had all been honored, it was time for the specialty of the house. Nancy Reagan stepped up to the mike.

Four years ago, it was hard for Mrs. Reagan to get through a "Hello, thank you, and good-bye." Now, campaigning for her second term of para-office, the First Lady held her security blanket, the 3-by-5 cards, but she was measurably more comfortable in front of a crowd.

Nancy Reagan began by telling the audience about her own private inauguration in January of 1981. As she stood beside her husband, "I caught the eye of a dear friend and knew that both of us were thinking the same thing: Nothing would ever be the same again."

In the beginning, the changes were pretty tough ones. The wife of the president never had a honeymoon with the press. She barely got a one-night stand. If First Ladies bask in reflected glory, they also get singed by the spotlight. The early returns on this First Lady were perfectly dreadful.

What Nancy describes now as her "nesting instinct"—a desire to get her White House life in order—looked a lot like a rich lady's decorating binge. We read about $200,000 of new china, $800,000 of renovations, free designer clothes, and not much else. Nancy took the reviews badly; in fact, she took them to the bathtub where she argued silently with the authors. As she says now, "I wouldn't have wanted to know that person they were writing about."

It's hard to pinpoint the moment Nancy Reagan's image started to improve. It's harder to know whether it's her image or her identity that's been changing. At some point, said a friend, "she stopped crying and started to cope." She began to show some humor. At the memorable Gridiron dinner, she came before the startled Washington press corps in tatters singing "Second-Hand Rose."

But the most important changes are substantive ones. Nancy Reagan has become less associated with Beverly Hills and more associated with an antidrug campaign. She has gone from donating her designer clothes to museums to donating her time in a campaign against addiction. The credits to her name are now on TV programs like "The Chemical People."

Part of the responsibility for the new Nancy has to go to Sheila Tate, her former press secretary, who professionally denies any major role. The country-club image was not exactly a political plus for the president, but, says Tate, "The idea that something was conjured up to help her husband is absolutely wrong."

What is absolutely right is that the position of First Lady sat there like a shoe or a seat waiting to be filled. Mrs. Reagan, a self-described worrier, is a fiercely protective wife of the president. The private role is legitimate, but so are the public expectations. As Tate reads it, "The day of a First Lady sitting home and cooking for her husband is over."

Today there is an amorphous but obvious pressure on First Ladies to become active—careful and, heaven help us, noncontroversial, but active. There is also something seductive about the power of this place. When a First Lady discovers what she can accomplish with a name and title, it changes her. With due apologies for the drug language, the power is addictive.

To this day, Ronald Reagan's wife draws mixed reviews and mixed emotions. The Nancy film played to the hall at the Republican Convention was positively cloying. The waving from Nancy on the podium to Ron on the giant videoscreen behind her drew laughter across the press work space.

In fairness though, feelings about First Ladies from Dolley Madison to Eleanor Roosevelt to Rosalynn Carter, are almost always mixed. We don't elect them, we don't pay them. We don't have a job description, but we have opinions about them. We even poll those opinions.

It's not without reason that Nancy Reagan still feels, "It would be nice to have a private life and not always feel like you're a punching bag." But watching her performance in these three years, it occurred to me that it isn't just presidents who can grow in office.

AUGUST 1984

MAUREEN REAGAN AND THE LOYAL OPPOSITION

WASHINGTON—Ensconced in her Capitol Hill office at Republican party headquarters, the president's daughter still seems nostalgic for the good old bipartisan days on the women's rights trail.

Back in 1977, Maureen Reagan remembers, she and Judy Carter were fellow travelers for the ERA. She still recalls the day when the leader of the Nevada Senate chamber "stood up and said, and I quote, 'It is my job to protect women who want to do the role for which God intended them. It is not my responsibility to help those women who want to go out and live in a man's world.'" The two of them, a Reagan and a Carter, were equally appalled.

"For years we [Democratic and Republican women] sat in the same rooms where if we'd ever gotten off the subject of women's rights, we would have killed each other," she says with her boisterous laugh. Then she adds, "What I am saying to you is that five years ago when 'A Woman' was appointed to the Cabinet we helped break out the champagne. There is no more of that bipartisanship."

Reagan, who is by blood and inclinations a highly political creature, isn't entirely surprised by the way that women and women's issues have become politicized. Both parties want their votes and allegiance. Women who come together for some issues may split on other ideological lines.

But what angers her is that the Democrats have tried to

put an armlock on women's issues. "The idea that only Democrats have answers, that only Democrats care, is ludicrous. If Democrats cared, we'd have gotten a whole lot more in the last fifty years then we've gotten," she says loudly and pointedly.

As a loyal daughter, feminist, and Republican, this energetic forty-two-year-old Californian ardently disputes the notion that women's rights activists were actually expelled by her party or her president. "My father," she protests more than once, "is not the problem." As for the Republicans, she counters, what about the Democrats?

In this frame of mind, Maureen Reagan has the formidable task of trying to make women's rights a bipartisan issue again. She is working for women candidates within the party and for the party with women voters.

You might call Maureen Reagan the Republican assigned to close the gender gap, but she prefers this description: "My job is to create a support mechanism for the Republican women candidates and officeholders within this party and to bring about a better dialogue with women."

A "support mechanism" includes getting party money and backing for women candidates. In the 1982 election, for example, Republicans Millicent Fenwick and Margaret Heckler lost the endorsement of women's rights groups to male Democrats. This year, Reagan hopes that a strong network of Republican women caucuses and councils in the states will be on hand—"women who can stand up at a press conference and say that we too are the women's movement and this is our choice; we won't get blind-sided."

At the same time, this president's daughter wants to encourage Republican women to follow her lead in loyal opposition: "What our women have to understand is that it is okay to not always agree. It's okay to not always agree with each other and it's okay to not always agree with the men and it's okay to not always agree with everything that our party does. You are allowed to say 'I'm for the Equal Rights Amendment and I'm a Republican.'" After all, she does it all the time.

Much of what this politically savvy lady says makes a good deal of sense. At the same time, she can sound wildly uncritical of her father. She defends the president's record on women, even the decision that replaced Mary Louise Smith and Jill Ruckelshaus on the Civil Rights Commission. She refutes the notion that his views of the fair sex are out of date. Indeed her only open criticism is that he is "sometimes a little too gentle, if you want my honest opinion."

But her main point is a solid one: "What we have to make sure is that the women's movement does not take itself out of the vote market, that no matter who is elected and no matter what side holds the policy position, there is advancement, however much, in every four-, five-, eight-, ten-year period for women."

In a two-party system, women can't afford to default on the Republicans. Women's rights can't become a totally partisan issue. The First Daughter is right about this. But why do I get the feeling that there's a gender gap between Maureen and her dad?

JANUARY 1984

DAVID AND THE KENNEDY CURSE

BOSTON—The news came over the wire in the early afternoon in April 1984. Twenty-eight-year-old David Kennedy was found dead in a motel room in Palm Beach. He hadn't made the plane home to Boston and a "Mrs. Kennedy" had called the motel to check. The secretary found him lying on the floor between two beds.

There was hardly time to shake a head, hardly time to say "What a shame" before the analyses started pouring in over the wires and airwaves. The word "troubled" was affixed to his name like a title. He was the "troubled son" of Robert Kennedy. He was the troubled son who had been deeply into drugs. He was the troubled son who was once mugged at a "bad-rep" hotel in New York, the troubled son who'd been hospitalized with a heart infection that can, they say, be related to drugs.

By the evening, everyone I met was speculating freely about why David Kennedy had gone down the tubes. It was because of problems without his father, problems with his mother, problems with his name.

Indeed the story that seemed to stick was as simple as a documelodrama. David's life had been saved the afternoon of June 5, 1968, when his father pulled him out of the surf. Later that night the twelve-year-old boy had watched him shot on TV. "David Kennedy," said a late-night commentator, "died the day his father died."

With the special alchemy that turns every private tragedy of the Kennedys into public drama, a new act was inserted into the national passion play. This was the "Kennedy Curse, Part 10, The Next Generation."

Well, forgive me if I don't tell you "What happened to David Kennedy," because I don't know. I don't believe that someone's life can be boiled down to a parable or a phrase. I'm not sure that it's truly finally "knowable."

We can follow clues to a conclusion. We can weave a tale from whatever threads are available in order to make, literally make, sense. But it's only partial sense. Until the day before David Kennedy died there were at least two story lines to follow. One that traced his own struggle for recovery, the other that ended on the motel floor.

If David Kennedy was a member of a clan, he was also an individual. If the traumas of his life were more profound than many and more public than any, we can't file away his life under the title "troubled" and under the curse marked "Kennedy."

I suspect that we analyze troubles in order to separate Them from Us and Ours. We look for a reason, a nice solitary reason for their disasters, one that could never happen to us. It's our safekeeping.

But no amount of explanation can solve what is essentially a mystery: the way in which one particular human being deals with one life. There were eleven children born to Ethel and Bob Kennedy. The Kennedy cousins number twenty-nine. They include cousins who have been in trouble with drugs and driving, cousins who are lawyers and broadcasters and students, cousins who work with the handicapped, the poor, the abused.

David's father was killed but so was sister Kathleen's, and she lives, practices law, and mothers. David suffered a horrendous loss, but so did cousin Ted when he gave a leg to cancer. David experimented with drugs, but what of others in and out of the family who were not trapped the same way?

I don't dismiss this Kennedy's pain; it was monumental. But if we could figure out what makes one kid survive and another go under, I swear I would bottle it and hand it out to every parent who ever stood at a grave or a drug clinic or a psychiatric ward.

David Kennedy himself described 1970 as "the point in my life when everything began to turn against me." He was fifteen that year. Anyone with kids in that earthquake stage of life knows where the fault lines are. Many of our kids are shaken at one time or another. Some of them are more fragile than others. Some of them have stronger foundations. But there is no single Richter scale to measure the effect.

The Kennedys seemed more sad than surprised by David's death. It was clearly the end of a long, long road for all of them. But neither they nor we can really fathom the way one psyche is shattered or strengthened by life. We cannot psychoanalyze this mystery, and file it far, far away from us under the heading, "Kennedy."

This twenty-eight-year-old was not finally a troubled son, a member of a clan, a victim of a curse. He was a soul who got lost. And that seems like an occasion for less analysis and more comfort.

MAY 1984

PAUL TSONGAS: COMING HOME

BOSTON—I met Paul Tsongas once on a late-afternoon flight from Washington to Boston. The senator from Massachusetts was traveling light that day. No bags, no briefcase, no aides. All he had with him was a daughter.

It was rare enough to see a man alone on a plane with a preschool child. But Tsongas' reason was even more unusual. He was going to Boston for a meeting and he wanted to spend some time with his middle daughter. So he was taking her along for the ride. Together they would get the late plane back.

I've thought about that scene a dozen times, with mixed feelings of admiration and poignancy. Here was a father struggling with the demands of work and family. Here was a father who had to capture minutes with his child, on the fly, at 35,000 feet.

This scene, repeated over and again in Tsongas' life, seems somehow symbolic of a whole generation of men and women: parents with schedule books. It is barely even a parody of the way many of us cram work and children into calendars that won't expand to fill the needs, into lives that cry out for more hours. Tsongas was one of us, trying to make it all fit together.

But in October 1983, the senator and father of three young girls discovered something that wasn't on his agenda. He had a tumor that was "not benign."

The mild lymphoma that Tsongas has is not life-threatening in the immediate sense. The statistical average life expectancy for those with this disease, as he related it, is eight years and he is planning for more. Many of his political colleagues are given shorter sentences by the actuarial tables.

But Tsongas decided not to run again. He is coming home to Lowell, Massachusetts, and home to his family in a way that politics doesn't allow.

Until that moment of diagnosis, Tsongas, like most of us, had carried his ambivalence through his political career the way he carried his child between cities that winter afternoon. Tsongas never forgot the older colleague who stopped by his table when he was a freshman congressman and said, "Let me tell you one thing. I was in your shoes. I was here and I really devoted myself to my job and I ignored my kids and they grew up and I never knew them. It makes me very sad. Whatever you do, don't do that."

When a New York reporter asked him his major accomplishment as a senator, he said spontaneously, "Keeping my family together." As his wife, Nikki Tsongas, a former social worker and law student, campaign partner, and now full-time parent, said: "What is the point of a life that is professionally successful if twenty years from now you have unhappy children who can't cope?"

He had to hear the words "not benign" to finally focus on priorities, on mortality, time itself. "I used to ache when I had to leave them," said the senator. "Now that won't be a problem. The illness forced me to do thinking that would not have taken place."

What of the rest of us who suffer, as the senator did, from midlife bulge, the years of small children, and big career plans? Tsongas lived at the outer edge of ambition and expectations where it's harder to keep any sort of juggling act in shape.

But there are times when we all end up completing a day or a week or a month as if it were a task to be crossed off the list with a sigh. In the effort to make it all work, it can become all work. We become one-minute managers, mothers, husbands. We end up spending our time on the fly.

"If you care about your children and you care about your job and you take it very seriously, something gives eventually," said the senator. Sometimes, what gives is pleasure. Not all of us are forced to confront our own deadlines, the reality that we are, as Tsongas put it, "all terminal."

It's not that we should all live urgently under some threat of execution. It's not that we should go home and play chutes and ladders with our children for forty-eight hours. But it's worth paying attention from time to time to the way we drift, function, fill time, spend time, lose time.

Tsongas now talks about eight years or more. In eight years, a newborn becomes a third-grader, a first-grader becomes an adolescent, a ten-year-old becomes a voter. In an inattentive life that takes time for granted, those eight years can slip down as easily as Jell-O.

By early 1985, Nikki Tsongas was back in law school and Paul in a new job. Their lives have slowed to the normal hectic level of the average two-career family. The peculiar thing is that they've gained some real time.

JANUARY 1984

MARGARET MEAD: DEBUNKING
THE FOUNDING MOTHER

WASHINGTON—There have been moments this spring [1983] when I thought we were all the jurors in an intellectual custody suit over Samoa. Every week someone else took the media witness stand to testify on behalf of either Margaret Mead's description of the island culture or Derek Freeman's vision.

The apparent issue—if you have been off on a tropical island—has been which anthropologist portrayed the real Samoa. Was it Margaret Mead, who in 1925 saw a culture that was relatively peaceful with a guilt-free love under the palms? Was it Derek Freeman, who in the 1940s and 1960s saw a culture obsessed with virginity and rife with rape? Is it any wonder that an exasperated prime minister of Samoa said this week, "To be frank, I think that both anthropologists were all wrong."

Having now waded my way through Mead's original *Coming of Age in Samoa* and Freeman's recent *Margaret Mead and Samoa*, I have a somewhat different view of the controversy. This is not a custody suit over Samoa. It's a case of arrested rebellion.

Derek Freeman has become the Gary Crosby or the Christina Crawford of the anthropological family.

It was daughter Christina who first told us that behind Joan lurked a Mommie Dearest. It is son Gary traveling about the country explaining how Great Guy Bing called him Bucket Britches and drove his mommy to drink. Now Derek Freeman is on the media circuit stating that the Founding Mother of modern anthropology was the dupe of a bunch of adolescent girls who lied to her about their sex lives.

Like the other descendants of superstars, Freeman is the master of the posthumous attack. Neither Joan nor Bing nor Margaret is around for a good solid "other side of the story." At no point in his book does Freeman explain why he waited so long to publish research done in the 1940s and 1960s.

It's not that Freeman's critique of Mead's early work is entirely wrong. It's been clear for decades that Mead's work was limited by poor knowledge of the Samoan language, by the relatively short length of her visit, and by her inexperience. She was young and so was her profession. Others, particularly Brad Shore of Emory University, have disagreed with her before. Their work was an advance on Mead's, not a repudiation.

But Freeman is also limited by his sources, and surely his prejudices. There is no proof, for example, that Mead was duped. As anthropology associate professor Michael Lieber of the University of Illinois has noted, "Mead's conclusions were based on her observations of adolescent girls, Freeman's on his close association with the Samoan male power hierarchy. If a foreigner asked American high-school girls to described America, he'd get a different picture from what corporate executives would present. This is the essence of the Mead-Freeman controversy."

As spring and the arguments wear on, Freeman's research is being contradicted point by point, article by article. But the tone of the book is more offensive than the details. It is just one academic shade short of nasty, full of the muckraker's delight in portraying Mead as a fraud, and more than a little patronizing.

He suggests among other things that Mead was also the pawn of her professor, sent out to prove his theory. This attack prompted even Mead's first husband, anthropologist L. S. Cressman, to rise to her defense in a moving letter, calling this "utter nonsense."

"If Margaret, in going to Samoa, wanted to prove some preconceived idea, it certainly was not the nature of adolescence in a Samoan village ... but that a woman, she, Margaret Mead, could be a professional anthropological field-worker as well as any man."

Freeman poses as a brave man willing to take on the Mead Myth for the sake of truth. Gary Crosby has said the same thing. But in fact there's nothing brave about it. The public loves a good unmasking.

What is behind all this is not an intellectual argument about Samoa or even human behavior, unless it's our own human behavior. There's a touch too much glee in watching people whack the great off their pedestals.

There's an added glee, I fear, when the towering figure is a woman. After one lengthy article on the controversy, Mead's daughter, Amherst College anthropologist Mary Catherine Bateson, noted that *The New York Times* had referred to "Professor" Freeman and "Miss" Mead.

Indeed Professor Bateson was one of her mother's greatest defenders that spring. Margaret Mead was at least lucky with her real child. Too bad about Bing.

MAY 1983

SALLY RIDE: ANOTHER FIRST WOMAN

BOSTON—It is Day Five for the First Woman and all is well in space and in print. This mission is under control but, more surprisingly, the media are under self-control.

To the best of my knowledge, there has not yet been a single headline about "Sally Ride, Girl Astronette." Nor have I seen a story about the spatial primping of our li'l gal Sal.

Twenty years ago, when Valentina Tereshkova went into space, she was followed by an appalling trail of words. The Russians' "smiling cosmonette" and "dimpled space sister" had "her feminine curves hidden in a clumsy space suit" although "the muscle she displays in a bathing suit would be the envy of many males." You get the idea.

Ride, in turn, suffered through some dismal chauvinistic foreplay before she went up in the Challenger. Johnny Carson quipped that the launch was being postponed until Sally could find the purse to match her shoes. A *Time* magazine writer asked if she wept when things went wrong. Assorted others inquired about her reproductive organs, her underwear, and her maternity plans.

We were even treated to the information that NASA had installed a candy-striped privacy curtain around the toilet, thus fulfilling every fantasy about equal rights and unisex bathrooms.

By lift-off, however, the media were just about as (1)

tamed, (2) repressed, or (3) enlightened as we could have hoped. Indeed, it was Sally Ride's name which seemed to provide more twists, puns, and plays on words for the headline writers than her sex. To wit: "Ride, Sally Ride," "Sally Rides High," and "Sally's Joy Ride."

Still, what we are witnessing is a classic case of First Womanitis, a social disease that comes with prolonged exposure to the spotlight. Sally Ride, First American Woman in Space, is taking this trip right into history while her male companions are destined for the trivia shows. ("For ten thousand dollars and a complete dinette set, name one of the four astronauts who flew with Sally Ride.")

She is also, willy-nilly, like it or not, joining a large sorority whose ranks include Elizabeth Blackwell, the first woman to be graduated from an American medical school in 1849, and Ruth Wilson, the first woman hired as a street cleaner by the Philadelphia Sanitation Department in 1976. Its membership numbers every woman who ever entered a mine or a boardroom or a courtroom where none had been admitted before.

When all is said and done, Sally Ride is just another First Woman.

Ride is luckier than any of the others in this sorority. People are rooting for her, rather than against her. But the initation rites are by now familiar.

As a First Woman, she is watched and called upon to explain her very existence in a way that her co-travelers are not. She is asked opinions on everything "female"—from fashion to feminism—and everyone offers opinions about her from her fashions to her feminism.

Nearly all of the select have felt this glare of extraordinariness, even in their more earthly pursuits. Nearly all of them have sighed, at some moment, as Ride did, "It may be too bad that our society isn't further along and that this is such a big deal."

But most First Women share something else: a special conflict. There is the desire to be accepted as a self-made woman, a person who was and is judged on individual merit. There is the realization that each carries a load of other women's frustrations and hopes.

First Women bear a special responsibility to those who didn't come before them and those who may—or may not—come later. It comes with the title.

Sally Ride's résumé makes Neil Armstrong look like an underachiever. At times she would prefer to be just one of the crew, but she, too, has taken an extra load into space.

Ride has borne the disappointments of women such as those would-be astronauts of 1961, the dozen whose space futures were canceled out because "the times" were not ripe. She has also taken on the hopes of a generation of young girls in search of heroines. I don't know if there are special ways in which this unique sorority handles pressure and attention, but maybe Ride is typical of the survivors. When it all gets to be too much, she flips "the switch marked 'oblivious.'" Maybe First Women wear that switch like a sorority pin.

In any case, Ride is now initiated. She's learned the rules. Being a full-fledged First Woman means carrying your self as a second job. Being a First Woman means taking every step for womankind. It's not easy, but the company is fine.

JUNE 1983

THE "MORAL TURPITUDE" OF VANESSA WILLIAMS

BOSTON—It's been years since I was able to work up a snit over the Miss America Pageant. The pageant has faded in that gentle world of camp where the tiara is worn by The Divine Miss M.

At a moment when a woman can be a Supreme Court justice, an astronaut, or vice president, it isn't as troublesome to see one make it on her measurements instead of her credentials. Just a bit silly.

But the sad and seamy saga of Vanessa Williams' abdication did a good deal to refresh my memory. This elaborate commercial venture called the Miss America Pageant is perhaps the last vestige, the social appendix of an era when women had only one virtue to sell: sexual promise titillated by purity.

The Miss America Pageant, for much of its sixty-four years, drew a line that was much more narrow than the runway in Atlantic City. It was an arbiter of what Nice Girls do and don't do, of what is wholesome and what is not.

A contestant had to be an exhibitionist to parade her body in bathing suit and high heels before an audience that rated her. But at the same time, she had to have the aura of modesty. Exposed except for the distance from chest to thigh she was a model of look-but-don't-touch sensuality.

"Miss" America was, in short, a virginal sex object, available but innocent, alluring but inexperienced. This scrubbed-up sexuality wasn't an easy role to perform. It took a Doris Day to do it on the screen.

Those women who grew up in the fifties, trying to find a safety zone in the triangle between the images of tease, or prude, or slut, remember all this. Every piece of behavior, every piece of clothing, was a potential trap. You had to grow up learning the rules, like some elaborate code of chivalry that could only be absorbed through years of apprenticeship. The distance between pedestal and pornography was never that far.

The times have changed more than Miss America, but the rules are still as vague as the words in Williams' contract—"moral turpitude." In 1968, sponsors almost booted Miss Iowa for go-go dancing. In 1983, Debra Sue Maffett was criticized as impure after reports of plastic surgery on chin, nose, and breasts. In 1984, eighteen inches of bathing suit stripped Vanessa Williams of her title. So, much more graphically, did the photos of her and another woman making love instead of history.

It has often been a matter of inches—ankles, knees, cleavage—that make for mortal turpitude in the beauty-queen world. Had her body been photographed for "art," had she and another woman shown up in silhouette instead of full relief, in *Vogue* instead of *Penthouse*, she might still have her crown.

If Vanessa Williams has been honest with us, she was indeed an innocent. At nineteen, she did what the photographer told her to do, and then believed that he would keep those pictures private. Photographers don't take pictures for their files. As a former associate said about this charming fellow, "He is very, very greedy."

This was one hour in her life. The very best interpretation is that she displayed naiveté along with her body, or a passive willingness to perform. She attributes it to curiosity and the sort of terminal trust that makes women malleable in the hands of photographers or pageanteers: Do with me as you will. The worst interpretation is that she was all too eager for exhibition.

In the fall of 1983, Miss Williams told a reporter fervently, "I am more than a piece of good-looking meat on a stage." But Pageant and *Penthouse* are both in the flesh biz. A beauty contest displays a woman solely as a body; a pornographer subdivides that body into its parts. Both make their subject into an object, both offer her up for the pleasure of the devouring public. It was with great joy that *Penthouse* publisher Bob Guccione transformed Williams from beauty queen to porno queen.

Abdication was inevitable. There is no way for this young woman to go on making personal appearances without being harassed at every stop. There is no way to speak with pride when your privacy has been violated and your private parts have been exposed to five million magazine readers.

Vanessa Williams made at least two mistakes: posing for the photographer and posing for the pageant. She lost the balance you need to wear this commercial crown. But let he who has never turned a *Playboy* magazine to the centerfold cast the first stone.

JULY 1984

JIGGLING WITH GEORGE GILDER

BOSTON—I met George Gilder before he had become the author most in demand by the supply-siders, before *Wealth and Poverty* had hit the best-seller lists.

In those days, David Stockman was an ex-divinity student. Ronald Reagan was an ex-governor and George was a bachelor.

This last fact was not, I hasten to add, extraneous. George had just finished a dreadful little book called *Naked Nomads*, a postscript to *Sexual Suicide* in which he set out to prove how miserable single men were. They were prone to everything from poverty to pornography, psychosis to syphilis. Those who were not violent to others were likely to inflict violence on themselves.

What I remember most about our interview was that George arrived wounded. He had cut his unwed chin while shaving. As he talked about the self-destructiveness of single men, a small piece of tissue kept jiggling ominously along his wound.

George was ardent in his belief that women should devote their lives to rescuing poor, needful men. Jiggle, jiggle. He maintained that if only women would stop being so damnably independent and would follow nature—see Lionel Tiger—all would be right with the world. Jiggle, jiggle.

Frankly, I thought Gilder was a bit dippy. By then, as I recall, I'd already heard the stories. Heard about his uncanny ability to lose overcoats. Heard about the time he'd driven to Philadelphia to see a track meet, flown back to Boston, and gone looking for his car.

It never passed through my mind that he would become a darling of presidents. I mean, who would trust the economic philosophy of a man who can't keep track of his overcoat?

But I must be kind about this. I chauvinistically assumed that Bachelor George would do what he said all men do: straighten out as soon as he got married.

However, here he is six years, one wife, and two children later, and lordy, the man is still at it. Once again in his book about hope, faith, charity, and the capitalist system, he bases his beliefs on some mysterious, mystical sexual powers.

"Civilized society is dependent upon the submission of the short-term sexuality of young men to the extended maternal horizons of women," he writes.

This time, capitalism, as well as mental health and crime prevention, rest on the ability of a woman to get her man and keep his nose to the grindstone. "This is what happens in a monogamous marriage: The man disciplines his sexuality and extends it into the future through the womb of a woman. The woman gives him access to his children, otherwise forever denied him; and he gives her the product of his labor, otherwise dissipated on temporary pleasures. The woman gives him a unique link to the future and a vision of it; he gives her faithfulness and a commitment to a lifetime of hard work."

Gilder identifies the enemies of this blissful romantic-capitalistic union as (1) women who allow sex without marriage, (2) working wives, (3) women with independent means, (4) government programs which in any way support (1), (2), or (3).

The basic point about family and the economy is that a man needs a thoroughly dependent wife and needful children to become a dependable, upwardly mobile worker. The woman (or government) who undercuts the male role as provider merely produces another naked nomad, as the capitalist system goes kapooey.

Jiggle, jiggle.

Gilder is blissfully unconcerned about what happens to the dependent wife and children when a man's nose is not permanently attached to the grindstone, or when it is not permanently attached to a wife. He's blissfully unconcerned about women who are not wives and mothers.

Under his plan for fun and profit, the only decent thing for a women to harbor is a fund of trust for her man, rather than, say, a trust fund. Under his plan a woman is supposed to provide, rather than to have, a meaning for life.

All this would be amusing, in a dippy sort of way, except for the fact that Gilder's mystical philosophy has been officially dubbed "Promethean in power and insight" by David Stockman. The ideas underlie the budget plans of the former divinity student and the former governor.

It is no accident that the Reagan cuts are aimed at any programs—welfare, child nutrition, food stamps—that would "undermine the motivation of men" by helping women and children. It was all in the works years ago, in the mind of the man with the tissue on his chinny, chin, chin.

MAY 1981

RAISA GORBACHEV: FIRST WIFE OF THE SOVIET UNION

BOSTON—On the whole, Moscow watchers in this country are a lot like their comrades at the Audubon Society. They need a trained eye and a lot of patience to see anything new. Even then, they don't always get what they are looking for.

This has been a week when the watchers kept their binoculars handy. The third Soviet leader in twenty-eight months died; the fourth, Mikhail Gorbachev, ascended, full of fifty-four-year-old "youth and vigor."

But the true event of this Soviet season was the early and scattered sighting of The Wife. For the first time in modern memory, we have this rara avis: The Wife of the Soviet leader. Her name is Raisa, and she was shown not once, not twice, but three times on a network news announcement of her husband's new job.

Of course, Raisa Gorbachev is not the first wife in Soviet leader history. Stalin had one. Brezhnev had one. Andropov had one. So did Chernenko. If, however, you can remember the name of any one of these women, you may move six spaces ahead on the Trivial Pursuit board.

The wives of the top Soviets have been as camera shy as a coppery-tailed trogon. No one was sure that Andropov's wife was even alive until she was seen at his funeral. If the Mesdames Brezhnev, Andropov, and Chernenko were put in a police lineup, and the average Soviet citizen had to match the names and faces "or else," there would be a lot of "or else" around.

The stereotype of a Soviet leader is a man in a heavy overcoat, a fur hat, and no visible neck because he donated it to the war effort. The stereotype of a Soviet woman is one who poses for the socialist realism pinup calendar in basic black.

But Mikhail's wife Raisa was dubiously dubbed "Bo Derek of the Steppes," by the British press. She is said to be a fifty-one-year-old professor at Moscow University, a mother of two, and a grandmother of one. Her plumage was what won Western attention, especially during her December flight to Britain.

The *Daily Mirror* said of Raisa, "What a chic lady is Mrs. Gorbachev. And what a contrast to the previous glimpses of other senior Russian wives . . . who looked as though they should be building dams in Siberia." The media covered Raisa from her gold-lame sandals to her short and curly brown hair. The *Daily Mail* even labeled the Gorbachevs "The Gucci Couple." The implication was that as a duo they would charm détente back to life.

I confess to being amused by international public relations. There is nothing that the Western world finds quite so reassuring as when the socialist world behaves like us.

When a beauty contest is held in Canton, it's proof of a warming trend. When the Soviet Union shows off a First Lady, it might as well be a heat wave.

It is not unusual for Americans, like the Britons, to pick the Western portents out of the Soviet life-style. Our nightly news features a Moscow aerobics class or a rock-music craze as proof of the popularity of things American. One book after another on the USSR details the Soviet passion for goods. They document the ordeal of a citizen who wants to buy a tomato in Leningrad in March or a car in Minsk in 1985.

We do it reflexively, the same way the Soviets keep publishing pictures of street people sleeping on grates in

New York City. It is the true, but incomplete, information that reinforces our sense of superiority. It's rather like finding out that Stalin liked jazz or the early reports that Andropov played tennis and listened to Glenn Miller.

The irony, I suppose, is that many Americans think the ultimate attraction of this democracy isn't free speech or elections. It's style, it's shopping. There is the quintessential scene in *Moscow on the Hudson* when a Russian on tour in America impulsively defects in the middle of Bloomingdale's. He is converted by shopping. At some deep level, many Americans believe that the Soviets can also be converted by the lure of commercial goods.

There is a comforting subtext to all the stories on creeping Westernization. Americans presume that given time and the choice, the citizens of the socialist world will inevitably become just like us: a people with a supermarket. This is probably as true and as false as the communist belief that if people keep sleeping on grates, class warfare is inevitable.

What, then, of the newest Soviet version (dare I say imitation?) of Western "life-style," the political wife? Any patient, experienced Moscow-watcher worth a pair of binoculars knows that answer. The first Raisa has been spotted. It takes more than one to make a thaw.

MARCH 1985

Part 3

THE REAGAN YEARS

SAY GOOD-BYE TO SELF-DOUBT

BOSTON—The era of self-doubt is over.

The president proclaimed this historic moment in a speech last week to the graduating class at West Point. As a footnote to the times, he added that we also have stopped looking at our warts.

Well, I don't know about the rest of you, but I have been waiting all weekend for a sense of relief to flood through my weary veins. After all, I can now say bye-bye to the birdie of self-doubt and so long to the warts of worry.

But to be perfectly frank, it isn't working out. I find myself worrying about people who do not worry, and having acute doubts about those who have no self-doubt.

It's not that I'm surprised by the president's announcement. He is not a man plagued by introspection. In many ways, his charm, his sense of ease in the world, appear to come from a remarkable lack of inner conflict.

I am not sure how people get to his age without experiencing turmoil, but there is something reassuring about his manner. He has the capacity to say even the most frightening things in the calmest way.

At West Point, for example, he injected gallons of personal warmth into Cold War words. The mix always seems a rather pleasant lukewarm. At other times he reminds me of the old poster: If you are keeping your head while all about you are losing theirs, maybe you don't realize the seriousness of the situation.

It's not that I totally disagree with the president. Excessive self-doubt, the inner dialogue that criticizes and judges every possible action, can be paralyzing. It can make any person or any country impotent and depressed.

But there is a whole lot of room between Hamlet and Haig.

Reagan told the cadets that he had lived through three major American wars. He knows, then, that there is no one more sure of his right, his purpose, his patriotism than the aggressor. He must know that the human race has gotten into a lot more trouble because of certainty than uncertainty.

Even the excesses of the 1960s—that era Reagan still looks back on with distaste—were not brought on by wallowing self-doubters, but by people of utter, even blind, self-confidence. As for the "Vietnam syndrome" Reagan described, the cause was our initial arrogance, not our belated anxiety.

Today, of course, doubt is unpopular at home as well as abroad. The reemergence of authoritarian religion, politics, and pseudoscience is a kind of personal testimony to the difficulty and distress that come with ambiguity, contradictions, complexity.

It is much easier to believe than to discover, easier to take leaps of faith than make excavations into truth, easier to be told than to choose.

With relief, some people give up the quest to understand, to criticize, to figure out what is right and wrong. If you do not believe that, think about how easily we rationalize injustice.

So I don't share the president's low opinion of self-doubt, because it ultimately is the best goad to creativity.

In one of Rollo May's smaller books, *The Courage to*

Create, he explored the relationship between doubt and creativity. Utter conviction, he wrote, "blocks off the user for learning new truth. . . ."

The most creative people neither ignore doubt nor are paralyzed by it. They explore it, admit it, and act despite it. As May wrote, "Commitment is healthiest when it is not without doubt but in spite of it.

"It is infinitely safer to know that the man at the top has his doubts, as you and I have ours, yet has the courage to move ahead in spite of these doubts."

In his speech, Reagan was talking about patriotism. "We've stopped looking at our warts and rediscovered how much there is to love in this blessed land." He described a choice: Either we look or we love, either we criticize or we praise.

But I don't accept these old "America: Love it or leave it" choices. Reagan was right, "There is a . . . hunger on the part of the people to once again be proud of America, all that it is and all that it can be."

The hunger comes from self-doubt, from wart worrying. It can be nourished with change. But the notion that it can be fed with denial, satisfied with rhetoric about our perfection, is . . . doubtful.

JUNE 1981

MARRYING FOR MONEY

BOSTON—For those of you who have been worrying about how to succeed under Reaganomics, there is boffo news from the Big Apple.

There in the heart of capitalism, a few hardy, brave entrepreneurs are teaching the one true way for the average working girl or boy to still make it big, yes, even in today's bleak business world.

For a mere $21 investment, more than 200 souls are spending an occasional Wednesday night in a school gymnasium in Manhattan's West Side learning how to realize the updated American dream. They are taking an adult education course called "How to Marry Money."

What is so marvelous, so wonderfully refreshing about this educational endeavor so few miles from Wall Street, is that at long last someone has discovered and is willing to share the secret of making it in the Reagan era. People no longer teach how to follow Horatio Alger's route to the top; they teach how to meet Horatio now that he's up there.

Marrying for Money has the symbolic course (of action) for the eighties.

To begin with, there is the perfect teacher. Who could be more appropriate for this class than a woman who earned a master's degree in social work in 1973?

Today, social work is the auto industry of the professional world. As the antipoverty programs of the seventies turn into the antipoor programs of the eighties, a lot of us have wondered what on earth would become of the social workers without a society to work in. Joanna Steichen, the "professor" of How to Marry Money, is a role model in the recycling effort. By just a slight change of perspective, this soul has landed a teaching job—no mean feat in itself—and a job that gives hope to the hopeless.

Of course, the whole class works only because greed has finally come out of the closet. Not long ago, people would have been too embarrassed to actually sign their own names at the registration desk.

Now the motto of the day is "My Money is O.K., Your Money is O.K.," and spouse shopping seems no more outrageous than mortgage shopping. As a female computer consultant and student told a reporter in the classroom: "I'm here because of plain old greed. . . . I can't think of a better hedge against inflation than money."

There is a woman after your own pocketbook.

This is not just an isolated event, a single class, I am sure. Marrying "up" fits the new Reaganomics too perfectly not to catch on. This is the ultimate financial-planning program. Moreover, it takes place exclusively in the private sector and depends solely on private enterprise. It is even, you might say, a volunteer self-help effort.

A highly practical economic idea, it isn't mucked up with all sorts of liberal emotionalism. And it has a certain traditional support. Who, after all, can forget the grandmotherly advice of past centuries: "It's just as easy to fall in love with a rich man as a poor man"?

But what is most important about this pilot program is that it offers the only possible method left under Reaganomics for the redistribution of wealth. If you can't tax 'em, marry 'em. It is clearly in the public interest to support the intermarriage of classes . . . as often as possible.

If a graduate of How to Marry Money meets one of the

Fortune 500, we can only approve their marriage. If they argue, we can only applaud their divorce, preferably in a community property state.

Having thus halved their wealth, with any luck each will meet other members of the lower classes and start all over again, until the Fortune 500 are the fortunate 50,000.

There are, of course, some flaws with this brilliant solution to the economic woes of the average American. Premarital agreements, for example. And love. The rich, you see, can still afford to marry for love. All too often, they have unpatriotically chosen to fall in love with each other.

But not to worry. We are all rooting for a stronger America. Surely even the rich realize that the only place money really trickles down is over the sacrificial altar.

FEBRUARY 1982

NUCLEAR FOLLIES: I

BOSTON—In case of a nuclear warning, according to my handy civil-defense booklet, I am to calmly pack my car with a list of essential items, including extra socks, a plastic drop cloth, shaving articles, and my credit card.

Thus supplied against the worst, I am to drive in a leisurely way to my designated "host community," Laconia, New Hampshire, where the people will be eagerly awaiting my arrival along with the rest of the fleeing urban hordes.

Together with the citizens of Laconia (presuming they have not also chosen "The Relocation Option" and driven leisurely with their credit cards to Canada), I shall build a new shelter or share the already well-stocked "pre-planned snack-bar shelter" of my hosts.

If, despite all of this protection, some of us in the snack-bar shelter suffer from radiation sickness, I need not worry. All I have to do is follow the first-aid hints: "If the patient has headache or general discomfort, give him one or two aspirins every 3 or 4 hours (half a tablet for a child under 12)."

I share all of this information in a public-spirited way in order that you, too, may feel comforted in the knowledge that your government is worried about public safety in this, the hazardous nuclear age.

As T. K. Jones, deputy undersecretary of defense for strategic and theater nuclear forces, told Bob Scheer of the *Los Angeles Times*, "Everybody's going to make it, if there are enough shovels to go around. . . . Dig a hole, cover it with a couple of doors and then throw three feet of dirt on top. It's the dirt that does it." There you go; nothing to it.

When I first began leafing through my booklets from the Federal Emergency Management Agency (FEMA) and "camera-ready newspaper columns," I couldn't decide whether to giggle or shiver. The calm, chatty descriptions of how to survive nuclear war with just a touch of inconvenience had what Yale professor of psychiatry Robert J. Lifton calls "the logic of madness": "Each step follows logically, but is all wrong and utterly unrelated to what would actually happen."

To evacuate urban populations, for example, as Tom Halstead of Physicians for Social Responsibility puts it, "You have to have: (1) days of warning time, (2) receptive host communities, (3) a docile and cooperative evacuation population, (4) nice weather, and (5) cooperative enemies."

This is why the seemingly innocuous, if somewhat dippy, plans of FEMA have become the focus for such a furious and emotional argument. They have become the testing ground between those people who believe that nuclear war is survivable and those who think it is suicidal.

It's not surprising that the Reagan administration, which talks increasingly of nuclear-war fighting as another option, is in favor of beefing up civil defense. Nor is it surprising that opposition groups think civil-defense planning is worse than absurd, it's immoral.

One side believes that nuclear weapons are just another big bomb; the other believes that they are the weapons of annihilation. One puts its energy into survival, the other into prevention.

Jones, the fellow with faith in shovels, told the *Los Angeles Times* that the United States could actually recover from a nuclear war in about four years if we develop a civil defense like the Soviets. This is, I am sure, news to the average Soviet citizen. The favorite underground joke in Russia about civil defense goes like this:

"What do you do when the warning siren goes off, Ivan?"

"Wrap yourself in a white sheet and walk slowly to the nearest graveyard."

"Why slowly?"

"So you won't cause a panic."

The absurdity of the civil-defense posture is even blacker than Russian humor. As Lifton, the author of *Broken Connection*, puts it most articulately, "Civil defense is part of the fundamental illusion about nuclear war: The illusion of surviving. The illusion of recovery. It's massive denial."

More ominously, he adds, "Civil defense tends to coincide with belligerence and preparation for nuclear war. In itself, it seems like a natural and appropriate thing to do. But it increases the possibility of nuclear way by making it more acceptable. That's why it's immoral."

Any rational look at "nuclear-war fighting" tells us plainly that it's overwhelmingly hard to limit, impossible to win, improbable to survive, and therefore essential to prevent.

Laconia, New Hampshire, is a nice place to visit. But frankly, I don't want to evacuate there.

FEBRUARY 1982

NUCLEAR FOLLIES: II

BOSTON—Yes indeed, ladies and gentlemen, just when the script was getting stale, we are offered a new act in the National Nuclear Follies. A hearty welcome, please, for "FEMA and The Farmers."

When last heard from, you may recall, FEMA (the Federal Emergency Management Agency) was hoofing it up on center stage with plans for evacuating our cities.

Well, fans, FEMA is back. They've taken on the farmers and they're talking food. They have assessed the postnuke food situation and are here to tell us that the survivors are all gonna make it if there are enough cans to go around.

FEMA produced its new script as a briefing paper for the Cabinet last year. It was going to be a private showing, but Representative Tom Harkin (D-Iowa) put it into our national repertoire. Once again, the theme is upbeat: A large-scale nuclear war wouldn't devastate American agriculture.

For one thing, they assure us that livestock might fare better than people in the aftermath. Sure, the crops would suffer, but the amount of damage is hard to predict since young crops suffer more from radiation than more mature crops. With any luck the nuclear war would take place in August rather than June. Summer stock time, as you know.

But FEMA's basic scenario is that, "The land and the work force would be available under even the greatest calamity—nuclear attack. . . . Sufficient production seems assured to meet survivor needs.'

In part, the planners are counting on the availability of migrant labor. There would be plenty of urban migrants hanging around to help with the harvest, they say. No more help problems, no more illegals. Everyone will pitch in with the picking.

They are also counting on diminished appetites. The pressure to feed the survivors will disappear pretty quickly, along with the survivors. Following an attack which would eliminate half the population, FEMA notes, "those who are doomed to die will be consumers for [only] part of that time." No problem.

But back to the cans. The authors do admit there will be a problem with food processing and distribution: "Frankly the post-nuclear attack picture is not so bright in processing." What we seem to be missing is a plan for more containers.

Now I don't know about the rest of the civil-defense audience out there, but I have a feeling that these people could have cribbed their script from *The Day After*. The best scene in the film was the wonderful meeting between the bureaucrat and the farmers.

The bureaucrat, speaking from instructions probably produced by FEMA fantasists, tells the farmers to go out into the fields and scrape up the fallout and the contaminated top soil. This is a little like skimming a ten-mile oil slick off the ocean with a teaspoon. Only this time, we're talking dead dirt.

Frankly, I hate to pan such a sincere troupe. Lord knows, they win points for imagination. More to the point, FEMA and the farmers were just doing their job of postnuke planning. In an era when we name a nuclear missile "The Peacekeeper" and talk freely about first-strike scenarios, FEMA is just a doo-wop chorus for a headliner like Edward Teller.

But I keep remembering the words of Robert J. Lifton, the Yale professor of psychiatry who has written about the "logic of madness" in our nuclear thinking: "Civil defense is part of the fundamental illusion about a nuclear war: The illusion of surviving. The illusion of recovery. It's massive denial."

Lifton's point of view is that of a nuclear theater critic. "In itself [civil defense] seems like a natural and appropriate thing to do. But it increases the possibility of nuclear war by making it more acceptable. That's why it's immoral."

In fairness, the FEMA predictions may be accurate. If Carl Sagan's group of scientists is right, 10 percent of the nuclear arsenal can create an ultimate nuclear winter. In that case, there would indeed be enough food for the number of people: none.

DECEMBER 1983

ONLY TOUGH GUYS CAN CRY

BOSTON—The president's voice broke with emotion again last week. It was reported in the papers.

This time he was reading a letter from a woman whose daughter had been shot down in the Korean Air Lines flight.

99

The time before, he was giving out medals at a White House ceremony. The time before that he was, I believe, pleading for a young patient in need of a liver transplant.

There have been other moments in this administration, moments when he talked about someone who had been hurt or heroic. Moments when he was touched by someone young or helpless, and showed it.

In fact this president's voice breaks more often than any other in my memory. In fact, this president is allowed what few other men are in America: to be emotional in public.

Now, we all know, we've all been told, that in our country, real men don't cry. One man lost his bid for the presidency because of half a dozen tears mixed with the New Hampshire snow. Here politicians are ridiculed for lusting in their hearts, and eggheads come to Washington to prove that they are too tough to crack. And yet this president expresses emotion quite regularly and no pollster's scale registers a seismic effect on his popularity.

I find this a curious phenomenon. The way I figure it, Reagan's cracking voice bears some complicated relationship to the way our image of masculinity is and isn't changing. In times like these, no one is untouched, not even cowboy presidents who pride themselves on hard lines and tough politics—especially not these presidents.

For well over a decade, men have been encouraged to do something that is called in the literature "expressing your feelings." A great deal has been written—some of it sane and some of it silly—about the "new sensitive man."

But lurking in our psyches and in our society is some uncertainty. It isn't always clear whether the role being offered is that of "new sensitive man" or "wimp."

There are surely more men who suffer from fear of wimphood now than women who suffer from fear of success. If a man avoids a confrontation with the thug on the street is it because he is too sensible or too afraid? If he picks up and moves once, twice, three times for his wife's job, is he a good husband or a sucker? If he chooses to negotiate with children or co-workers instead of issuing orders, is that because he is sure of his values or unsure of his authority?

In any transition, our gut reactions may be out of sync with our reason. Many men deal with their role confusion by going through some two-stage process, some rite of passage. Many have to prove their masculinity under the old terms before they feel free to look the terms over. They have to wrestle first with the fear of wimphood.

There is a parallel or perhaps exaggerated version of this identity conflict in society. We say that we want leaders who are strong but not macho, emotional but not weak. But in real life, those who have impeccable credentials for their toughness are given more permission slips to express feelings.

There are limits, of course. Even the tough ones must display the right degree of emotion. A lump-in-the-throat kind of emotion. But those who have ridden a horse or a tank or a spaceship, those who have proved themselves somehow or other male in the most traditional sense, have some immunization against our fear of wimphood.

I am not nominating Reagan as the New Sensitive Man. Hardly. There is a point at which duality is self-deception, or pretense, or the sentimentality of a hard heart. It just won't do to excise hope from so many lives and then express pity for the chosen few.

But Reagan carries a long résumé of old-fashioned, hard-core male qualities and one public, persistent exception: the voice that breaks with his emotion and without our judgment.

There is a paradox at this moment in our history. Today, real men may be the only ones who ARE allowed to cry.

OCTOBER 1983

101

THE GOOD OLD WARS

BOSTON—Somewhere in the middle of the president's trip to the Far East, in between the canned speeches and the photo opportunities, there was a spontaneous moment. During a television interview in Japan, Reagan talked for a moment about the good old wars.

"Once upon a time," he said, "we had rules of warfare. War is an ugly thing, but we had rules in which we made sure that soldiers fought soldiers, but they did not victimize civilians. That was civilized. Today we've lost something of civilization in that the very [nuclear] weapons we're talking about are designed to destroy civilians by the millions. And let us, at least, get back to where we once were."

Now maybe, just maybe, we should be reassured by his comment. At least the president has noticed some difference between nuclear war and conventional war. But frankly, I find this thinly veiled nostalgia for the glory wars of a mythical history bizarre and telling.

There have surely been moments in world history when the brutality and horror of war were necessary to defend civilization. But never in my memory has a leader called war itself "civilized."

It was well that Reagan began his remarks with the phrase "once upon a time," because his vision of war existed only in fairy tales and screenplays. Perhaps war was civilized in the studio lots of Hollywood, in the rules and restraints operating over screenwriters.

But was it civilized behavior on that July in 1863 when 50,000 Americans died or were wounded at Gettysburg, and wagons carted away hundreds of amputated arms and legs? Was it civilized on July 1, 1916, when 57,000 Britons died in the Battle of the Somme? Was it civilized war that took the lives of 58,000 Americans in Vietnam?

These casualties were "just" soldiers, of course, and Reagan made a distinction between the sorts of wars that only involve military men—do we still call them cannon fodder?—and the wars that involve civilians. But this, too, is a distinction that exists only on the cinematic jousting fields of Camelot. War, real war, conventional war as we label it now, doesn't just take place on front lines.

We don't have to go back as far as Genghis Khan to list victimized civilians. In World War II, seven million Russian civilians died in addition to eleven million soldiers. More than 70,000 British citizens died in the German bombing. About 135,000 German citizens died in the Allied bombing of Dresden. The Japanese to whom Reagan was speaking killed 100,000 Chinese citizens when they took over Nanking.

Of course if you prefer more recent figures, they are also available. About 14,000 Vietnamese citizens were killed during the Tet offensive of 1968. And if you prefer smaller figures, 22 residents of My Lai were killed by one American soldier. Those were the good old days, and, as the president says, "Let us at least get back to where we once were."

Am I making too much of a single exchange on a Japanese television program? I don't think so. Whenever Reagan comes out from behind a prepared text, it's time to listen. This is the real Reagan, on his own with neither a speech writer nor a poll taker to direct his action.

This time, after all the written peace speeches, the man personally expressed not so much a desire for peace as a frustration with the restraints of nuclear weapons. Nuclear war isn't fun, isn't "civilized."

Read through those lines, and you can comprehend the president's pleasure, and even the national support for the war in Grenada. Grenada made war fun again. Here we are, restrained from a big confrontation by the mutual suicide pact of the two superpowers. What a relief it was to discover that we can still whack someone small, still win one for the Gipper.

Bertrand Russell once said, "People who are vigorous and brutal often find war enjoyable, provided that it is a victorious war and there is not too much interference with rape and plunder. This is a great help in persuading people that wars are right."

The president of the United States went beyond explaining why war may be right. He told us that it may be civilized. What a long way we've come from the days when war was hell.

NOVEMBER 1983

SPILLING THE (MILITARY) BEANS

BOSTON—Two men came to the Senate last week to spill the beans about Air Force coffeepots.

The airmen, who worked on spare parts at Travis Air Force Base, said that a ten-cup coffee maker for a plane had cost the Air Force $7600. This did not include the stainless-steel pot or, for that matter, the coffee.

The men brought another goodie with them to the Senate subcommittee: a flashlight the Air Force had bought for $180. They didn't bring the aircraft armrest that cost $670, but said that it could be manufactured for between $5 and $25.

The coffeepot, the armrest, and the flashlight will be added to the infamous $436 hammer and the $1188 plastic stool-leg cap. The names of Robert Greenstreet and Thomas Jonsson will be added to the list of whistleblowers and national heroes.

But I for one refuse to pin a medal on these two men. It's just too easy to laugh at the military these days. It's like picking on someone who is suffering from a problem he can't control: forced feeding. Today's military budget is rather like a tub permanently placed in the throat of the armed services, into which they mercilessly pour money. The $7600 coffeepot is merely its foie gras.

Remember what happened in 1981 when budget officers found out that the administration was going to ask for an increase of $32 billion? As Nicholas Lemann reported in the *Atlantic*, the first question facing the officers was "... What can we think of to spend all the money on?" A man working on readiness accounts said, "Carter had given us a lot. The Weinberger team came in and said, 'Add more. Find room to add. Find places to put more money.'"

It was, as they say, a tough, dirty job, but somebody had to do it. The mandate according to Weinberger was to outspend the Soviets.

It was an article of faith among the Reagan people that the Soviets were outspending the United States. Indeed, it had to be an article of faith, since there simply is no way to estimate the Soviet budget, let alone compare it to our own.

The government says that in 1982 the Soviets spent $257 billion to our $196 billion. But of course the Soviets don't spend any dollars, they spend rubles. How do we compare these apples and oranges of two economic systems?

The CIA has devised some wonderfully fanciful ways of doing this. They count beans, and I don't mean coffee beans. They count up each piece of equipment and each military personnel and then figure out what it would cost us in dollars to have what they have. This leads Weinberger into Wonderland. A Soviet private, for example, is paid in rubles worth about $100 a month, while an American private is paid $573 a month. But we calculate the Soviet privates at American wages. When we give our men and women a raise, we give one to the Soviets. (They should be so lucky.)

That's simple compared to what we do for equipment. We take a photo of a Soviet missile or plane. We then ask our own defense contractors to tell us what it would cost their companies to build the same missile or plane. We have no way of knowing whether these contractors will budget $670 for each armrest in the mythical Soviet plane. But when this whole bizarre process is over, we take the figures from Hughes Aircraft or whomever and charge those to the Soviet side of the ledger.

As Andrew Cockburn wrote in *The Threat*: "The bottom line is that no one has the faintest idea what the real costs of Soviet defense are and the tremendous efforts that go into finding a figure are solely for the purpose of helping drive up the U.S. defense budget."

But have a little sympathy for the military. Faced with this bogus accounting system, and pressure from the administration, the poor beleaguered men still have to figure out some way to outspend the mythical Soviet military budget. If the Soviets were listed, for example, as spending $50 on their hammers (they are probably inefficient enough to do that without financial fandangos), then the least we could

106

do for the sake of our country is to spend $436 on our hammers.

Spending here, spending there, spending, spending everywhere. It's pretty tiring stuff. Frankly, after a long, hard day spending, I think the officers in charge deserve a nice $7600 cup of coffee without getting roasted for it.

SEPTEMBER 1984

"NYET PROBLEM"

BOSTON—For most of 1984, I have been engaged in foreign policy. It began, as many of these things do, with simple curiosity. Here I was, a citizen of one of the two countries that might actually finish off civilization, and I knew little about the other one. I wanted to see and write about the Soviet Union.

It is not possible for an American journalist to call up a travel agent, book a trip to Moscow, and wander around the streets interviewing people. So, around January, I began the process of gathering permission slips for a journey.

Over the next months, I studied the language from an engaging tutor, and the bureaucracy from a pleasant Soviet official in Washington. From both men, I learned the word "zaftra," which translates into Spanish as "mañana."

The trip I had originally tried to schedule for March and which was rescheduled with "nyet problem" for June has now, after innumerable calls, been "postponed" indefinitely. Explained my contact, "There are so many journalists who want to go at this time, we cannot make for you such a wonderful trip right now."

Here we get into the foreign policy part of the story. From my thoroughly trivial rebuff, I got a sense of how indirectly the U.S.A. and U.S.S.R. deal with each other today. I also learned something about the nature of negotiating in a time of mistrust.

After my "Nyet for now," I immediately discounted the official explanation. So I was left to figure Soviet motivations without any help from the Soviets. Was my budding trip nipped by the big chill? Was it something I said? Wrote? Am? Should I take this personally or professionally? Or was it just their way?

If this all begins to sound like the ranting of a person who's been stood up by a date, I hasten to say that this is how we conduct foreign policy these days: by international analysis. We don't say what we mean or what we really want. Instead, each country tries to psych out and out psych the other. To the best interpreter go the spoils.

The Soviets withdrew from the Olympic games, claiming personal danger. We rejected that notion and came up with our own. It was, we figured, tit for Carter's tat. It was fear of defections in Los Angeles. It was just plain obstinacy. In the absence of plain talk each side withdrew behind its most paranoid theory.

Then there was the MX fiasco. In May, the House of Representatives passed a compromise bill to fund fifteen MX missiles unless there were arms negotiations before April 1985. The supporters explain it as a "bargaining chip." Sitting near the international relations couch, they say that this will get the Soviets back to negotiating. Never mind that American detractors call it insanity on the part of the government, or even vanity on the part of Representative Les Aspin (D-Wis.), who drew up the misguided "compromise." The Soviets must analyze it, simply, as hostile.

In the arms race as well, each country figures the behavior of the other. Each then draws up a real defense against their imaginings. Are "they" trying to influence U.S. elections? How can the United States best "show them"? Does Reagan call the USSR an Evil Empire? How can they best show us? Can we scare them back to the table? Can they scare us into the election booth? How can we avoid making them believe that we are, gasp, weak?

Both countries end up contemplating what we think they think we think that they think. Instead of talking to each other we read their signals and send signals. Afraid of tipping our hand, we both clasp it over our mouths and then try to decipher the code of international mumbling.

Both countries behave rather like a couple in a bad marriage. They can no longer communicate but can still try to manipulate. Reluctant to use our mouths and ears, we try to read minds. It would all be pathetically amusing, if the messages that we need to psych out weren't so bleak.

As for the postponement of my own excursion into foreign terrain, the man in Washington has suggested that we try for January 1985. The last person who was invited to Moscow in January was Napoleon. I'll have to figure out what this means.

JUNE 1984

HIGH-TECH WAR

BOSTON—If there is a favorite fantasy for those of us who share the four-o'clock-in-the-morning fears of nuclear war, I suppose it is the fantasy of some ultimate safety, some impenetrable self-defense. It must be the same fantasy that fueled the imagination of those who once built castles, moats, city walls, even the Great Wall of China.

To calm the jitters of our own nuclear generation, our fantasy would have to include a shield for our whole country, our whole continent. And indeed it has.

In Reagan's "Star Wars" speech, he had a vision that day of a "future which offers hope," a program of self-defense. He led us to believe that we could create a protective guardian way out there in space to shoot enemy missiles out of the sky.

At the time, I found some videogame humor in the idea, but also some comfort. Why not spend some money on defense, instead of offense, for a change? Maybe it would work. Surely it's harmless.

But I'm not comforted anymore. Nor am I convinced that this fantasy, which has become defense policy, is so harmless. It seems to me now that the whole Star Wars project maintains the truly central fantasy about war: that it is the business of technicians, a question of the right hardware.

Harold Brown, Jimmy Carter's secretary of defense, once

said, "Our technology is what will save us." Recently, *The New York Times* ran a long story about the young Star Wars technicians at the Lawrence Livermore National Laboratory in California who believe they'll be our saviors. They were nothing if not believers.

"We're working on weapons of life," said one of these young men who is convinced that he is in this research to end nuclear war. "Why not find technical solutions to a technical problem?"

I understand the psychology behind his question. Scientists generally have more faith in technocracy than in bureaucracy to solve world problems. Physics is purer than politics. Science promises the concrete answers than elude the students of human and foreign relations. It engages scientists in seductively interesting intellectual pursuits: the Manhattan Project, the Star Wars Project.

I am sure there is something pleasing to the military as well in the idea of a Star Wars peace. It suggests that we don't really have to negotiate with the Russians. It promises that we can become invulnerable without giving up a single advantage.

The high-tech peace wouldn't mean a nickel less for the Pentagon budget. A high-tech protection, after all, is so much more expensive than a low-tech conference. The arms race could go on without fear of resolution until we were utterly bankrupt.

There is something fundamentally perverse about pinning our hopes for the future on hardware. It prevents us from resolving conflicts, discourages us from thinking about the real reasons for this arms race.

Thomas Powers wrote in the *Atlantic Monthly* about his attempt to discover what the arms competition between the Soviet Union and the United States is finally, actually, about. Our political differences don't explain the risk of annihilation. There is no victory or conquest in nuclear war.

111

So he asked over a hundred people a deceptively simple question—"What is it about?"—and rarely received more than a blank stare from Americans or Soviets engaged in thinking about the arms race. "It was questions about hardware that interested them . . ."

Powers finally came to the conclusion that "it" was about fear, fear of each other's power. "We fear each other. We wish each other ill," he wrote. "All the rest is detail."

Is there a technological solution to fear? Of course not. Even if we could make nuclear bombs bounce off our national chest, a wildly dubious proposition, our mutual ill will could take the form of chemical warfare or "conventional" warfare.

The notion that we will be safe—that we can forget about the Soviets, that we can have our war games and security at the same time—is a dangerous delusion. The reality is that we are stuck here on earth with the most human of problems: how to save ourselves. Our only weapon is that familiar and flawed software called the human mind.

FEBRUARY 1984

MR. REAGAN MEETS YOUNG AMERICA

BOSTON—Have you been up nights wondering what exactly it was that Reagan put into the time capsule? Have you been unable to sleep because you so desperately want to hear what Reagan was going to say about young people before he was cut off?

Well, I have.

The debate closed on a cliffhanger. In the rambling, bedtime story that doubled as Reagan's closing statement, we the people were offered a picture of the man cruising down the Pacific Coast Highway pondering a letter that he would write to be opened in a hundred years. But he never did get around to saying what he wrote. Was he afraid he'd kill the suspense?

Then we were told about the wonderful experience he had this campaign season meeting young America. But what did he think of young America? The great communicator was disconnected by the moderator.

I don't think we will ever know what was in the letter, or for that matter, whether there really was a letter. The bulk of investigative reporters in America are too busy trying to locate criminal records of Geraldine Ferraro's great-grandparents to worry about this sort of trivia.

However I was greatly relieved the next day when Reagan finished his thoughts about the young. Stand back! Here they are: "Your generation is something special."

On first hearing, this comment may sound ambiguous. It reminds me of my father's tactful remarks to the star-struck parents of newborns: "Now THERE's a baby!" Even Abbie Hoffman thinks this generation of young is something special. When asked about college students of the eighties, the sixties activist said, "They have designer brains."

But, in all fairness, the candidate who has run his campaign like a pep rally for U.S.A. High has gotten the bulk of cheers from the eighteen- to twenty-four-year-olds. There are as many theories about the affinity between Reagan and the young as there are theorists. One correspondent from Cambridge, Massachusetts, maintains that her generation just plain loves "winners." Another regular writer from California says that Reagan is a grandfather figure (this writer is a psychologist, of course) and that every generation of young allies with Grandpa.

I would add an alternative theory to the current list. I am convinced that it's the Reagan philosophy of individualism that is most appealing to the newly emancipated. They are the target audience for a Republican message which insists that anyone can make it on his or her own, indeed must make it on his or her own.

The entire child-raising ethic of the country is geared to produce independence in our children. We treat them as unique, nurture them as "special," encourage their individualism. We imbue them with our own anxious understanding that sooner or later they have to stand on their own two feet.

By the time they reach voting age, the young, according to our developmental timetables, have begun to strike out on their own. They are more likely to live alone, less likely to be a member of a functioning family than at any other time in their lives. They are at the peak of unbridled interest and investment in themselves, in their own separate futures.

Anybody who deals with young people witnesses the single-minded concentration, the self-centering process, the worship of the Great Can-Do Spirit. Many of these young are not interested in caution signs or bleak prognostications of the future. They want to feel in control of their lives. It is a necessary, energizing tool of youth to believe you can make it on your own.

I also think that these new adults are often the least willing to see the government as a necessary helper because they do not want to see themselves as needing help. Adulthood is still raw, memories of childhood dependency too strong. They are not yet caretakers of aging parents or of their own babies. They are not mindful of the uncertainties of life.

Call it youthful selfishness, if you will, but selfishness, self-interest, independence, and individualism are all on a continuum. The optimism of Reagan comes over like the effusive encouragement of a loving grandparent, and never mind realism. Mondale's alarming talk about the national debt and the arms race must sound like the warnings of parents when they hand over the car keys.

There is one other thing that many of the young share with this particular elder: They are both unencumbered by facts and untethered by history. What if there were a time capsule buried with memorabilia from this election? What message would the Reagan/Youth campaign of 1984 leave for their descendants? Ten thousand balloons?

OCTOBER 1984

THE NEGATIVE DOWRY

BOSTON—Bill Bennett spent his first weeks as secretary of education striving for an 800 on an achievement test in Outrageousness. By now his description of student life on borrowed money has been immortalized. The guaranteed-loan student of the 1980s is a car-owning, stereo-buying, beach-hopping youngblood with books, a variation on the theme of the Cadillac-driving welfare mom.

According to Bennett, the profligate young won't join the truly suffering if the proposed budget cuts are enacted. If a cap of $4000 a year is put on all federal student aid, some would merely trade down from private colleges to public. If the family-income cutoff is lowered to $32,500, families would just "tighten the belt."

Alas, nobody has yet devised a competency test for Cabinet members. But it appears that cooler heads may yet prevail. A chorus of students, families, and private colleges joined a refrain of complaints. The Congress seems to have heard them.

What has been lost in all of the high-ed hullabaloo was any serious critique of what debt does to students. At the moment, about 60 percent of the full-time undergraduate students at four-year institutions borrow money for tuition. The average amount they borrow is about $2200 a year, or $8800 per degree. The average medical student is nearly $40,000 in debt by graduation.

For the most part, we have approved this deficit financing of education in the name of equal opportunity. Schools have been the centerpiece of the dream of equality. We pride ourselves on the notion that Americans who begin life on different economic footing can educate themselves up to the same starting line.

But as the debt burden grows, the concept of education as the great American equalizer shrinks. Frank Newman, president of the Education Commission of the States, says that loans are also "the great unequalizer." The student who leaves college with heavy debts—$10,000 or more—is hardly starting off on the same footing with the student who leaves free. Loans may just push the inequity off four years.

Anyone with a friend or a child starting postgraduate life with a serious financial handicap is conscious of the cost. Arthur Levine, a veteran researcher and innovative president of Bradford (Massachusetts) College, says bluntly: "The system has got to change. Debts are just killing some young people." Not just killing their bank accounts, but killing their idealism as well. Debts are calculated into the decision to go on to graduate school, to take one job instead of another, even to marry. Loans have become known as "the negative dowry."

Frank Newman suspects that debt feeds into the anxious

self-centeredness of people in their twenties. Some have more motive to pay off the bank than to pay back society. He has, for example, been asking medical students about their obligation to others. "What you get back is real anger. 'This country didn't help me; I helped me.' If you have too heavy a set of loans, I really think it adds to the whole me-firstism."

All this may sound like a good rationale for dumping the student-loan program. But that's a bit like barring a patient from the hospital because the medical bills would run too high.

We have become too dependent on loans. Certainly too dependent to cut them off at the Reagan pass. The system has to be changed to reduce the debt burden on students instead of reducing the number of students.

People like Newman look favorably on two models for financing college: work and service opportunities. They want to expand the work side of the financial equation. The Education Commission of the States has proposals for service opportunities coming out soon that are based on the concept of the GI bill: "You serve your country and the country helps you in return."

There are other plans around. In one, the government could grant students financial aid in return for a fixed percentage of their income for a certain amount of time. This might alter the incentive that students feel right now to abandon professions such as teaching in favor of more lucrative ones.

Few of these alternatives are big federal money-savers. But in the end, the programs that may cost the government most are those that use the tax system. One new book for middle-class families is titled succinctly, *Nearly Free Tuition: Let the IRS Pay for Your Child's Education*.

There is widespread agreement among people in and out of the government that the financing of higher education is a mess. Secretary Bennett, however, managed to portray students as members of the leisure class. The problem is that they are members of a debtor class.

FEBRUARY 1985

COMMENCEMENT 1983: SHARING THE "REAL WORLD"

BOSTON—By now the annual academic harvest is nearly over. The black robes have been returned to the rental companies. The clarions used to call seniors have been hung up for another year.

Soon, the last of the new crop of graduates will be gathered in. The long winding procession of hundreds of thousands of men and women, all decked out in commencement clothes, will have moved over that border from the academic world to the "real world."

For as long as I can remember, adults have made a sharp distinction between undergraduate and postgraduate life. We have thought of college students as young people planted in a secure but distant place called academia. At times, we believed that their concerns were as unrelated to ours as Sanskrit is to accounting. We have called our own world the "real" one.

Yet having watched two commencements recently, seen two groups of students emerge from their black husks as fully certified graduates, the line that separates their lives from ours doesn't seem so solid anymore. This generation of young people has had to operate under remarkable stress.

118

They are less like we were at their age and more like we are now.

When my cohorts, as the demographers like to describe us, were graduated from colleges two decades ago, there was a place for us in the world. We assumed that we would be welcomed into the adult community.

Ours were not the good old days, but there was a sense that if you followed a predictable course, you would be eligible for predictable rewards. There were ladders to be climbed and anyone coming out of college had already gotten a few rungs up on the rest.

It's not the same for this generation. The degrees that I saw awarded cost $40,000 apiece. But no guarantees came with the pricey diplomas. These seniors didn't go to college to become upwardly mobile, but as a defense against downward mobility.

On their way to commencement, they heard the advice of their elders in stereophonic sound. In one ear, there were concerned parents talking about tangible results, rewards for the educational "investment." In the other ear, there were concerned teachers trying to encourage them to pursue some unquantifiable love of learning.

If their heads were full of mixed messages about their own futures, they were equally uneasy about THE future. According to the polls, most of them, like most of us, believe a nuclear war is likely to occur in the next decade.

Surely they aren't the first generation to live with the bomb. In the fifties, we were led into the school bomb shelters and taught how to "duck and cover" if a mushroom cloud appeared over the horizon. We had our own nuclear nightmares.

But we also had a greater measure of faith in authority. Even our naiveté served the purposes of a comfortable youth. Today's college generation is far more cynical about the notion of nuclear-age national "security."

This crop had clearly been raised in less-settled weather. What they were asked to do isn't easy: to go for the degree in the midst of doubts about its value. To plan for the future in the midst of doubts about its reality. To create their own lives, their own sense of purpose, their own plans without the guideposts, the predictable rewards.

Yet, in an odd way, it has been pretty good preparation for postgraduate life. The fact is that out here, in "the real world," we, too, have learned to function in the midst of doubt.

In the real world we, too, have learned to go through life adjusting and readjusting the course, questioning its values and our value. We have learned—or tried to learn—how to balance instant gratification with postponement, fun with work, the short run with the long run. We have learned to resist the paralysis that can come with ambivalence.

Today's commencement is less and less of a demarcation line between childhood and adulthood. Today's undergraduates, graduates, and postgraduates sound more and more alike. I guess we are sharing "the real world."

JUNE 1983

COMMENCEMENT 1984: IN SEARCH OF A "BALANCED LIFE"

BOSTON—Somewhere, behind the relentless refrains of "Pomp and Circumstance" that dominated commencement season in 1984, there were echoes of the 1960s. An occasional armband tied around the sleeve of a black robe. A political message pinned to a mortarboard. A single protest on a placard.

The echoes were dim (as in diminished), sometimes ironic and sometimes even forlorn. On the West Coast, Mario Savio, a forty-year-old father of two who once founded the student free-speech movement in Berkeley, got his degree summa cum laude. On the East Coast, an almost-protest was launched at Harvard because the hats for the twenty-fifth-reunion class members were made in South Africa. These moments were duly recorded by those who will always compare students to The Students.

On the podiums, a thousand commencement speakers exhorted the graduates of this more dutiful, less involved generation to make commitments, to believe in something, to change the world. In private, one member of the noisy class of 1969 said of the quiet class of 1984, "They are afraid of being suckers."

In or out of commencement season, it's impossible to spend much time on campuses without feeling the wariness, the holding back from cause or commitment. These are the young who watched the course of illusions and disillusionment run by the formerly young. From their post in the mid-eighties, it's understandable if they regard the idealism of the sixties as reckless and see their own reservations as a safety precaution.

Or they may indeed feel that deep political commitments make suckers. Or, more gently, they may just be struggling to create a life that balances public and private ideals and pleasures. It isn't easy to create balance out of passion.

In *The Big Chill*, that movie about sixties people living in the eighties, we saw the campus radicals who had toned down their idealistic passion and become successful: a lawyer, a gossip journalist, a manufacturer of running shoes, and a TV star. Yet they were all somewhat uneasy with their apolitical lives.

In contrast, the stars of Rosellen Brown's deeply textured novel, *Civil Wars*, are sixties activists who went on trying to live their political ideology. Jessie and Teddy, the flip side of *The Big Chill* cast, are somewhat uneasy with their personal lives.

Civil Wars is too rich, too wonderfully layered and complex a novel to reduce to a paragraph or an idea, but some difficult questions about living with political passion are woven through the plot. What happens during big, chilly years when, as one character in the book says, being a civil-rights organizer "feels like we're making horseshoes or piano rolls or something these days. . . ." What happens if you are a confrontation hero who cannot adapt to "a long quiet time of unflamboyant action and behind-the-scenes tinkering. . . ."?

What happens when there is a conflict between political and personal commitments? In *Civil Wars*, Teddy retreats from a difficult, needful family life into political action, saying that, "I'm teaching them there are larger groups than the family that you can swear loyalty to." But his wife, Jessie, believes he is deserting them: "What about this world right here under your roof?"

The current generation of students has spent its life in such civil wars of the past twenty years. They know something about the conflicts between the ideal and the real. The conflict between cynics and suckers. The conflict between work and pleasure, public and private life.

If they don't suffer from ambivalence, perhaps they suffer from maturity, or prematurity. They talk more about this "balanced life" than any young people I can remember. It is a life that includes many parts, is enriched by multiple ingredients. If they are wary of making deep, plunging commitments, political or personal, it may be part of their own elusive ideal, that easy, comfortable balance.

Thinking of these graduates, I am struck by a scene in

Civil Wars which said a good deal about the passage from one generation to another. The son of a black woman who fought for her rights through the heat of the sixties and the chill of the eighties turns to his mother and says, "You got a son who's going to learn to settle for a few good things and relax."

In some ways, he is an honorary member of the class of '84.

JUNE 1984

WINNERS AND LOSERS

BOSTON—Now that the '84 election is over, I find myself thinking less about who won and who lost than about how we have changed the concept of winners and losers.

In July, New York governor Mario Cuomo told the Democratic Convention a tale of two cities, one rich and one poor. All fall, the Democrats talked about a nation increasingly divided into haves and have-nots. The brilliance of the Reagan campaign was in redefining the haves as the winners and the have-nots as the losers.

The resounding cheer of this election, "U.S.A.! U.S.A.!" was more than a sound track for grandstand patriotism. It was an Olympic call to middle-class Americans to root for the strong, the wealthy, the healthy, the independent—to side with the winners.

Once, the people who lived in the Other America were called the needy and regarded as victims. But there is a line, a fault line, that separates the old "victim" from the new "loser."

In our political dictionary, a victim is blameless while a loser can only blame himself. In our political landscape, we may ask the government to lend a hand to victims, but not to waste handouts on losers. The "needy" may elicit guilt and help from more affluent neighbors. But losers only get scorn.

If I had to write the subliminal script for this campaign, it would include at least one responsive Republican reading:

What do you call a black who cannot make it into the middle class without a government program? A loser.

What do you call a single mother who cannot succeed without child care or job skills? A loser.

What do you call an elderly person who didn't put away enough for a comfortable old age? A loser.

The Democratic party became the party of these losers, those who admitted need, those who looked to the government for help. In his concession speech Mondale said, "Tonight, especially, I think of the poor, the unemployed, the elderly, the handicapped, the helpless and the sad. . . ." They were the only economic group that gave the Democrats a majority. The middle class stayed away from their cause, afraid of being infected by those they now regard as society's untouchables.

Much of the emotion behind this win-lose event was fear. The Republicans offered themselves as the party of optimists, of a bright, unlimited future, of morning in America. But optimism lies in ideals. In a vision of a society with room for everyone. In the notion that we can give to others without taking away from ourselves.

This was not an optimistic election year. It was, rather, the prototype of a campaign in an era of limits. The middle class in America knows that the gap between rich and poor is growing. The young see the slide of downward mobility.

The momentary high of this economy was as seductive as the man who gave us a choice between identifying with the haves or the have-nots.

In this campaign, anxiety spoke. The anxiety of people trying to hold on to what they have. This is not the stuff of "selfishness." I never liked that "selfish" name-calling in this campaign. The poor voted for the Democrats for selfish reasons. The rich voted for the Republicans for selfish reasons. The problem was that Mondale never convinced the middle class that he was in their best interest. The people in the middle didn't trust the Democrats with their money.

Americans are not fundamentally ungenerous. Show us hunger in Ethiopia and we respond to the victims. But in an era of limits, people think of their own survival first. In the scramble up the side of the haves, the people in the middle of this growing gap are much less willing to share. Fear tightens the purse strings.

The success of the Reagan campaign is that he legitimized this tightening and salved our collective conscience at the same time. If we are going to limit opportunities for those stuck in the Other America, it is much easier to think of these people as failures. If we are going to chip away at social programs for the have-nots, it is easier to name them losers.

We used to call this blaming the victim. Now we call it winning.

NOVEMBER 1984

ABORTION AND THE "BIG MO"

BOSTON—In the midst of all the heated rhetoric about abortion that choked the news recently, there was one sentence that still echoes in my mind. It was the message transmitted from the man in the Oval Office to the pro-life demonstrators on the Ellipse: "The momentum is with us."

I wanted to dismiss his words as the optimistic cheer of a fan. Go get 'em, tiger. There is no evidence, after all, that public opinion has moved an iota closer to his anti-abortion stance. Instead it seems to have frozen in place. The constitutional amendment that would ban abortion has stalled and the Supreme Court has reaffirmed the basic right to choose abortion.

But Ronald Reagan knows his business, and his business is political communication. The "momentum" he talks about is a word that comes out of that specialized dictionary. The "Big Mo" is a political term used to describe the direction in which the pack is traveling, especially the journalistic pack. Within that definition, the president is right: The Big Mo is with the right-to-lifers.

In recent months, I have been struck by the success that the antiabortion movement has had in reframing the questions and the arguments, in producing the action and the news in this long public debate. What is "news" this season is the clinic closed down by a bomb or a bomb threat. What is news is a sonogram videotape of a fetus being aborted.

What is news is the medical technology and bioethical dilemma of the middle trimester.

By contrast, the oldest story in the world is that of a pregnant woman. It's the story "we've already done," the story that's been filmed and reported a thousand times.

It's not that the media have turned pro-life, or pro-choice for that matter. The essential bias of my profession is pro-change, pro-newness. It's this bias that has subtly and fundamentally shifted the coverage from the woman to the fetus.

You do not need to be a full-time media watcher to chronicle this. One *Newsweek* cover story on abortion was cast "in the context of a struggle over helpless beings." The "beings" were those in the womb. The piece described aggressive pro-life tactics and "moral disquiet" and scared politicians. There was no space devoted to the life of the carrier of those beings.

The television networks focused their lenses in much the same way of late. Questions about the life of a fetus dominated the talk shows. Bernie Nathanson's sonogram of a fetus being aborted was replayed on the news with hardly a word questioning his premises.

In the passion for "newness," the pregnant woman was as invisible in the argument as she was in the sonogram. The media looked straight through her. As Nanette Falkenberg of the National Abortion Rights Action League asked one reporter in frustration, "Do you think the fetus is housed in a Tupperware jar?"

What has happened to the other side of this difficult story? Half of all Americans know someone who's had an abortion. More than 1.5 million women a year choose abortion. Where were these women, most of them young, most of them unmarried? They were the absent, the disappeared victims of the Big Mo.

Those who have struggled to keep abortion legal and

available are very conscious of the shift in attention. Falkenberg admits, "Our folks feel beleaguered. The president talks about abortion in his inaugural address. Our clinics are getting blown up. This propaganda [the sonogram videotape] gets shown on all networks. We have really noticed a total absence of any focus on the woman involved."

She predicts a struggle to recapture the Big Mo. "We had a conscious desire to de-emotionalize this issue and I don't think we can play it that way anymore. We think it may be time again for women to publicly tell their own stories. We have to say, 'You want emotion, we'll give you emotion. You want real life stories, here they are.'"

Most of us in the media are uneasy with this, uneasy providing—even grooming—an emotional battleground of such intensity. But as surely as the pendulum swings, we lean toward the new story, go where the action is, build the momentum.

So the president is right about momentum. The story of the unwanted pregnancy is as old, as rumpled, as dull as yesterday's news. And yet it is also as fresh, as new, and as unique as the life stories of the thousands of women who will face that crisis tomorrow for the very first time.

FEBRUARY 1985

HOPE FOR THE NEW YEAR

BOSTON—It is a new year and so it comes with all sorts of human rituals—promises, resolutions, fresh starts, beginnings. For at least a while, until 1985 becomes a familiar number to write on a check or read in a newspaper, we are supposed to feel a surge of new possibilities. We are even supposed to entertain hope.

Well, I am not so sure that we are ready for that. Hope was not the best guest of the 1984 social season. It was so meager, so parsimonious, such a downer. I'm not sure we want to entertain it again.

Last week, last month, last year, Hope for Peace went party hopping and raised a very odd set of toasts. The hardline hopes for the future were pinned on Star Wars. The peacenik hopes were pinned on, of all things, nuclear winter.

We were all there when Caspar Weinberger said that the president would never abandon his vision of that videogame defense against the enemy, a plan to shoot nuclear missiles out of the air. "It offers too much hope," explained Weinberger deadpan. "It's the only thing that offers any real hope to the world. And he will not give that up."

At the same time, a legion of new scientists and advocates of arms reduction signed on as believers in the theory of nuclear winter. They agreed that just a fraction of our arsenal of nuclear weapons would produce the ultimate cloud of dust, the final frozen wasteland.

This knowledge, the nuclear winterites believe, will force governments to rewrite the suicide pact of war. As Thomas Powers wrote in the *Atlantic Monthly*, "To me, recognition of the nuclear-winter problem, awful as it is, seems a piece of immense good fortune at the eleventh hour and a sign that Providence hasn't given up on us yet."

This, I tell you, is what passed for hope in 1984. This is what people try to pass off as hopeful for 1985.

From one group, we are offered the possibility of a multimultibillion-dollar Chinese wall to try to keep out the nuclear-missile hordes. From the other, we are offered the possibility that governments can be brought to their senses by the belief in doomsday.

I have tried to wrap myself in the silver linings they offer us. I've tried to find the comfort in nuclear winter and instead found myself shivering. I have tried to imagine a defensive shield against airborne missiles and instead envisioned nuclear weapons delivered in suitcases.

It is too hard to believe in a technological fix from above, too hard to believe that we can beat our fear of nuclear winter into hope. I find these a peculiar pair of miserly hopes to welcome the new year. "Hopes" that have this much in common: pessimism, a long negative view of history, of governments, perhaps even of human nature.

I have the sense that these two contenders for public attention agree that humans are "naturally" hostile. They envision governments so eager for a fight that they can only be either scared out of a lethal battle or technologically shielded from its effects.

These most sophisticated debates about national security inevitably come back to old arguments about human nature. What's unusual is to see how clearly pessimism dominates the argument right now.

Perhaps I am not the one to best counter this pessimism. At this turn of the digital calendar, I find it much harder than usual to make a case for a better, brighter, new, improved year. The change I see looks like more drifting.

But my own view of human nature is at least mixed. We are fundamentally, "naturally," neither aggressive nor passive nor anything except a mass of possibilities and decisions. And that is where the real hope comes in. Not the glamorous stuff of star warriors and nuclear winterites, but of human beings and fresh starts.

If I may contradict Mr. Weinberger, "the only thing that offers any real hope to the world" is a belief in the variety of human nature, a belief that peace has as much place and potential in our nature as aggression. If we are going to hope this year, and that's an open question, we'd better not look in the stars but in ourselves. That's where we'll find the signs that "Providence hasn't given up on us yet."

JANUARY 1985

CONTRA CHARLEY AND THE PRIVATE WAR

BOSTON—Charley doesn't look like the sort of fellow the kids would normally bring home from college during spring break. Maybe it's the bullet belt over his sleeveless T-shirt that sets him apart. Maybe it's the M-16 in his hands that seems just a bit menacing, even for the punk crowd.

But let us keep an open mind here. Charley is, after all, the campus poster boy of the College Republican National Fund. He is the new star of a fund-raising campaign to encourage college students to adopt their very own Nicaraguan rebel.

In a macabre twist on the theme of the Save the Children Federation, the fund is telling students that for a mere $16 a month, only 53 cents a day, they can buy one contra meals and medicine; maybe they'll even get a letter back describing how much better the murder and mayhem are going.

The poster pitch goes like this: "My name is Charley and I am a Nicaraguan Counter-Communist. A Contra. A Freedom Fighter.

"I have taken up arms against the Soviet Empire and its satellite government in Nicaragua and I need your help.

"Last year your Congress cut off our funding. . . . Please help me and my fellow patriots. We haven't got long." It closes with the sort of ecological plea that always attracts the young: "Save the Contras."

Frankly, I find this tale of Charley and the contras a perfect story for the 1980s, and I don't say this merely to keep Charley from getting angry with me (although I would feel better if he took his finger off the trigger). This Republican fund-raiser is a logical extension of policymaking in the age of Reaganomics.

After all, this is an era when domestic policy is rapidly becoming a private affair. Why not foreign policy? The days of privatization began back when Reagan first started cutting social programs. He maintained that donations and charity would take up the slack. Individuals would do what the government wouldn't do. It didn't happen that way, but everybody got the hint. The public sector was going to do less, the private sector was supposed to do more.

So we have gone private, at least in the sense of service. We now have a growth industry in private security systems, a new supply of private jails, and a bumper crop of private hospitals.

In New York, where the public-transportation system is

creaky and sometimes spooky, there is now a private bus company. In cities where the public-school systems are impoverished, many head for private schools. Social policy has been reduced to one basic principle: You can get anything you are willing to pay for.

Sooner or later this was bound to spill over into foreign affairs. If Congress refused to fund the contras, then it was natural to turn to the private sector, at least to those private citizens who regarded Charley as a home-team player. Representatives Jim Leach (R-Iowa) and Mel Levine (D-Calif.) introduced a bill last week to stop this sort of private military funding, but they're just trying to keep an old-fashioned government monopoly going.

The rest of us can now enter the era of Free Enterprise War. Each American citizen can have the wonderful opportunity of choosing sides and sending their nontax dollars to whatever armed forces they find cute enough to adopt. Like the looks of an Afghanistan mullah? Give him a couple of bucks a week. Sick of Marcos? Have an auction for the opposition. If you prefer Iran and your neighbor likes Iraq, why fight about it when each can adopt his or her own soldier for a mere 53 cents a week?

The beauty of this free choiceism is that we don't have to hold foreign-policy debates, we don't have to arrive at any sort of consensus, we don't even have to agree. In fact we don't have to fund any government at all.

Why, for that matter, stop with building private armies? While we are in the business, let us encourage the Reagan administration to return the tax dollars slated for new weapons systems and let private citizens, in all their disparate wisdom, take over. We could begin by holding a bake sale for the MX. I have a swell recipe for chocolate-chip cookies.

MARCH 1985

PETTY ETIQUETTE

BOSTON—There are times when history makes such an awkward guest. It hovers around some current event like a garrulous elder, interrupting the people who are trying to maintain decorum. It tugs on the sleeves of the guests, ruffles the diplomatic calm, whispers gossip from the old days.

See those two friends? asks history. Once they were mortal enemies. See those enemies? Once they were allies. See that righteous country in the corner? I knew it when.

History simply refuses to obey the rules of international etiquette. If it has one great social flaw, one unforgivably rude habit, it's this: History remembers.

This is a perfect spring for history to make its mischief. We are about to celebrate the fortieth anniversary of V-E Day, the victory over Nazi Germany. But we are trying to do it without offending any Germans.

Today, our country is on the best of terms with its old foe. It's the Soviet allies who have become the "evil empire." So the question for the genteel diplomatic world is how to commemorate a big win without insulting the losers.

The U.S. government has come up with a politically polite solution to this social dilemma that would satisfy Emily Post. The president will make a pilgrimage to West Germany in May, but he has decided to skip the guilt-trip to the concentration camps.

Reagan explained his motives this way: "Instead of reawakening the memories . . . maybe we should observe this day as the day when forty years ago peace began and friendship. . . . I felt since the German people have very few alive that remember even the war and certainly none of them who were adults and participating in any way, they have a feeling and a guilt feeling that's been imposed upon them." He wants to keep history under control—to give it limited access to the party.

Well, Reagan's math is off, but not as far as his moral compass. There are a lot of German veterans, like American veterans, who are alive, well, and indeed younger than the president. The current chancellor, Helmut Kohl, was, as he reminds people regularly, only fifteen at the end of World War II. But Holocaust writer Elie Wiesel was sixteen when his death camp was liberated.

There is a statute of limitations on national guilt. Young Germans have no more responsibility for Nazism than post-Civil War Americans had for slavery. But they do have the responsibility to remember. And so does the world.

What radically separated World War II from the other wars, what made the Allies liberators rather than mere victors, what firmed American belief in this "good war" was the Nazi technology of evil. The camps. If a presidential visit to these murderous shrines would embarrass the ally, ignoring them shames our own sense of values. Even the memory of these victims is sacrificed to politics.

The Germans themselves have wrestled with the difficult task: How do you tell a postwar generation about the millions of people murdered by their elders? It wasn't until 1962 that German schools began to teach the Holocaust. Not many parents and grandparents tell their grandchildren stories about what they did in the war. There is a strong motivation to forget. Even this spring, it is said that the West German media concentrate more on the bombing of

German cities and the advance of Soviet troops from the Eastern Front than on the Nazi regime.

But if our friendship with West Germany requires that we tiptoe around the past, then we have given up too much. If allegiance requires that we delicately avoid mentioning the deepest shame of humanity, it's a sham.

History is a troublesome guest because it reeks of truth. Let the Germans join this celebration, especially the young Germans whose feelings our government is worrying about. They were also liberated from the evils of Nazism on V-E Day. But we can't let history be barred from its place by etiquette's petty amorality.

APRIL 1985

Part 4

OF WOMEN AND
MEN IN TRANSITION

CASUALTIES OF COMMITMENT

BOSTON—The announcement comes over the phone, from West Coast to East, a long-distance obituary to a longtime relationship.

I listen as my old friend, a poet, mourns her loss, eulogizes her broken connection. Her words are so familiar to me that they might have been uttered at a hundred other such wakes: "In the end, he couldn't make a commitment."

This is the third time recently that I have been called upon as pallbearer to a love affair. Some strange spring fever seems to have proved fatal to these couplings.

In each case, the man came up to the threshold of promise. In each case, he experienced it less as a doorway than as a line drawn in the sand. A line he couldn't cross.

By the time I hang up the phone this long evening, I share my friends' pain and frustration. I want to say something about men and their troubles with the thing we call commitment.

I know that three life stories do not make a class action or even a generalization about men. I am surrounded by exceptions, in my home, my family, my friends, my reading.

Yet when I look back over space and time, I see more men who were skittish about permanent connections than women, more men who were frightened about commitment, more men who were anxious about marriage.

I am not talking about men who subscribe to *Playboy* magazine and its philosophy. I am not talking about musical comedy "guys" who fear being housebroken by marriage-minded "dolls." I am not just talking about 1950s bachelors who try to avoid the tender traps.

These are men who have relationships on which they work. These are men who may regard their reluctance to make a commitment as a problem. When pressed though, they may tell themselves that the problem will disappear with "the right woman."

Nor do the women in their lives lay traps anymore. They do not fill hope chests or talk about men as good catches. They, too, have relationships on which they work.

Still, sometimes I wonder how much things have changed between men and women. The dimensions of the commitment problem, the description of it may be different than in the days of the tender trap, but what about the origins, what about the feelings?

We still, men and women, grow up differently. It's not just a matter of dolls and building blocks, though there is some of that. We are taught in this country that people have to break away to become mature. People have to become independent, a condition we confuse with being alone. In real life, these people are men.

We teach men in a thousand ways that relationships are encumbrances that hold them back, trap them, catch them. It's the men, almost always, who become our lone rangers.

Women learn another double message. We are both urged toward independence and encouraged toward caretaking. We try to grow up without growing away, thinking of ourselves and our lives as connected. And fearing isolation.

What happens then when we come together expecting love? Men who equate maturity with independence meet women who equate it with connections. Our fears collide.

Most of us break through this difference, but not all or always or without pain. Often, there are casualties along the way.

I spoke with one of the three men who had caught this spring fever. It was hard, he said, but he would get through it, tough it out. I had the sense that he regarded this breakup as a challenge.

Reenacting some primal scene, he was again a real man, alone. In some odd way the new bad feelings felt right.

In the next few weeks or months, this man will use his considerable strength. He will use it to prevent himself from crossing the threshold. He will use it to deal with his loneliness. It will be easier for him that way, making no commitments.

APRIL 1983

LOVE, INCORPORATED

BOSTON—More than fifty years ago, when Sigmund Freud was asked the prescription for a healthy life, he came up with two simple ingredients: work and love. But what the doctor had in mind was an integrated personality, not an integrated work force.

The corporate executives of today may also believe wholeheartedly in love and work, but they appear to be wary of love AT work. Since Mary Cunningham and Bill Agee became a case study in how not to mix business and pleasure, a torrid interest has grown around the subject of love between executives.

Now the *Harvard Business Review*, which caters to the classiest of corporate leaders, has come out with some advice on dealing with dalliance at the top. In this month's issue, senior editor Eliza Collins concludes, after studying the business dynamics of four affairs, that "Love between managers is dangerous because it challenges—and can break down—the organizational structure."

The new coalition, the love coalition, makes everybody anxious, she says. It threatens to exclude others, makes subordinates worry about the judgment and the fairness of bosses who are blinded by love.

Having analyzed this, Collins makes some fairly bold recommendations. The senior executive should intervene in the executive love affair because "of the high degree of stress in the corporation."

"If the company sees rats in the basement they've got to get them out," said Collins in an interview. "It does have a responsibility to run an environment in which people can work."

Short of hiring a pied piper, then, the best interest of business is apparently to separate love or at least one lover from work. Collins suggests that the senior executive persuade "the person least essential to the company" to leave. She advises this reluctantly because the less important person is still "in almost all cases a woman."

Much of Collins' description of how a love affair can disrupt the office environment is astute. But her generalizations and recommendations are somewhere between offensive and dangerous.

For openers, a piece like this in the prestigious *Review* feeds into the wave of literature on how women are confronting the corporate world with all "their" messy little problems. The *Wall Street Journal*, for example, has been running an apparently endless series on the woes of young executive mothers. Apparently there are no young executive fathers.

Now the new women are mucking up the structure, by bringing love relationships into the boardroom, instead of keeping them where they belong, say, in the steno pool. The notion is that executives are so freaked out by their love that they cease functioning rationally at work. Love comes in and business school training goes out.

But there are others, like Anne Jardim, a dean of the Simmons Graduate School of Management in Boston, who remain unconvinced of Collins' basic premise. For every bungled relationship, Jardim can count another "in which the people involved handled it with discretion, became scrupulously fair and survived."

More to the point, she says it is probably unnecessary and insulting to call in "Big Daddy" to separate adult executive lovers.

Rosabeth Kanter, professor of sociology and management at Yale University, suggests that senior executives handle love affairs the way they handle alcohol. Do nothing until there is an issue in job performance. Perhaps, she suggests, there should be a checklist for problem lovers that asks: How is this showing up at work?

The reality is that there are all sorts of special relationships between executives, all sorts of political and personal alliances in the corporate power structure that are untinged by sex. Kanter is not convinced that sexual love between executives is either widespread or disruptive enough for the sort of radical advice Collins has offered.

"People can behave in absolutely adolescent ways," says Kanter of executive lovers. "But it doesn't last that long in that stage. If we can indulge people when they are going through divorce or alcoholism, then we can indulge them with love."

What is most unsettling about the new advice on executives in love is that, once again, the business world is being fed the illusion that they can and, indeed, should manage emotions by removing them from the workplace. The prime candidate for emotional excision is, as always, love: first, family love and, now, sexual love.

In this case, the solution Collins recommends would effectively remove even the "carrier" of love in this society: women. We go back again to the notion that a healthy business personality is different from a healthy human personality. The message? If you want to get ahead in business, keep love off the books.

SEPTEMBER 1983

PARTNERS IN DIVORCE

BOSTON—When they announced "Here's Johnny" the other night, most of the audience knew where Carson was coming from: the lawyers. The estranged Mrs. Carson had just asked for $220,000 a month in temporary support.

Here, indeed, was material for a monologue. While his lawyers cringed, Johnny picked up his cue.

Once in childhood, he explained, his hero had been Babe Ruth. Then, as a young professional, he had looked to Jack Benny. During the past week, however, he had latched onto a new hero: Henry the Eighth.

Now, under the circumstances we can understand Carson's nostalgia for the good old days when a man could sever his attachments so neatly. Henry after all had six wives. Johnny has had three. Two of Henry's wives ended up beheaded, while one of Johnny's will end up heading her own fortune.

The catalog of expenses Joanna Carson claimed are enough to support a minor principality, or princess-ipality. The most stunning revelation is that she is used to spending $37,000 a month in jewelry and furs and $5000 a month for clothing. I cannot figure out how you spend that much on furs without buying an entire zoo, but there it is.

The request for $2.6 million a year surely makes Joanna Carson a candidate for the hit parade of top ten spenders. Who can resist the temptation to award her the title of money-grubbing divorcée of the year?

But if this is going to be a dialogue instead of a monologue, someone should present the other side. In the role of devil's advocate—although I would get paid more as either of the Carsons' advocate—allow me to suggest this: If the Carsons were still married, we would regard her as no more than the overindulged wife of an overindulged performer. It is only upon divorce that the wife of a rich man is reclassified as a greedy harpy who is "trying to take him to the cleaners."

Is it more outrageous for Joanna to be awarded $220,000 a month by Johnny than for Johnny to be paid $1.5 million a month by NBC? If the wife of a pauper is a partner in his nothingness, isn't the wife of a millionaire a partner to his millions?

What is at stake here isn't just a fur allowance but a conflict in our attitudes toward the economics of marriage. This conflict runs through the recent study on *American Couples*, by Philip Blumstein and Pepper Schwartz.

The two researchers asked lots of questions about the role of money in couples' lives. They report that couples who are truly committed to a future with each other are more likely to pool their money. Indeed, they concluded, "If we were going to use one major indicator to determine when these couples became solidified as a unit it would be the point at which they joined their resources." At some moment money was no longer yours and mine, but ours.

At the same time, the researchers note, "the amount of money a person earns—in comparison with a partner's income—establishes relative power." Each person may continue to keep track of his or her share in "our" money.

Whatever conflicts lie latent in marriage tend to surface immediately in divorce. It's not just the former couple who experience them, but anyone observing the messy process.

On the one hand we think of long-term marriage as partnership, two people working as one mutual fund. If they split, surely the fund should be split. This theory is the law in California.

On the other hand we understand the way the economy works. Whether we are Johnny Carson or Johnny Carson's chauffeur, we are being paid as individuals. The weekly paycheck bears one name.

In the end, I favor the partnership theory, but not because of what happens when people separate. I favor it because of what it takes to hold a marriage together. As the authors of *American Couples* said, "There are many centrifugal forces that tug at relationships. To endure, couples need countervailing forces. One is financial interdependence."

We still need to maintain marriage as a shared venture, something which people nurture together, something that is larger than one or two paychecks. That's true whether the joint income is $15,000 a year or $1.5 million a month. We can only support that ideal by treating it like a partnership when it dissolves.

As for Johnny Carson, if Henry the Eighth is his role

model, he better hustle. Henry died at fifty-six. Carson is fifty-seven and only ending his third marriage. Is there a fourth Mrs. Carson in the wings? If so, somebody better lend her a history book.

OCTOBER 1983

PROMISES, PROMISES

BOSTON—For years, maybe decades, I used to see a romantic ad in the magazines that pictured a man, a woman, and a perfume bottle. The ad always had the same tag line: "Promise her anything, but give her Arpege."

I never could figure out how this ad sold perfume. It sounded to me like Arpege was the booby prize of broken promises. Promise her a Rolls-Royce and give her a lousy bottle of perfume? Promise her the moon and give her an ounce of smelly stuff? What were they doing, promoting duplicity?

I suppose I was just a skeptical child. Certainly more skeptical than Vicki Morgan or Lee Perry. These two women in the courts, and in the news, are portrayed as champion believers. But when their romances fell apart, they decided that they wanted a lot more compensation for broken promises than a bottle of perfume.

Each of them has followed Michelle Marvin's well-worn path to the law courts.

In July 1982, Vicki Morgan, that self-proclaimed "other woman" in the life of the late Reagan pal, Alfred Bloomingdale, filed suit against Bloomingdale for $5 million. She claimed that he had welched on his promise of lifetime support in return for her attentions, and what she described as "therapy" for his Marquis de Sade complex.

That not being enough, mistress Vicki went on to sue wife Betsy for another $5 million because she alleges that Betsy had the gall to put an end to the payments. Then, in September, a scant month after the death of Bloomingdale, Vicki Morgan filed a twenty-page declaration in court of promises, promises, broken promises.

Lee Perry's story is more complicated. She isn't a "model"; she's an assistant professor at Harvard. She alleges that Richard Atkinson, the head of the University of California at San Diego and a married man, impregnated her in 1977, and then persuaded her to have an abortion. Lee Perry maintains that she only agreed to the abortion because he promised that they would conceive a child again.

Last week Atkinson denied that he had impregnated her or ever tried to convince her to have an abortion. But Perry is suing him for "fraud and deceit," seeking $1 million in damages for broken promises. So much for free love.

What is going on here in the brave new world of chutzpah law is as simple as it is seamy. Vicki Morgan, we are told by her original lawyer, Marvin "Palimony" Mitchelson, is out to establish the principle of "mistress' rights." "We believe," said Mitchelson, "this is the first suit where the other woman has sued the wife." Hip, hip, hooray.

Lee Perry, who went to the same lawyer, is said to be out to establish the right of motherhood. "Not every lover's promise is binding," says Mitchelson, "but this woman has a right to have a child, and he misrepresented his intentions."

I always find Mitchelson's role in creating this area of the law intriguing. His women are invariably posed as hapless victims of male duplicity: women who have been loved and abandoned; women who are more to be pitied then censured. He then overlays this most ancient of honorables onto some fairly updated turf: housemates, mistresses, other women. He treats them as if they were buyers not able to beware.

But unless Vicki Morgan's brain was addled by twelve years of Marquis de Sade therapy, I don't see her as dumb enough to have believed that Bloomingdale's unwritten contract was more binding than society's unwritten contract. At least, she was mentally up to firing Mitchelson, because of "continued and fundamental disagreements."

Nor do I see Lee Perry as a proper victim. A woman with a curriculum vitae that runs four pages, a family therapist for five years, a doctor in counseling psychology, a teacher of human relationships—along the way she should have learned something about taking responsibility for decisions.

Whether or not it was Atkinson who impregnated her, she had, and made, the choice of abortion. Should a man be required to fulfill this sort of "contract" by doing it again? Can any one of us be sued for breach of seduction? Can those who swore "I'll love you forever" be sued for deception and fraud?

No, these are not issues of rights. Both women were into the murky area of promises, promises, broken promises. They were in high-risk affairs, totally uninsurable. The attempt to recoup their losses in court is outrageous.

There is a strange odor about these two law cases, but it isn't Arpege.

SEPTEMBER 1982

A MEANINGFUL RELATIONSHIP
WITH SUPERMAN

BOSTON—I don't usually take movies personally, but I was worried about Lois Lane from the minute the credits started rolling.

I mean from where I was sitting, this guy she got involved with was just another 1980s Everyman. Strip away the red cape and the blue tights and he was a flying mass of role conflicts.

One day he was a man with weaknesses and feelings. The next day he was an honest-to-gawd Superman. On Monday he was happy at work with nary an aspiration and on Tuesday, whammo, he felt compelled to go out there and save the world.

Someone as smart as Lois should have seen this guy coming around the corner. Sure, he was cute, but the morning after the night before he was going to be out the door. It just wasn't going to work out.

But there it was, once again, the fatal attraction of the Semiliberated Lady for the Traditional Man Who Is Trying to Change. You see it all the time.

Aside from the X-ray vision and a few other eccentricities, Superman was a case study of traditional malehood. He grew up on the ultimate performance trip. He never rebelled. He never racked up the car. He was a regular duty-first doo-bee. It's for sure that he never cried.

But like a lot of other urban professionals, he tried to

keep up with the times. This is, after all, an era of partnership marriages and meaningful relationships and open feelings. Sooner or later, he got the open feeling that he ought to get with it. When he decided to meaningfully relate to Lois, he WANTED to change.

What could be more irresistible to a gal like Lois? We've all known a Lois or two in our life, a lady stuck between time zones with all the messages from the past and present.

One minute she wants to stand on her own two feet and the next minute she wants to be swept off them. She may be Ms. Independence on the job, but in her personal life she only falls for the guy who could take her up, up and away from it all.

The Semiliberated Female is a pushover for the He-man Who Is Trying to Change. She thinks she knows who he *really* is. She thinks she can dig down to his core, bring out the softness in him.

So what happens to this couple? I could have predicted it. Superman gives up his dominant ways in order to live in equitable earthly bliss with Lois. Thus wooed up to his place, they spend the night in prenuptial PG-rated bliss.

But soon he finds that life as Mellow-man has its problems. For one thing, he can no longer hide his true identity. He's no longer defended by the mysterious powers. He's just a regular guy. Maybe even a person.

Not-so-super-men bleed. They get backaches. They lose fights. They trade in the awe of women for friendships and sharing. They exchange adventure for affection.

And while they are struggling to work it all out, the whole world gets nervous without its supermen. If the strong and good and the brave get domesticated, then the strong and the bad and villainous take over the world. That particular fantasy isn't just Hollywood property.

At the first alarm, faster than you can say kryptonite, Superman drops all this trendy sex-role-changing business and gets back to the man's job of saving the world. And just as I figured, semiliberated Lois accepts the guilt for ever having taken away her lover from his Important Work.

"It's sort of like being married to a doctor," she says with a sigh of depression.

The Man Who Wants to Change turns out to be just another male recidivist. He slips back to the days when Supermen were powerful and women panting as if his old role were an old slipper. The semiliberated woman is easily tricked back to her bad old days, eternally pining for the flighty guy with the Big S.

I wonder if this is what they mean by conservative backlash in the movies?

JULY 1981

IN THE MALE DIRECTION

BOSTON—There was a time in my life, I confess, when I thought that the only inherent differences between men and women were the obvious ones.

In my callous youth, I scoffed at the mental gymnastics of sociobiologists who leaped to conclusions about men and women from long years spent studying bugs. I suspected the motives of brain researchers who split the world of the sexes into left and right hemispheres.

But now, in my midlife, I can no longer deny the evidence of my senses or experiences.

Like virtually every woman in America who has spent

time beside a man behind a wheel, like every woman in America who has ever been a lost passenger outward bound with a male driver, I know that there is one way in which the male sex is innately different from the female: Men are by their very nature congenitally unable to ask directions.

The historical record of their unwillingness was always clear. Consider, for example, the valiant 600 cavalrymen who plunged into the Valley of Death . . . because they refused to ask if there wasn't some other way around the cannons.

Consider the entire wagon train that drove into the Donner Pass . . . because the wagon master wouldn't stop at the station marked Last Gas before the Disaster.

Consider even my own childhood. My father—a man with a great sense of humor and no sense of direction—constantly led us on what he referred to as "scenic routes."

But for centuries we assumed that this refusal was a weird idiosyncrasy. We never dreamed that it came with the testosterone.

In recent years, I have from time to time found myself sitting beside men who would not admit they were lost until I lit matches under their fingertips in an attempt to read maps in a box canyon.

One particular soul would consult an astronomical chart for his whereabouts before he would consult a police officer. Another would use a divining rod or a compass before he would use a gas station attendant.

In the 1970s, people believed in roles instead of genes, and I assumed that this behavior came from growing up male in America. I figured that males were taught that being lost was a challenge and seeking help was a cop-out. I assumed that the lost highwayman thought of himself as the Daniel Boone of Route 66.

Finally, however, the new breed of scientists is offering us new insights, not into upbringing but into biology and brains.

The male brain, according to researchers, is organized differently than the female. Men have better spatial abilities; women have better verbal abilities. Thus, we see the problem: Men read maps and women read people. The average man uses instruments. The average woman uses the voice.

Due to this fact, the husband who is able to adequately drive into a toll booth and roll down the car window is handicapped with the inability to then ask the question: "Where is Route Twenty?" A man who can stick-shift and double-clutch, using his right hemisphere, is handicapped by his left hemisphere when it comes to asking, "Do we take a right here?"

It isn't his fault, you understand. It has to do with our Darwinian roots (what doesn't these days?). The primeval hunter couldn't ask a highway patrolman which way the antelopes were running. He had to shut up and follow the tracks. A good berry picker, on the other hand, could follow advice.

These primitive differences have all the value of the appendix. They are likely to rupture in modern life. In my own life, the differences between the sexes have led to all sorts of misunderstandings and midnight hysterics. In other cases, they have led to deserted roadways, and divorce instead of doorsteps.

It is time for the female who finds herself in the passenger seat on a scenic tour to take the wheel or to be more understanding. After all, anatomy may not be destiny—but it has a lot to do with destination.

SEPTEMBER 1981

MAKING THE PROS

BOSTON—Two scenes out of recent newsreels are stuck in my mind: images of friendship and competition, winning and losing, and caring.

The first scene was a page one photo of Pam Shriver walking off the court at Forest Hills, arm in arm with Martina Navratilova—the victor comforting the vanquished. The two friends who had just battled each other would soon again be doubles partners.

The next scene was relayed to me secondhand. It took place in the Senate chamber where Bob Packwood was standing alone, filibustering against the Helms antiabortion amendment. As he read from James Mohr's history of abortion, Jesse Helms entered. The senator from North Carolina put his arm around the senator from Oregon and together they walked around the floor as Packwood continued to read. Even in conflict, they rubbed shoulders.

If I were a photo editor, I would have written the same caption under these snapshots: No Hard Feelings. They were pictures of two people, on opposite sides of the net, on opposite sides of a political battle, reassuring each other that they could still get along, walk along.

They were, in that sense, portraits of pros. It's pros, after all, who learn how to fight wholeheartedly without feeling angry with the opposition. Without taking it personally.

This is a tough business for the bulk of us "amateurs."

Few can manage it without training. Certainly not as kids. In my own childhood, when I disagreed with my father, he thought we were debating and I thought we were arguing. He sounded philosophical and I sounded angry. Only I took it personally.

Even today, I think it's hard for a lot of us to see competition—for points or points of view—without assuming personal conflict. An opponent is after all, someone out to "beat" you, someone you are supposed to "beat."

Maybe it's especially hard for women, raised to put relationships above games. In that context, even winning can seem mixed. As accomplished a victor as Pam Shriver had to say, "I have mixed emotions. I'm thrilled for myself, but I'm sad for Martina."

Politics are much more subtle than racket sports, but no less intense. In the Senate, Packwood and Helms are disagreeing about something more fundamental than who has the stronger serve. They disagree about human values.

The old admonition, "Don't take this personally," breaks down when the issue is truly personal. I remember to this day the man who calmly explained to me the theory of women's inferior intelligence telling me, "Don't take this personally." How should I have taken it? As if I were a frog?

Human values are also "personal." There are times when it may seem inappropriate for senators to disagree so politely about such heated subjects. Most of us at one time or another have wondered whether coolness was really a lack of caring. Most of us have questioned people who are able to separate their emotions from their behavior.

Looking again at my mental photograph of the opposing senators walking the floor together, I also wonder: Is this sane or phony? Are they behaving as gentlemen or old boys, civilized or clubby? Or just pragmatic?

By now I vote for pragmatism. Packwood and Helms,

156

Navratilova and Shriver, after all, have something in common. They travel in the same circuit. They are opponents one day and partners another. There is more than the usual reason to keep the competition focused on making points rather than enemies. More than the usual reason to take it impersonally.

Eventually I think most of us have to learn this skill. In my own profession, people who wildly and publicly disagree with each other's point of view in print ask about each other's children in private.

In corporations, people who compete for position, who argue about goals and power, talk pleasantly in the hallways and the elevator. Even in that most personal arena, family, we may vote for different people and still make dinner together. Most of us struggle to make our differences reconcilable.

This lesson does have its emotional costs. It takes self-control to drain our confrontations of their personal venom. It also takes some understanding and some perspective to live with differences, even competition, without feeling personal conflict. I guess it takes a pro.

SEPTEMBER 1982

"WHERE DO YOU WANT TO EAT?"

BOSTON—They are going out to dinner.

He turns to her and asks, "Where do you want to eat?"

From his point of view it is a simple matter for which there is a direct answer.

She hears him, holds his question in the air, and looks it over.

From her point of view it is the opening line of an exploration, the beginning of a process.

Slowly, she runs through her Rolodex of local options. One place was too crowded last time, another too expensive, a third she liked but he thought too "veggie."

Three or four possibilities finally present themselves before her mind for screening purposes. She responds to his question with her questions: "What about Chinese food? Are you in the mood for pizza? How did you like the fish place last time?"

"I'll go anyplace you like tonight," he repeats. "Where do you want to go?" There is an edge of impatience now lining his voice.

The woman senses something familiar about this dialogue. They have been here before. She begins to see a choreography to the way they make plans. She remembers now all the other performances, prompted by all the other questions: What time should we leave? Which movie do you want to see? Which color do you like?

As a rule, he thinks that she has trouble making up her mind. As a rule, she thinks that he is impatient.

But this evening, she finally realizes how different their goals are, how different their minds are working. He is always looking for a decision. She is always searching for a consensus.

What do you want for dinner? He is asking, literally, for the name of a restaurant. She on the other hand wants to find out what he feels like eating, what she feels like eating, what their first choices are, what their second choices are, is there a choice that will satisfy him, her, them?

His question is simple; hers is complex to the point of absurdity.

She thinks now of the women in her family. To make a

date with her mother, sister, or aunt requires at least two, possibly three, phone calls. As a group, they can barely compose a menu for a family dinner without the services of a polling agency. They are famous for conference calls, drive each other crazy in the need for agreement.

It happens even with her women friends. They are not, individually, uncertain. One makes editorial decisions about national policy with confidence; another makes plans for natural conservation with aplomb; a third makes a career of challenging conventional wisdom.

But put before them a question—Your place or mine?— and they begin to waffle. "What do you want to do?" "I don't know, what do *you* want to do?"

The woman is, of course, exaggerating, but not by that much. There is a problem, somewhat endemic to her sex, about this kind of decision making.

The way she figures it, women are, as a whole, more likely to consider relationships in making decisions. They think in context. A choice as simple as the restaurant is recast as a concern about pleasing everyone.

Like members of some Japanese quality circle, they prefer to spend the time reaching agreements, rather than writing directives. At worst, their pursuit of consensus ends in paralysis, or stifled differences.

Their men, on the other hand, often regard this process as interminable and chaotic. At worst, their pursuit of decisions ends in bossiness or submission.

Of course there are other movements in this dance of indecision. An arabesque of martyrdom, a plié of self-sacrifice. Sometimes, under the guise of pleasing others, the women she knows waltz away from conflict and responsibility. If the movie is lousy, if it rains at the seaside, if the pizza is cold, it won't be their fault.

Her own motivations are, probably, one part thoughtful, one part self-protective, one part chicken.

The woman considers all this. She has, as usual, gone too far. They are only talking about dinner, after all. One dinner. No one will arrest her for selfishness if she chooses the restaurant. In fact, the consensus is that it's her turn to make the decision.

JULY 1982

MS. UNDERSTANDING

BOSTON—The little girl doesn't understand.

A boy in her first-grade class has selected her as his recess quarry. All week he has pursued her, capturing her scarf, circling her with it, threatening to tie her up.

The look on her face as she tells us this story is puzzled and upset. She has brought home similar tales of playground encounters since Monday and laid them out across the dinner table.

My friend, who is her mother and amused by it all, explains again to the girl, "That's because he likes you." But she still doesn't understand.

Finally, the mother turns to me, because I have been through it before, seen the tears of another first-grader, offered the same motivations. "Tell her," says the mother in frustration.

I begin to form the analysis in my mind. I will tell her how the boy wants attention, doesn't know how to ask for it, only knows how to grab for it, confuses aggression with affection . . .

Then suddenly I stop.

I hear an odd echo from the words inside my head. What is it? An echo of a hundred generations of women interpreting males to their daughters? An echo of a hundred generations of women teaching their daughters the fine art of understanding human behavior?

All at once I find myself reluctant to pass on this legacy. I am wary of teaching this little girl the way to analyze. I am not so sure at this moment that we should raise more girls to be cultural interpreters for men, for families.

I look at my friend. This woman is admirably skilled in the task of transmitting one person's ideas and feelings to another. Indeed, she operates the switchboard of her family life.

The people in her home communicate with each other through her. She delivers peace messages from one child to another. Softens ultimatums from father to son; explains the daughter to her father. Under her constant monitoring, the communication lines are kept open; one person stays plugged into the next.

But sometimes I wonder whether she has kept all these people together or kept them apart? Does she make it easier for them to understand each other, or does she actually stand between them, holding all the wires in her hands?

I watched Katharine Hepburn play the same role magnificently in the scenes from *On Golden Pond*. She placed herself between the angry, acerbic, viciously amusing husband (Henry Fonda) and the world. She was his buffer and his interpreter—to the gas station attendants, the postman, the daughter.

"He wasn't yelling at you," she tells the boy who comes to live with them. "He was yelling at life. Sometimes you have to look hard at a person and remember he's doing the best he can . . . just trying to find his way, like you."

Her caring was wondrous, inspiring, full of energy and

161

love. But it was only when the boy confronted the old man, dialing directly, shortcutting the switchboard, that the man changed.

In Gail Godwin's novel, *A Mother and Two Daughters*, there is another aging mother, still negotiating between her two "children" who are now turning forty. She is like the woman in many of our autobiographies—the mother, or grandmother—behind the scenes.

How many families only know each other through these women? Some mothers, like the one in this movie and this book, have been forced to occupy the stormy fulcrum of family life, and others have chosen to be the power broker of human relationships. Some actually keep people at peace, others keep them at bay. Sometimes the endless interpretation, especially of men by women, keeps couples together. Other times it keeps men from explaining themselves.

I know it is a skill to be able to understand and analyze one person's motives and psyche to another. It requires time, attention, emotional dexterity to run these switchboards. Yet it can also overload the operator and cripple the people from talking across their own private lines.

Today, anyway, I feel peculiarly unwilling to explain the first-grade boy to the first-grade girl, peculiarly unwilling to initiate the six-year-old into this cult of communication.

I offer only friendship and sympathy. These are things she doesn't have to struggle to understand.

FEBRUARY 1982

GOING COED

BOSTON—On one of those June days that serve as lush background scenery for white graduation dresses, I found myself in a procession walking beside a trustee of a small private school.

It was something of a special occasion on this campus, because this was the last year for an all-girls graduation. The school was completing its merger. Next year even commencement, the last remnant of separate histories, would be coed.

"It will be kind of a shame to lose this," the trustee next to me said as the songs and speeches—the special events of this female ceremony—continued. His assumption, unspoken and unquestioned, was that next year the girls would become a part of the traditional male ceremony, that the females would give up their own rituals to gain access to male rituals.

I have thought of that day often since. The trustee wasn't wrong in his assumptions. In fact, over the past dozen years, "going coed" has often meant the admission of women into existing and unchanging male institutions. The merging of men's and women's organizations has often resulted in the submerging of women.

You can see this in the business world, where women are allowed in, even up, if they'll play by men's rules. You can see it in the professional organizations, when the acceptance of women into men's groups has meant the end of the women's organization.

But it's most stark in the college world. Men's colleges like Yale, Princeton, and Dartmouth admitted women, believing that they could, indeed should, be treated the same as men. Brother and sister colleges like Brown and Pembroke married, and the women lost their names. Once I went to Radcliffe College; now women go to Harvard.

Among women's colleges the urge to go coed (in 1960 there were 298 women's colleges, today there are 116) slowed and then virtually stopped as this evidence mounted. Separate was sometimes better for women's equality. Women's colleges are now less carried away by proposals, more interested in contracts.

I suppose the latest chapter in this curious history of coeducation was written by Barnard and Columbia colleges.

Barnard, like so many other women's colleges, came into existence because Columbia wouldn't accept women. Almost one hundred years later, Columbia ardently wanted women. But Barnard was reluctant.

This wasn't just a case of bad romantic timing. Barnard has, many believe, the best of both worlds. They have their own faculty (59 percent female), their own curriculum, their own finances. Admissions are up 51 percent; they are operating in the black. Yet they can also share Columbia's dorms and dining rooms, libraries and courses.

As Barnard's president, Ellen Futter, put it carefully: "One might describe as ideal the notion of two single-sex institutions with a relationship." But it was not ideal to Columbia. And as Futter said, "There's a difference between what is structurally ideal and practically ideal."

Columbia wanted women for its men and its classes; Barnard wanted a measure of independence for its women and itself. There was talk of merger and suspicions of sub-merger.

164

In the end they made what President Futter called "a long-term stable arrangement." Others might call it a curious arrangement. Like two lovers who can't reconcile their separate needs, Barnard and Columbia will go on together, but Columbia will be free to go looking for other women.

Barnard will survive as a private liberal arts college with a special affiliation to Columbia (and more control over faculty tenure). Columbia will admit women it can call its own.

Both colleges profess pleasure at this arrangement. Barnard will survive. Columbia will get its women. They will all live happily ever after in the same dormitories and dining halls.

But there is something odd in this, a peculiar example of the times, of ideals. Columbia longed for an intimate relationship, but never offered partnership. Barnard was wary of compromise.

Now, young women applicants can choose between the female institution of Barnard, separate but dedicated to equality, and the male institution of Columbia, integrated but not yet equal.

Somehow or other their choices seem familiar.

JANUARY 1982

THE CULT OF MIDLIFE BEAUTY

BOSTON—For those of you who missed it, Sophia Loren turned fifty in 1984. We are told that she celebrated her birthday publicly in a shopping mall in Atlanta. What glamorous errand had brought the Italian movie star to the mall? Had she run out of candles or panty hose?

No, Sophia Loren had joined the bustling ranks of certifiably older women promoting beauty. By now it appears that nearly all the women who are pumping and primping, selling their shapes and their books on the circuit, are more than halfway through the average life expectancy.

Joan Collins, at fifty, wrapped her body in nothing but boas for *Playboy*. Before that Jane Fonda, forty-six, began bumping and grunting on thousands of videotapes. Now we have Raquel Welch writing and posing as a forty-four-year-old yoga pinup queen and Sophia Loren hustling for Coty and a book of beauty tips. Middle age is so popular that soon a younger woman may have to lie to get a publisher, or endorse a face cream.

Frankly, I don't begrudge Jane her biceps or Joan her pectorals or Sophia her everything. By all accounts, women like these are supposed to offer hope for the Ghost of my Christmases Future. But I'm not sure how I feel about their kind of middle age.

When I was a kid, the only older women who won prizes

for their physical preserves were Greta Garbo and Marlene Dietrich. Even they were looked upon with suspicion, as if there were pictures of Doria Gray hung up somewhere in their closets. Most of us assumed that at some point past thirty, you just quit. It was a vaguely unsettling but also reassuring idea.

After all, it was hard enough trying to look like a model in *Seventeen* when you were a teenager. How many of us suspected that we would be compared to Linda Evans at forty? Indeed, think of the women who have spent five decades being measured against Sophia Loren. Is it any wonder that they are fans of Elizabeth Taylor?

The central notion of the middle-aged, show-and-sell routine is that if SHE can look that good at fifty, so can you. Just follow the directions on the package or the book. This is a bit like saying that if Shirley MacLaine can dance at fifty, you can dance at fifty. (Dear Diary: Can I look like Catherine Deneuve at forty-one? Dear Writer: Did you look like Catherine Deneuve at twenty?)

The sales pitch of beautydom is generally accompanied by a charming disclaimer about youth. Ms. Loren, for example, writes in her new book, that "this mature approach to beauty . . . does not depend on possessing the dewy cheeks of a teen-ager. . . ." The secret in this advice is that Sophia Loren apparently had "dewy cheeks" as a teenager. The rest of us had zits. A few of us may have had muscles in youth; the rest had premature cellulite.

The new role models of midlife assure us that they, too, were really awkward and unattractive in their youth. "I wasn't always considered beautiful," writes Loren. "When I was 13, my nickname was Toothpick. . . ." Raquel Welch goes a bit further, saying, "For the most part I see myself as a well-proportioned wimp."

But if you really think of Loren as a toothpick and of

Welch as a wimp, then I have some books, a line or two of beauty products, and a lot of exercising just waiting for you.

As far as I can tell, not one of the new breed of midlife beauties is going to make their peers feel good about themselves. It's Rosemary Clooney in a muumuu who makes them feel good. What Loren, Fonda, Welch, etc., have done is to raise the threshold of self-hate faster than the age span.

We no longer look forward to letting go at thirty. There is no thought of aging gracefully at forty. At fifty, we are faced with a prospect of daily regimens to soften our skin and tighten our thighs. The end result of all this is that those of us who failed to look like Brooke Shields at seventeen can now fail to look like Victoria Principal at thirty-three and like Linda Evans at forty-one and like Sophia Loren at fifty.

When Gloria Steinem turned fifty, she updated her famous line from forty. She said, "This is what fifty looks like." With due apologies to the cult of midlife beauty, allow me two words: "Not necessarily."

OCTOBER 1984

A WORKING MARRIAGE

BOSTON—I have two friends who have just passed the couples crisis, a kind of midterm exam for commitment in the 1980s. The crisis began, as it often does, when each part of this unmarried pair was offered an ideal job in another city.

These long-distance callings forced them to evaluate what they had assumed for the past year: their desire to be with each other. Neither could be absolutely sure that their own bond was strong enough to resist the centrifugal force of their work lives.

In the course of this crisis, two "I's" were put on the table, balanced against one "we": two jobs against one relationship. The tangible rewards of professional advancement—money, status—against the intangible rewards of a personal connection.

The crisis was even harder because my friends are still in their twenties, still young in an era when work comes first chronologically, and often emotionally. Nevertheless, these two concocted an elaborate plan of action including many basics in two-career coupledom—a one-sided move, followed by a time of commuting, and then reunion.

When the crisis had passed, I was not surprised to hear that they had decided to get married. After all, they had already done the hard part. The pair had hammered out a compromise. Instead of demanding a sacrifice of each other, they had worked their way to a place of mutual consent.

The details were less important finally than the process. These friends—lawyers in love, with due apologies to Jackson Browne—completed their prep course for marriage in an era when the "institution" is really an open-ended negotiation.

I don't know quite how to chronicle this new pattern of negotiation. Not that long ago, in the peak days of traditional marriage, the family unit spoke with one dominant voice or one veto. Decisions about careers and geography were largely a game of follow the leader. In everyday life, household chores were also divided by hormones. Nearly every piece of work—from kitchen duty to car repair—was pre-labeled his or hers.

But in marriages between equals where tasks are acquired

169

instead of inherited, everything is up for grabs. Two people with two jobs, two schedules, and two egos place a much greater strain on the day-to-day skills of communication and compromise.

I suppose that's why the early pioneers of "liberated marriages" tried to reorganize their lives with household contracts. They wanted to protect themselves against backsliding but also against uncertainty. The contracts sometimes read like transcripts of legal proceedings for joint custody of washers and dryers. Roles were set according to days, weeks, and months instead of by sex, but they were set.

Now it appears that what keeps marriages between equals together are not rigid formulas of fairness, but a tolerance for change, flexibility, a lot of give-and-take and negotiating.

When roles are no longer separate, they overlap and open up gaps in the everyday life of couples. When there is no single permanently assigned Milk Buyer, a family refrigerator can hold two bottles or none. On any given day, both, either, or neither spouse may be in charge of the children's schedule or the laundry stubs or the social calendar. Over time, regular chores, such as bill keeping or gardening, may belong to husband or wife, but the only permanent system that evolves is one for trade-offs.

This kind of marriage geometrically increases the amount of decision making. He does not buy the car and she the rug; they do. She doesn't worry about the school system and he about the mortgage rate; they do. It triples the chances for a bad marriage to flounder on power struggles, misunderstanding, and mutual withholding. It also enhances the chance of a good marriage to thrive on connection, the sense of joint venture, mutual gratitude.

I don't know what will happen to my lawyer friends now, a pair who settled the trial of their premarriage so professionally, so personally. Surely they were lucky to find a solution to this contemporary crisis, and luck is a good sign for any couple. But their eagerness to negotiate, their willingness to work it out is even more promising. It is a proper way to begin a working marriage in every sense of those words.

MARCH 1985

Part 5

SCIENCE AND NON-SENSE

THE O-RING SYNDROME

BOSTON—Frankly I try not to read about airplane accidents while I am in the air. So I was not tickled to learn about the precipitous plunge of an L-1011 over the Bahamas, while I was buckled into the seat of a 727 somewhere over Illinois.

I have quite enough paranoia without worrying about engines that shut down and a plane that drops like a stone for 12,000 feet. I am, you see, still working off my DC-10 phobia. I can't even bear chatty pilots who conduct guided tours from the cockpit when they should be watching the instrument panel.

Still there was something familiar about this particular near-catastrophe. For want of three small O-rings, an L-1011 was nearly lost. For want of three oil seals, a jumbo jet and 172 people almost ditched in the ocean.

As the Eastern Airlines officials explained in public hearings in Miami, the fate of the fanciest technology came down (almost literally) to two maintenance men who hadn't done their job properly. A planeload of lives was in the hands of humans who simply hadn't read the company memos about the new procedures. Anybody could make a mistake.

What we have here, it seems to me, is a thoroughly modern mortality tale. Call it The O-Ring Syndrome.

Back in the seventeenth century, when George Herbert first reported about the battle that was lost for want of a nail, it was a rare event. Herbert was writing in a decentralized, rural economy about people who were relatively independent. They only got together to go to war.

Today, you don't have to be in battle to have your life hang on the work of some cobbler. You can be riding in a plane or walking down the street or drinking a glass of water. At any moment when a lot of lives are at the mercy of a few, they may be suffering from The O-Ring Syndrome.

The O-Ring Syndrome was, for example, in full swing at Three Mile Island, Pennsylvania, when a near-catastrophe was caused by, among other things, valves left open by maintenance men. It was in operation at Times Beach, Missouri, where a single waste hauler named Russell Bliss sprayed the streets with dioxin to keep the dust down.

It was evident even when the Tylenol murderer was lacing the medicine bottles of Chicago. One person's evil intention, after all, can be as disastrous as another's accident. An unknown crazy killed seven people and nearly killed the product as well.

It's not that the rate of human error or malevolence is any greater today than it ever was. But the instruments are more powerful, and we are more easily targeted.

A hundred years ago, when someone didn't attach a carriage wheel properly, the lives of half a dozen people were threatened. Today when someone screws up an L-1011, up to 300 lives can be lost, and when someone sprays a street of one small town, 2500 lives are affected.

The potential for disaster in mass transit, mass production, mass destruction, has grown geometrically. We are much more vulnerable to the single computer byte gone awry and the sole terrorist gone mad. The more centralized our world, the easier it is to sabotage. The more powerful our weapons, the more dangerous.

Our very survival on earth depends today on the people who keep military computers running. Somewhere, I am sure, there is an O-ring on a nuclear missile.

We deal with this vulnerability with a safety mania. We buckle up. We hold hearings. We issue instructions. We demand standards. When a single person adds cyanide to Tylenol we counter with a billion safety packages. We try to match each anxiety with a code of protections in some escalating cycle.

As the certified owner of a pair of white knuckles, I know how we comfort ourselves with safety notices. The more powerless we feel in any situation, the more we long to believe in the competence of the people or technology in control.

By now, I am sure there isn't a maintenance worker in the business who isn't checking the oil seals. But the rest of us are stuck here, in the age of the O-rings, with all the shaky symptoms of The Syndrome.

MAY 1983

THE SCAPEGOAT COMPUTER

WASHINGTON—For a while on a Thursday morning in December 1983 I had something in common with the astronauts: computer failure. Never mind that the six of them were in a space lab and I was in an earthly office, never mind that they were worrying about their landing and I was worrying about my credit rating. We were both chatting with the specialists, the troubleshooters.

Single-handedly, I had just completed a twenty-day orbit around a bill collector. The bill had been paid long ago and yet the notices kept arriving, threatening to repossess Christmas and cut off my plastic life-sustaining equipment.

Finally the specialist had gone to the root of the problem. All fixed up, he said proudly, and then proceeded to explain what had gone wrong. You guessed it: "It was a blip in the computer."

Now I don't know about the rest of the hi-tech consumer world out there, but I have heard this one too many times. When this explanation comes over the telephone or over the television, when I hear it from the space-lab *Columbia* or the District of Columbia, I harbor a small nagging suspicion about the role that the computer is playing in society. I think the role is called scapegoat.

Remember back when that Iowa woman who was declared dead by Medicare, although otherwise in fine fettle? What killed her? Computer error. Remember when thousands of customers at Merrill Lynch became overnight paper millionaires? Who had fiddled with their accounts? Why, they said, the computer. Remember the Massachusetts man who was ticketed for a car that he didn't own on a street where he'd never been. How did it happen? The computer. Virtually everything that goes awry in our earthly lives—aside from lost love and a fallen soufflé—is now blamed on some computer or other. In the whodunit of modern life, the computer is the butler. The silent butler.

Frankly I am not so quick with a judgment of guilty against the computer anymore. At least on this planet, some of the mistakes are just too whimsical or charming for the mind of a machine.

Was it really a computer error that sent a Moral Majority membership card to Ted Kennedy? Is a computer mischievous enough for that?

Was it a computer that sent about 20,000 San Franciscans to the wrong polling booths? If so, was it a Democratic or a Republican computer?

What about the Texas computer that listed a funeral home in the Yellow Pages under the heading "Frozen Food— Wholesale"? Was it programmed with a sense of humor?

We have gotten so used to the explanation "computer error" that we think of software as a dybbuk, a household ghost that goes through our daily lives rattling the pans and screwing up the bills.

But more often than not, the glitch is a human one. After all, for every computer program there is a computer programmer.

Not every business even has its computer. Not long ago, a friend's furniture was sent about 240 miles to the right of its destination—which was her living room. She called the warehouse and got the usual explanation: the computer-dunit. But this dingy warehouse, I am convinced, is run by dusty people in green eyeshades wielding quill pens.

More than once, I have called an insurance company for information only to be told that the computer was down. "The computer is down," a friend informs me, is another way to spell "coffee break."

In Seattle, I once sat next to a bank officer who told me of complaints people made about their computer money machine. They put the card in, but they didn't get the money out. A huge number of these complaints mysteriously disappeared when the banker said that the transactions were all videotaped.

I'm not suggesting that the computers never make a botch of things. The one that I write on for example has produced some terrible spelling errors from time to time.

But it's too handy a victim. The computer can't yell. It has a cursor but it can't tattle. It can't even file a suit charging defamation of character.

What we need here is a Computer Legal Defense Fund to separate human error from computer error, garbage in from garbage out. In the spirit of civil rights, we need a user-friendly legal system that helps us to know when the computer did and didn't dunit. In a country like this, every computer deserves a lawyer. After all, who wants a scapegoat that's all byte and no bark?

DECEMBER 1983

DR. GOD AND HIS JUNIOR PARTNER

BOSTON—My friend went to the doctor's office expecting to find God. The doctors she knew always played God, except on Wednesday afternoons, when they played golf.

But what she discovered was that Doctor-God-Sir, the professional keeper of the Temple of the Body, was not available. Instead a new doctor sat down before her, opened up her chart, met her eyes sincerely, and asked her to think of him as her "junior partner in health care."

This somewhat abrupt transfer from God to the junior partner had a startling effect on my friend's blood pressure. But she had discovered the latest trend of the medical profession: God is dead, or at least dying out.

The whole history of Doctor-as-God began way back when medicine men were merely priests. Eventually, they got academic degrees, and demanded a promotion—although there were some who thought that God was a little high.

Medicine still remained a profound mystery to the laity. Such is the way with all religions. It was conducted in Latin or Medicalese, which was Greek to the average person. The patient/suppliant was required to have faith, hope, and a little something to put on the plate when it was passed.

We were expected to submit to such rituals as the knife and to such magic as pills. Few of us ever saw the appendix that was removed or understood how antibiotics work. But we took penicillin as a kind of oral penance for illness: four times a day for ten days, and bow to the east three times.

Somewhere along the way in this skeptical, secular era, the medical laity became less worshipful. The best and brightest of the young apprentices were also less willing to pretend omniscience.

And so we have now entered the era of the Junior Partner in Health Care.

What are the characteristics of a junior partner? First of all, an aura of humility. You can tell a junior partner by precisely how many times he or she uses the expression: "We really don't know. . . ." Junior partners believe in sharing, especially in sharing doubts.

You can also identify junior partners by their passion for education. This friend called her J.P. recently when a bee sting had blown her arm up to the size of a large thigh. "What do I do?" she asked. He answered, "First let me tell you something about bee stings."

All junior partners have been educated by the full-disclosure, informed-consent school of medicine. Gods give out proclamations; J.P.s give odds. The odds that you will get better, the odds that you will get worse. Along with every prescription comes a description of side effects. If just one Manchurian lost an earlobe or a belly button from this cream, you will hear about it.

Consider the true story of a woman who discussed the possibility of surgery with her J.P. After listening to his explanations, she tried to recap the pros and cons. "So," she said, "the worst that can happen . . ." "Oh, no," he interrupted. "The worst that can happen is that you'll die from the anesthesia." After peeling her off the floor, he admitted that this possibility was fairly remote, one in 30,000. This is called overinformed consent.

The most basic thing to remember for your next encounter with a J.P. is that he or she will not tell you what to do. Gods give commandments, but J.P.s only lay out options. It is up to you, the Senior Partner, to take responsibility for your health decisions. (This fact is on a poster in the J.P.'s waiting room, near stacks of pamphlets on fiber in the diet.)

It is still possible, of course, to find God. But he is likely to be (1) he, (2) older, or (3) a specialist in heart or brain surgery. The life-and-death stuff still seems to fall into the hands of you-know-Who.

Should we be surprised by the takeover of the junior partners? After all, isn't this what we all wanted? We wanted doctors to stop treating us like children. We wanted them to talk to us, tell us the whole story. We wanted them to stop acting like gods. We wanted them to admit their fallibility.

Isn't that right? Absolutely. Positively. I swear to God.

JULY 1984

DYING TO GET INTO SPACE

BOSTON—I know a lot of people are dying to get into a space program but I never thought it would go this far. The government actually approved the launching of the ashes of ten thousand into eternal orbit.

The aerial burial—a contradiction in terms if there ever was one—is the scheme of a Florida firm called the Celestis

Group. They expect to charge a fairly celestial price of $3900 for anyone who wants room in their 1900-mile-high mortuary. The capsule of "cremains" will be boosted into place by a private company headed by an astronaut from the Mercury days, Donald K. Slayton. You've heard of astropoliticians? Slayton is the first astromortician.

This business venture was approved by the Department of Transportation, the federal boosters for free enterprise in outer space. According to the DOT, you can put anything (or in this case, anyone) into space as long as it doesn't jeopardize national security, international treaties, or human health and safety. And we don't have to worry about the health of these passengers.

As far as DOT is concerned, this postmortem is "just another aspect of a very well established industry." As a friendly spokesperson, struggling to contain the giggles, said, "It's really no weirder than scattering ashes over an ocean."

Frankly, the whole thing's a bit freaky for my taste. I don't want my final nonresting place to be in orbit, even if the capsule is outfitted with reflectors so that my descendants know when I'm watching over them. (Twinkle, twinkle, little Grandma.)

But what's most startling about this space hearse isn't its cargo. The glare coming off the capsule reflects the diminished idealism of our own star-struck days.

In sixteen years, we have gone from putting a man on the moon to putting his cremains in orbit. The most lofty notions about a mission in the universe have literally turned into ashes. Talk about your small steps for mankind: We are now on a new frontier for hucksterism.

The same sort of thing is happening in a minor way at NASA, where the shuttle program has been suffering an identity crisis. They want to be a glamorous pioneering space operation and a reliable transportation company. NASA hopes to be self-supporting by 1990. The conundrum is that the more they attract the private trucking business, the less they attract the glitter of public support.

Imagine what would have happened if NASA had contracted to haul up this payload. Can you picture the network correspondents counting down for this macabre uprising: "This is Lynn Sherr at the Johnson Space Center in Houston. It's three minutes until the first celestial resurrection." NASA has gotten enough grief for hustling Senator Jake Garn to the heavens. What if they were shuttling his ashes? The launch would be about as glamorous as jump-starting a hearse.

The problem with this postmortem lift-off isn't just profit. Columbus' trip had a profit motive. But the space sale is the most ghoulish extension yet of the consumer ethic that promises us that we can buy anything as long as our check matches our whim. The sky is the limit. Or is it?

This is the same ethic that puts up a billboard on a mountain. It's the same egotism that claims ownership to a lake or a piece of seashore. It's the same marketing mentality that is ready to sell first-class tickets on any ego trip.

Maybe this is the way the Wright Brothers would feel today about Supersavers. But it is depressing to believe that all that research paved the way for a celestial cemetery; it's rather like discovering that the DNA double helix could be used for a corkscrew.

Remember in 1961 when Jack Kennedy gave the moon program its send-off? He said, ". . . No one can predict with certainty what the ultimate meaning will be of mastery of space." Somehow I don't think he expected that the ultimate meaning would be a trivial pursuit. But today a piece of the sky has been sold off to the morticians. The rest cremains to be seen.

FEBRUARY 1985

ORGAN FOR SALE

BOSTON—When my daughter was small, I used to sing an old, bittersweet lullaby about life and death. There was a line of fatalism that ran through this folk song: "If livin' were a thing that money could buy, the rich would live and the poor would die."

I remember that line because living often is a thing that money can buy. When food and medicine make the difference, the rich may live and the poor may die.

We see this not just in photographs from the Third World but sometimes in stories from our own world. Lately, we have witnessed it in moments of high drama when communities from Massachusetts to Wyoming tried to raise funds the way they once raised barns, for a neighbor who needed a lifesaving heart or liver transplant.

But never has the relationship between rich and poor, life and death, been so crassly presented as in the venture of a Virginia doctor who set up a business to broker human kidneys. Under this scheme a person who needed the money could literally sell a kidney to a person who needed the organ, and the doctor would get a fee for services.

I suppose it was inevitable in this world of supply and demand that someone would seize such a ghoulish business opportunity. Not long ago, in Maine, a man set up a short-lived plan under which people could have their organs sold after death and the benefits sent to a beneficiary. A *Wall*

Street Journal columnist suggested that private and government health insurance agencies pay the closest relatives some money for the organs of the deceased.

Now more than 6000 people are waiting for kidney transplants, more than 4000 awaiting corneas. The next logical step of the free-enterprise system would surely allow a live person with two kidneys, two corneas, a mess of debts, and an edge of desperation to sell what he or she owns. Whose body is it, after all?

But there are limits to what is tolerable. To some degree our society has permitted the buying and selling of bodies. We have supported prostitution, allowed the purchase of sperm and blood, and witnessed contracts for ova and rental of wombs. But we have not yet permitted human beings to be stripped of organs for profit, never accepted the notion that the have-nots should become a source of spare parts for the haves.

As Daniel Callahan, the director of the Hastings Center, which deals with questions of medical ethics, says, "In theory there ought to be no laws that would stop competent adults from selling whatever they want. But the potential for abuse is just too great."

The fundamental abuse is, of course, exploitation of people so desperate that they would sell half their sight, or kidney function. But there are other troubling questions. If a person is competent enough to sell a kidney, is he or she competent enough to sell a heart? If an organ is up for sale, should it go for the top dollar?

"Our system of values isn't supposed to allow the auctioning off of life to the highest bidder," says Representative Albert Gore, Jr. (D-Tenn.) "It erodes the distinction between things and people. It's not too difficult to conjure up some great problems in the future if we place a bounty on human organs."

For these reasons Gore has added a prohibition against

buying or selling organs from live or dead people to a bill that he is filing in Congress on the whole subject of organ procurement. But he knows that these bizarre market schemes are emerging only because of the intense need, and competition for, transplants.

In the current scramble for organs, the gap between the rich and poor isn't the only one. There is the gap between those who have access to publicity and those who do not.

And there is the fundamental gap between the large source of potential donors and the small number of actual donations. Each year there are about 20,000 potential donors—people who have suffered brain death—and only about 2500 provide organs for transplants. The latest Gallup Polls show that 95 percent of us know about the shortage of organs, but only 24 percent of us would give permission for our own organs to be donated.

The notion of a free market, a business enterprise in merchandising organs, is an unseemly and inhuman one. But in the end, the problem isn't whether we can buy life, but how we can be persuaded to give it.

SEPTEMBER 1983

BABY FAE AND THE BABOON

BOSTON—The headlines announcing her death were classics of the genre. "Baby Fae Dies," read one, "but Doctor Sees Gain in Science."

The words relayed from Loma Linda, California, dressed this tiny casket with a silver lining of progress. Dr. Leonard L. Bailey, who oversaw the twenty-one-day drama in the thirty-two-day life of the girl with the baboon heart, called her and her parents "pioneers." The university spokesman at the memorial service said solemnly, "Baby Fae has not lived in vain, nor has she died in vain." Even the mother, we are told, gave one last wish, to the doctor for his experimental work: "Carry it on."

By the time Baby Fae is laid to rest, the choreography of this public medical ballet will have been complete and completely familiar. We have been through this enough to see the shape of a ritual drama.

The plot opens and concludes with "hope." At the beginning, the doctors announce that they are trying to save a patient, a life. The technique is new, daring, promising. There are risks, yes, but Barney Clark may yet be back on the golf course with his artificial heart and Baby Fae may turn twenty with her baboon heart. The story ends with a claim of victory for "science"—and a funeral.

Each time the curtain rises, the public audience suspends a bit of its disbelief in preference for medical magic shows.

We have watched so many impossible cures become routine treatment that even when faced with a baboon organ beating inside a human body we do not want to be considered antiscience, antiprogress, pessimistic.

"What if it works?" we say. After all, when Christiaan Barnard did the first human transplant, the patient lived for only eighteen days. Now, 65 percent of transplants done at Stanford live a year, and half are alive after five years. Yes, Barney Clark may have died after 112 days, but Dr. William DeVries announced that he is ready to try again.

We don't know whether "frontier-blazing" experiments like animal-to-human transplants are headed down dead ends or onto new paths, whether we are talking Laetrile or penicillin. We don't know if Dr. Bailey, who fits the alluring image of the buccaneer scientist, is a committed crank or unrecognized genius. So, the human and the editorial response is that this situation "bears watching," and "raises questions."

But I don't think we have to be quite so reticent to judge this medical event. The issue of experimenting on terminally ill human beings has not always been handled honestly. Dr. Christiaan Barnard admitted in his memoirs that he lied to the first transplant patient. Dr. Bernard told Louis Washkansky the strong odds in favor of survival; he did not tell him that these were the odds of surviving just the operation.

Dr. Barnard describes the state of mind of terminally ill patients who become subjects for experiment quite accurately: "If a lion chases you to the bank of a river filled with crocodiles, you will leap into the water convinced you have a chance to swim to the other side when you would never accept such odds if there were no lion."

We have all known people chased by the lions of cancer or heart disease. Barney Clark signed an eleven-page consent form for an artificial heart, and leaped into that water.

He had the right to do so.

Here the question is whether a parent has the right to throw a child in. All the medical evidence of this case—except for the original boasting testimony of Dr. Bailey—suggests that this infant had no chance to survive into toddlerhood, let alone adulthood. Given that, we have to conclude that Baby Fae's body was donated, alive, to science. The rationale, that she was "going to die anyway," implies that it is open season on the dying, that we can try even the most outlandish experiment on these human beings.

Dr. Bailey, who called this transplant a "tremendous victory," is planning to do it again. It is entirely possible that he found what he was looking for, a reason to go on tinkering with newborns and baboons. But whatever rationale there was for the first experiment—the idea that a newborn with an undeveloped immune system could absorb a foreign body better than an adult—there is none for a second experiment.

Those we cannot give consent should be the last, not the first, people we use for experiments. It may be difficult to stop at the shoreline when the lion is gaining on your child. But when the crocodiles are hungry and the baby can't swim, there is no mercy in throwing that child in the water.

NOVEMBER 1984

WHOSE LIFE IS IT ANYWAY?

WASHINGTON—For a time, life has been imitating art in Riverside, California. The courtroom case of a twenty-six-year-old quadriplegic, Elizabeth Bouvia, is every bit as dramatic as the script of the movie, *Whose Life Is It Anyway?*

In September 1983, Bouvia admitted herself to the psychiatric ward of Riverside General Hospital with one goal in mind: to starve to death under their roof. She wanted doctors to give her only the medical attention needed to ease pain.

Unlike the character in the movie, Bouvia had been paralyzed since birth with cerebral palsy. Her grit was well-recorded in daily life and academic degrees. But after a failed marriage, failed attempts at pregnancy, and deepening depression over her future, her only determination was to die: "I choose no longer to be dependent on others."

Here is a case that pushes just about all the buttons on our finely engineered ethical panel. The right-to-life and the right-to-die buttons. The one that labels suicide as rational act and the one that labels suicide as a crazy act. The one that opposes medical intervention against a patient's will and the one that supports medical intervention to save lives.

It presents us with the dilemma that we've been edging up to slowly, case after case. Ever since Karen Ann Quinlan, we've debated whether a hospital could, should, keep someone "alive" after brain death. Today we discuss the ethics of "heroic" care for the terminally ill as well.

Slowly, we have also asserted certain rights to medical care. In 1973, in the case of a woman named Roe, the courts determined that a pregnant woman seeking an abortion had the right to privacy. Recently, in the case of a baby named Doe, the courts determined that parents could deny life-prolonging surgery to a severely handicapped infant. On our own we can refuse therapy, even maintenance therapy like dialysis, and willfully shorten our lives.

Meanwhile suicide, at least among the elderly or ill, has gained a certain odd legitimacy. In March 1983, the writer Arthur Koestler, ill with leukemia, committed suicide and his healthy wife, Cynthia, joined him. She was described as "devoted." A Florida couple in their eighties carefully killed themselves as a "solution to the problems of aging." The sheriff commented on how "thoughtful" they were.

In this atmosphere, Elizabeth Bouvia's request to be allowed to starve with painkillers and without force-feeding seems almost routine. After all, if the parents of Baby Doe have the right to deny treatment, then doesn't the patient herself have the right to refuse it? If Roe has the right to "control her own body," then doesn't Bouvia? Isn't suicide a civil right?

The reality is that the Bouvia case has pushed over the established ethical line. We are now entering into a moral arena where words like "rights" begin to lose their meaning.

"I'm not asking for anybody to kill me," this woman has said. "I'm asking that the natural process of death take over." But refusing food is no more a natural process of death than falling is when you jump off a bridge.

What makes this case different from other "right-to-die" cases is that, however miserable she regards her life, Bouvia is not suffering a fatal disability. What makes it different is that she is not just proposing suicide; she is asking for the help of doctors. Indeed, Bouvia checked into a ward that specializes in preventing suicide. There are, as Freud said, no accidents.

The California Superior Court judge made a proper distinction last week when he ruled that, yes, Bouvia had the right to kill herself—it is her life, anyway—but not "with the assistance of society." If she did not continue to accept nourishment, the judge would allow the hospital to force-feed her. Now, as I write this in December 1983, the young woman has refused sufficient liquid protein to sustain her ninety-five-pound body.

No matter how uncomfortable the idea, I think it is appropriate, even imperative, for the hospital to forcibly feed its despairing patient. Psychiatric wards are not suicide centers where people come for help in terminating their despair.

Deep down, I'm afraid it is too easy for society to "understand" the unhappiness of a quadriplegic instead of alleviating it. It's too easy for us to begin to regard suicides of the sick or the aged as "thoughtful" solutions.

If we support Elizabeth Bouvia's civil-rights stand, then sooner or later we would passively watch a woman step off a ledge and a man swallow sleeping pills. As we stood there, bystanders, would we then remind each other not to interfere? The "right to die" can easily become an excuse for our own unwillingness to reach out and help.

DECEMBER 1983

A VERY WANTED CHILD

BOSTON—She was the very model of good behavior at her first press conference. Maybe fourteen years later, she would storm out of a room yelling back at her parents, "I never asked to be implanted." But at three days old, Elizabeth Jordan Carr, the first American conceived in a dish, cuddled against her mother, held her own nose, clenched her own fist, and promptly fell asleep.

The most hardened opponent of in vitro fertilization had to be infected by the delight of the twenty-eight-year-old mother, Judith Carr. The most qualm-ridden professor with a list of ethical questions about "test-tube babies" had to smile at this scene of mother and infant.

Even a room full of reporters put aside their normal cool and applauded the existence of this very wanted child.

It was an odd televised ceremony that I watched from my living room, and a touching one, marking the difficult transition the Carrs had made from couple to family, formally introducing a child to the world. It carried more meaning than the usual show-and-tell of infancy.

"I hope they understand," said Judith Carr to the critics of in vitro fertilization. "We have our child and that's what we wanted."

It's not hard to understand that "want." Indeed, Elizabeth's costly life comes out of our empathy.

She is in some ways the creature of a system which

responds well to private needs, is engaged dramatically in producing happy endings to personal stories. We do better for individuals than for masses. We give more applause to the extraordinary than to the mundane.

Seeing Elizabeth in the spotlight, I couldn't help making comparisons between the haves and have-nots, between dramatic problems and routine.

Nine months ago, Elizabeth, then a small collection of cells, was inserted into a womb of sophisticated technology. Her birth was a tribute, as they say, to modern medicine.

Nine months ago, the infant mortality rate, which can be controlled by the common denominators of old-fashioned care, had risen in Washington, D.C., by 10 percent. The deaths were not a tribute to modern politics.

During the summer and fall, Elizabeth grew in her mother's womb. She was carefully nurtured, watched over by the accomplices in this creation.

During the same seasons, the federal program which had fed two million pregnant women and children, WIC (Women, Infants and Children), was tossed into a block grant and then cut. There will be less food money this year for these everyday pregnancies. This food has made the difference, all the research said, between a healthy baby and an "undesirable outcome."

Now, in the days after Elizabeth's birth, some scientists speculate about the risks of this fancy procedure. Much is already known about the risks of poor nutrition. As a people we are better at caring about a child than we are at caring about children. Better at performing feats of caring than routines.

It's not just Elizabeth. Tell us about an abandoned baby and we will call by the hundreds with offers of food, money, even adoption. Tell us about a child who will not survive without a fancy operation and we will set up a fund to buy its health.

But tell us about the 40,000 children who die every day in the world and our eyes glaze over at impersonal numbers. Tell us that thirteen out of a thousand infants will die in this country and it seems remote. Talk about nutrition for two million of the poor and pregnant and we do not find it ... urgent.

Perhaps, after all, we need a glossy magazine photo of each pregnant woman who promises to send baby pictures if we keep her in flour and cheese and milk.

After watching Elizabeth's performance, I went back to the *Natural History* magazine on my lap. I read an article about birds that only feed their offspring if they stay within the nesting circle. If one goes a foot beyond the invisible marker, the parents will ignore the cries of their own young.

Our society's a bit like that, I thought. We care for those who live within a certain circumference, or who capture our attention because they are extraordinary. We let some in and keep others out. And we don't ask ourselves often enough to expand the circle of caring.

JANUARY 1982

AIDS I: BETWEEN LIFE AND LIFE-STYLE

SAN FRANCISCO—Bill Kraus drives slowly by the bath-house parking lot and counts the cars. There are only eight of them tonight, eight cars in a lot that has room for at least thirty.

For Kraus, a congressional aide and a leader in the gay community, the evidence of bad business for a bathhouse—where sex with strangers is the major commodity—is a somber, welcome sign. The gay men in this city are beginning to respond to the threat that appears on posters and pamphlets almost like warnings on cigarette packages: the threat of AIDS.

Acquired immune deficiency syndrome is now a full-fledged epidemic in America, but particularly in the gay community. Of the 1641 confirmed cases, 1140 are identified as homosexual or bisexual. In San Francisco, where the homosexual community is the most concentrated and politically powerful in the country, and where the homosexual life-style is often highly promiscuous, 90 percent of the 250 AIDS victims have been gay men.

The people who have AIDS stare at a bleak set of statistics. All those who got it three years ago are dead. Seventy-five percent of those who got it two years ago also are dead. Indeed, earlier this day, Bobby Campbell, a lanky former nurse who came down with AIDS in 1981 when he was twenty-nine, described himself with bleak humor as "the AIDS poster boy," for the simple reason that he is still alive.

There is no way to overstate the effect of AIDS on the gay community. Nearly everyone knows someone who has it or died of it. Moreover, this minority group, persecuted for its sexuality, barely out of a closet full of demons, is now faced with a disease that is transmitted through semen or blood.

As Kraus put it, "When I first heard about AIDS, I thought, Oh, God, they've finally found a disease for the diseased. It rekindles in the psyche all the hateful propaganda that you are sick."

Many in the gay community share those vivid memories

and experiences of being labeled "sick" and "untouchable." In some terrible irony, they feel a medical stigma replacing the old social stigma.

The fear of being persecuted again, this time for carrying a "gay plague"—although the disease is not believed to be caught through casual contact—leads to denial and paranoia. Men such as Kraus who tried to convince gays of the need for precautions were labeled by some as "sexual fascists" or "homophobes." There are still stickers in the telephone booth near Castro Street, the heart of the gay district, insisting that AIDS "comes from a government laboratory, not your life-style."

But even for the majority of gay people who don't share "CIA conspiracy theories," the call to change their life-styles sounded ominously like a medical form of the old repression. The entire history of open gay life is short and tenuous. It's still less than a decade since the Twin Peaks became the first gay bar in San Francisco to have glass windows.

Among many gay men, "liberation" was defined or confused as the right to have sex without restraint. Their sex life included a series of anonymous sexual encounters. Now, as one man put it, "we have to choose between life and lifestyle."

Routinely, in one conversation after another, one man explains "the need to change my life-style" and another says he has "dropped out of the fast lane" and a third describes "the return of courtship and romance." The choices range from celibacy to monogamy to condoms, but they are the subject of incessant, almost obsessive conversation here, particularly among "the worried well."

"There's never been anything that has had such a dramatic impact on people's behavior," says a local writer. "A year ago a fashionable gay man in the Castro area was promiscuous and used drugs. Today those are the people you want to stay away from." As Kraus describes the change in his community, "It's sort of like going down the freeway sixty-five miles per hour and throwing the car in reverse."

Says thirty-one-year-old Bobby Campbell, who is living with AIDS: "Knowing someone's middle name does not protect you." But the reassessment of the culture seems to go beyond precaution.

Listening to gay men I hear a mild nostalgia for the old excess, as if those had been fraternity days, and yet a strong sense that it is better to move on. AIDS, like some fatal herpes, has given homosexuals in the fast lane a reason to grab the emergency brake.

"If there is anything positive about this horrible situation, assuming the great majority of us survive, it will have been a crisis that makes people stronger," says Kraus. "I see it detrivializing sex. I think that will be permanent. I think there's room in human society and gay society for people to be kinder and warmer to each other."

With luck and a cure, this may be the peculiar legacy of a dreadful disease.

JULY 1983

AIDS II: THE NEW LEPERS?

SAN FRANCISCO—Sooner or later, the word "leper" comes into any conversation here about AIDS.

Maybe it comes from a patient who describes how it feels to be shunned by former friends, and even nurses. Maybe it comes in a story about a man with AIDS who was hounded out of a gay bar the night they held a fund-raiser for his very disease.

Or maybe it comes in tales told by a healthy homosexual about a bus driver who wouldn't touch his transfer, or the straight friend who suddenly felt uncomfortable sharing dinner, or the couple who refused to be served by a gay waiter. But at some point, the word recurs: "I felt like a leper." "They're treating us like lepers."

To Dr. Mervyn Silverman, the public health director of San Francisco, there's a special irony in the leper analogy because, "You know, leprosy isn't very contagious. When you go back to ancient times and think of the person with all the terrible sorts of things that come with Hansen's disease [leprosy], you can understand the paranoia. But even when it was discovered that leprosy wasn't easily spread, you couldn't convince most people."

Nor is AIDS very contagious. The weight of medical evidence suggests that acquired immune deficiency syndrome is transmitted through blood and semen and not through casual contact. The high-risk groups are homosexuals and bisexuals, drug users, hemophiliacs.

Not a single one of the hundreds of health professionals who care for, clean, and feed AIDS patients has come down with the disease. Yet a gay man goes to work in San Francisco with nothing more than a cold and his colleagues make uncomfortable jokes. A man with AIDS shows up for jury duty here and the other jurors refuse to serve with him.

For Dr. Silverman, dealing with the second epidemic, the epidemic of fear in the straight community, is frustrating. "With all the talking I've done in interviews with the media," he says, "it seems that the paranoia grows rather than recedes."

Where does the fear come from? Uncertainty mixed with fatality and spiced with mistrust.

Both the cause and cure of AIDS are still unknown.

"When you have a disease for which we in the medical profession don't have all the answers, then people naturally say, 'Wait a minute, if you don't know what the bug is, how do you know that I can't catch it casually?'" says Dr. Silverman. "We are saying things like, 'Well, up to now it seems like, and it looks like, and it appears like...' The public isn't used to hearing that."

Public health officials can plot how a disease is transmitted even when they don't know where it comes from or how to make it go away. But that isn't easy to explain in a thirty-second television newscast. The anxious public is all too used to hearing the government protest the safety of dioxin or Agent Orange or Three Mile Island.

But there is something else that makes AIDS a particularly volatile disease. As a San Francisco writer tells me, "The fact that it's gay people who have the disease tosses gasoline on the fire."

The notion of a fatal disease spreading sexually through the homosexual community is rife with meaning among those who believe that homosexuals are "sick." The idea that it is catching, that it could spread to the straight world, is explosive politically and psychologically.

There are some diseases which carry enormous symbolic weight in our culture, far beyond their medical danger. This is one of them. We forget that the influenza pandemic of 1918–19 killed more people than four years of fighting in World War I. But we remember syphilis, the black death, TB. We will remember AIDS.

In her book, *Illness as Metaphor*, Susan Sontag noted that "Illnesses have always been used as metaphors to enliven charges that a society was corrupt or unjust." Before AIDS even existed, she wrote prophetically: "Any disease that is treated as a mystery and acutely enough feared will be felt to be morally, if not literally, contagious."

The cure for paranoia is ultimately in finding a cure for

AIDS. But in the meantime, a customer sitting in a gay bar watches to see if I order a drink in a bottle or a glass. In the meantime, Dr. Mervyn Silverman goes out to do another television spot saying that you can't get AIDS from a bus ticket or a handshake. In the meantime, a man with AIDS wonders whether he is society's new leper.

JULY 1983

CELEBRITY MEDICINE

BOSTON—Back in the 1960s, Andy Warhol predicted that everyone in America would someday be famous for fifteen minutes. The artist had in mind a glitzy, Studio 54, disco-till-dawn sort of fame.

It hasn't worked out that way. The way to become famous right now is not through the social columns, but through the medical annals, and not as a performer but as a patient.

Just look at the record, the hospital record. Barney Clark was a superstar for 112 days, Baby Fae for 20 days. Now it's Bill Schroeder's turn. He couldn't be a better health-care star if he came from central casting.

We know about his taste for beer and his choice of basketball teams. We know about his phone call from the president and his Social Security hassles. We've watched him ask people to feel his artificial heart, and read about the effects of his stroke. We have seen him up and seen him down, and rooted for him. Like the others in this peculiar medical lineup, he has become famous for what's been done to him.

My colleague at the *Boston Globe*, Otile McManus, calls this the era of celebrity medicine, and I think she is right. We take our hi-tech medicine personalized now. We prefer our innovations with a shot of hype. The latest in medical technology comes attached to a name and a story. It makes it much more interesting.

I confess to being uncomfortable with all this. It not only makes celebrities out of patients. It turns medical researchers into publicity hounds. Would Humana Hospital have volunteered to pick up the bill for a hundred hearts if they did not believe that their patronage would pay off?

The company spokesman was not ashamed to admit his hope that the artificial-heart program will make Humana "a household word in health care." Must every research project now come complete with a press kit and an attractive, articulate patient available perhaps for talk shows and certainly for evening news programs?

But that isn't my only reservation. It seems apparent that celebrity medicine affects the decisions we all make about how to spend health-care dollars. When a new technique or treatment is attached to a real-life story, it makes the single rescue, the frontier heroism, the flashy hi-tech medicine so much more attractive than the low-profile and low-cost tales of prevention and care.

As the dean of the Harvard School of Public Health, Harvey Fineberg, suggested: "Someone has to speak up for the thousands of people whose names are not on everybody's lips, who are dying just as surely as Mr. Schroeder and whose deaths are preventable."

I am not surprised or scornful of the fact that our public attention is captured most faithfully by a single life. It is easier to digest a human life than a statistic. But while

Humana sponsors the artificial heart, we are also cutting Medicaid payments for hospital stays, closing community health programs and watching infant mortality rates rise in some cities. The cost of extending one life attached to a machine could, we know, feed, inoculate, and save other people.

As Tom Murray, associate professor of the Institute of Medical Humanities at the University of Texas, puts it: "It is one thing to see a Bill Schroeder, and another to see a thousand women say, 'If we feed them, we're going to save maybe ten babies.' We don't see those babies."

I don't begrudge Bill Schroeder his artificial heart, nor would I shut down the artificial-heart program at this stage. But there is a kind of media and moral schizophrenia between the celebrity of a few and the anonymity of others. Do you have to have the right sort of "interesting disease" now?

In this age of hi-tech, celebrity medicine, how do we focus a spotlight on the people whose health issues aren't so glamorous? Must we put photographs of one pregnant woman a day in the paper? Must we put a schoolchild on television each day and talk about what it means to have lunch?

In the sad aftermath of Bill Schroeder's stroke, when his ebullience was drained and he had clearly suffered brain damage, a doctor at Humana said, "Don't give up on Schroeder." The doctor suspected how fickle the audience and how fleeting this sort of fame can be. After all, we've already given up on so many people whose names we'll never know.

DECEMBER 1984

THE KILLER BEE SYNDROME

BOSTON—The tree outside my front door is safe for now. It stands there, half its leaves brown and nibbled, looking like a banquet table deserted by guests in the middle of the salad course.

That's pretty much what happened. The guests—rude, greedy creatures—were gypsy moth caterpillars. They had just eaten their way in from the suburbs and begun on my tree when nature called them to their cocoons.

This time I was lucky. But looking at the leaves I remember the original gypsy moth immigrants, whose descendants have decimated the Northeast. They were brought to this country from France by a scientist who thought they would produce silk.

Anybody could make a mistake.

While my tree stands in Boston, the people in California are dealing with another imported pest, the Mediterranean fruit fly. The planes there sprayed people as well as land. The public's outrage there was palpable.

How did this new outbreak occur? In part because the 200,000 sterile fruit flies released to mate turned out to be fertile. "We got burned on a shipment from Peru," said a state official.

Sterile. Fertile. Anybody could make a mistake.

On both sides of the country, then, we have examples of that fun couple, scientific method and human error. Call it the Killer Bee Syndrome if you will. Someone sets out to breed a bee that will produce lots of honey; some technician unlatches the cage with the killer bees.

Anybody who could make a mistake usually does.

The most scientific system in the world with fail-safes and triple checks and computer backups is devised by people, run by people, used and misused and screwed up by people. To put it as simply as possible, the more dangerous the science, the more terrifying our fallibility.

This is something I would like to see cross-stitched on the walls when the leaders of all the major industrial countries get together in Ottawa. One of the chief subjects on the agenda is that ultimate killer bee, nuclear know-how.

For decades, America has been the chief exporter of the most dangerous scientific species. Not only have we built bombs and used them, we have passed out most of the nuclear information for what we used to call Atoms for Peace. We've exported uranium, exported sixty small research reactors, and lent $5 billion for seventy commercial reactors for energy production.

While the construction of nuclear plants has slowed in this country—by the sheer tug of public protest over safety issues—we continue to sell overseas, the same way we sell banned chemicals. We worry about our own technicians, our own safety standards, our own hazardous waste. But we regard "foreign" problems as if they had some private stock of air and water.

More to the point, each "peaceful" nuclear reactor produces the raw material for nuclear weapons. One 1000-megawatt reactor produces enough plutonium for more than twenty bombs a year. That is why Israel bombed Iraq's French-made plant.

The Reagan attitude toward countries that want to develop the bomb was expressed best in his campaign quote, "I just don't think it's any of our business."

That's changing now, but slowly. In preparation for Ottawa, the administration has come out with a stronger statement against extending the nuclear "family." But it also promised to remain a "clearly reliable and credible supplier" of nuclear technology for peaceful purposes.

The problem is that no one knows how to control the spread of nuclear weapons while expanding the market for nuclear energy. Even the Reagan government offers only some vague idea about monitoring or retrieving the plutonium from foreign countries.

In short, we still seem to be dealing with nuclear bombs the way we've dealt with handguns. I can almost see the bumper sticker: A-BOMBS DON'T KILL PEOPLE. PEOPLE KILL PEOPLE.

But the more bombs we build and store, and the greater the number of people involved, the greater the risk. The risk is multiplied by each country—with its own enemies and instabilities, its own leaders and technicians—that gets nuclear knowledge.

Surely, nobody wants to blow up the world. But, as I can tell from my tree, anybody can make a mistake.

JULY 1981

THE FATE OF THE DINOSAUR

BOSTON—I became a dinosaur groupie when I was eight years old. I still remember the colossal reconstructed skeleton of a brontosaurus in the science museum that first captured my imagination.

This wasn't a dramatic, life-changing event. I didn't run off to become a paleontologist. Nor did I run off with a paleontologist. But I was hooked. Over the years, when other members of my family worried about the extinction of whales and seals, I stuck to dinosaurs.

I suppose it was their size and fate that grabbed my attention. Children tend to equate the huge with the powerful. The larger something or someone is, the more impressive to a childish mind. These creatures were, by any definition, grown-ups, the biggest animals on earth. Yet they had all died. Here was a mystery that challenged my preconceptions.

Over time, I read all sorts of explanations for their extinction. The dinosaurs were big, but their brains were small. The dinosaurs couldn't adapt. Slowly, they died out while humans, the adaptable, thinking species, prospered.

There was a charming egocentricity to these theories. My dinosaurs were evolution's failure and we were its successes. There was some comfort in it, too. In the nineteenth century, Darwin's theory of gradual evolution upset the religious orthodoxy, but it offered an orderliness of its own.

Evolution drew a reasonable pattern in the universe. Over time, species grew better and better. In the rough justice of nature, the fittest survived.

But the theory didn't survive intact. A few years ago, another generation of scientists offered up evidence about my extinct subjects. The dinosaurs didn't gradually die of their evolutionary flaws. The scientists speculated that sixty-five million years ago an asteroid struck the earth and produced a worldwide crop failure that did them in. My giant vegetarian, the brontosaurus, was the victim of a climatic disaster, a cosmic accident.

Then, more recently, two scientists at the University of Chicago reported that such disasters have occurred like cosmic clockwork every 26 million years over the past 250 million years, wiping out huge numbers of life forms. The dinosaurs were just the biggest, most memorable of the victims.

Now when I look at the evolution of these theories, I wonder whether every era gets the dinosaur story it deserves. I don't mean to suggest that science is trendy. All theories are not equal. They are built on real, measurable knowledge.

Yet scientists are also part of their culture, their times. At one moment or another they are open to a certain line of questioning, a path of inquiry that would have been unlikely earlier on.

The scientists of the nineteenth century—a time full of belief in progress—saw evolution as part of the planet's plan of self-improvement. The rugged individualists of that century blamed the victims for their own failure. Those who lived in a competitive economy valued the "natural" competition of species. The best man won.

The latest theories may reflect our own contemporary world view. Surely we are now more sensitive to cosmic catastrophe, to accident. Surely we are more conscious of the shared fate of the whole species.

Today the astronauts travel into space and report back that they see no national borders. Environmentalists remind us that the acid from one nations' chimneys rains down on another. Most significantly, another group of scientists warns us that a nuclear war between two great powers would bring a universal and wintry death. One hemisphere is no longer immune from the mistakes of the other hemisphere.

In that sense, the latest dinosaur theory fits us uncomfortably well. "Our" dinosaurs died together in some meteoric winter, the victims of a global catastrophe. As humans, we fear a similar shared fate.

The difference is that their world was hit by a giant asteroid while we—the large-brained, adaptable creatures who inherited the earth—may produce our own extinction.

209

In these times, what a luxury it would be to only worry about the next "natural" catastrophe. It's due in fifteen million years.

JANUARY 1984

Part 6

A SENSE OF PLACE

ANYBODY HOME?

BOSTON—It is ten o'clock in the morning, and the suburb feels as empty as a factory at midnight.

If a camera panned this neighborhood from above, it would look like a Playskool world. All the single-family houses are neatly painted and furnished, all the yards landscaped, all the streets clean and tree-lined . . . and barely inhabited.

The postman makes his rounds here like a watchman. He leaves behind letters that will sit for hours until the return of Occupants and Residents. He meets only a sprinkling of people: a mother with a young baby here, a housewife there, a retired couple in one home, a baby-sitter in another.

The neighborhood has slowly lost its lived-in look. In fact, people do not live here anymore in the old sense. They spend weekends here. They sleep here. They pay mortgages here.

But at the sound of the Monday morning bell, they walk out: the shorter ones to school, the taller ones to work. In the daylight, the deserted houses stand as a reminder of a past culture.

The effect is eerie, as if some economic neutron bomb hit suburbia. That's not a farfetched image, not really.

In the earlier part of this century, the thirties and then the fifties, we were sold on the ideal of owning our own homes on our own plot of land. From Herbert Hoover's housing conference in 1931 to the GI mortgages and tax deductions of the post-World War II days, the government fostered this rampant architectural individualism.

It wasn't hard to do. The house in America fit our desires for security, and privacy, and ownership. House was home. House was, for many of us, the one space in the world we could control. We could nail pictures to the walls, play drums, cook cabbage. It was ours.

For decades, the house fit our pocketbooks and our lifestyles. It was a man's provision and a woman's occupation. If it was also a living arrangement that separated men from women and children, we didn't notice for a while.

Within a single generation, homeowning went from being a prerogative of the rich to being a middle-class way of life. Within two generations, it went from being an American dream to being an American assumption. By the seventies, when there were, finally, fifty million houses, when seven out of ten of us lived in single-family homes, the house had become the personification of private life.

Today, the house still circumscribes the domestic world, the personal space in an anonymous life. In every sense of the word, it is our shelter. But it is, increasingly, our taskmaster. That is the irony in the intense feelings about homeowning that we can see every daylight in the deserts of our suburbs.

A while ago, a husband bought a house and a wife ran it. Now couples have two incomes or often can't afford a mortgage. A while ago, a young couple chose a house for the children. Now a young couple often chooses between a house or children.

The woman of another era who married her architecture and became a housewife is now often a working wife with the double work load of a societal bigamist. Room to breathe is now room to clean.

The schoolchildren who were the special rationale of the suburban planners are now the special worries of suburban parents. The houses were carefully built so that children would remain in the care of their own families. Now these houses keep them isolated from any other care.

Children are the afternoon people of these suburbs. The parents who wanted a private connection with these children under a single roof now watch over them by telephone. To have a home, we must leave that home every day. We devote more time to the house and spend less time in it.

Should this teach us that the old center of family life doesn't fit the new realities? Probably. But instead, in some odd way, our frantic lives away from home make us value our private space all the more.

So we seem trapped in change between conflicting versions of the life we want to lead. We work away from our home, to hold onto our home. We diffuse our families to protect their center.

And in the daylight, our neighborhoods become still-life monuments to the powerful idea that only a house is a home.

OCTOBER 1981

THE COVE AND THE TIDE

CASCO BAY, Maine—The huge blue heron glides over our cottage roof and settles down gently, taking up his post at the mouth of the tidal cove. Standing guard on elegant long legs, he picks off trespassers who swim too close to the border. When he is through and the water begins to intrude again, he takes off, arcing out over the bay.

Every day since we arrived, the great bird has followed this pattern. He arrives at each low tide like clockwork—no, nothing like clockwork. Watching him at my own porch post, I cannot imagine anything more different than tides and clocks, any way of life more different than one in tune with tides and another regimented by numbers.

The heron belongs to a world of creatures who follow a natural course; I belong to a world of creatures who have fractured continuity into quarter hours and seconds, who try to mechanically impose our will even on day and night. But each year I come here, vacating a culture of fractions and entering one of rhythms. Like many of us, I need a special place, just to find my own place, my own naturalness.

It has taken me longer than usual this year [1984] to sink into the island life. My time here has been wrapped around those most certifiably "manufactured" events, political conventions. There was no internal logic or cosmic timing to the political clock. The quadrennial gathering of elephants and donkeys, the rituals of politicians, have no common purpose with the shifts worked by the heron. The contrast was jarring.

Even here, the outside world pursued us. One night, my husband and I stood on the porch watching lightning far offshore. As the sky between clouds and water lit up, we felt awe—and a gradual realization that somehow, subconsciously, we were waiting for the stem of a mushroom cloud. Even the most stunning natural spectacles are dwarfed by our man-made nightmares.

But finally, one morning I left my watch to wind down on the bureau. Life became simple again. I ate when I was hungry, slept when I was tired, woke when I was rested, did a great deal of the things we call nothing. This is what I will remember of my summertime here. And I will remember how hard it is in our human world to get back to simplicity.

The most basic of human rhythms disappears in our workaday lives, the way the sound of a cricket disappears in the city. Whatever is natural in our biological patterns gets knocked out of sequence by the metronome of our social existence. From the time we're small, we learn to wake up to alarms and work to somebody else's schedule. We have lunch when it's lunchtime, go to bed when it's bedtime. Sunrise and sunset are less relevant to our lives than 9 to 5. Hot and cold are less significant than thermostats.

Most of us work fifty weeks a year in order to have two for ourselves. We work thirty or forty years in order to have ten or more in which to retire. There is very little room on our shopping lists or weekly calendars for being natural. We need to literally vacate the premises of our ordinary life.

I suppose it's something of a miracle that, given time and environment, any modern urban dweller can still drift into his or her own nature. It's as if there is some center waiting to be rediscovered, one that we can touch when we are at rest. Maybe simplicity is a secular miracle today the way that Willa Cather's archbishop once described religious miracles: something that comes when our perceptions are made finer "so that for a moment our eyes can see and our ears can hear what is there about us always."

I don't know if I can take simplicity home with me tomorrow. Like multicolored sand carefully layered in a glass jar, it doesn't travel well. By the time I return to the city, the subtlety may be jostled away. But during this list-making, schedule-hopping, clock-abiding fall, I can retreat—at least in memory—to the cove and the tide.

SEPTEMBER 1984

WAVING GOOD-BYE TO THE COUNTRY

BOSTON—The weekend is over, and we drive down the country road from the cottage to the pier, passing out our last supply of waves. We wave at people walking and wave at people riding. We wave at people we know and wave at people who are strangers.

The island wave is by now a summer habit. It took me time to acquire this salute, but now it feels a natural part of life in Maine. Like year-rounders, we pass back and forth the visual assurance that anyone on our island belongs here, is accepted.

When we arrive at the pier, the boat is already crowded with the end-of-summer exodus. Island emigrants help each other stack cat carriers and lift bags onto the back of the boat. Crossing the water, everyone is patient with each other's dogs and children.

But by the time the three of us have transferred from the ferry to our private car and reached the turnpike, my wave has begun to atrophy. Before we cross the Maine border, my hand has entirely lost its training. As the hundred miles go by, even the tolltakers have turned from smiles to surliness. The jawline of drivers in other cars seems to set as the city skyline rises.

To ease my reentry into workaday life, I decided to walk the last mile home. I am left at a familiar safe city corner and, yes, almost immediately, my accent changes. I begin to "speak" in the city's body language: neutral and wary.

Suddenly conscious of my own adjustments, I notice how few eyes meet on this mile. Women do not look at men. Old people do not look at teenagers. Men do not smile at each other. People don't wave to strangers on these streets. They measure them.

A quarter of a mile from home, inevitably, I pass two young men who give their own obnoxious verbal greeting to every woman who crosses their stoop. By the time I reach my own door, I go over the threshold as if entering a haven.

This small pilgrimage from rural community to city is not unique. But today I am peculiarly aware of how my own trip seems to mimic American life.

Our whole country has moved from rural communities to cities, from towns where contact was reassuring to cities where contact may be threatening. In 1900, 60 percent of us lived in the country; in 1980, 74 percent of us lived in the city. We have exchanged being known in small communities for being anonymous in huge populations.

It is this easy public space that seems to shrink as the population increases. Millions of us have exchanged a street life in which we acknowledged each other for a street life in which we deliberately ignore each other.

I am not glorifying rural life. I know that in small communities people have to struggle to maintain their privacy, their individuality. The same society that supports people can confine them. The same people who help each other some days annoy each other on other days.

But in the city, people have to struggle to make a community. We have to recreate a world in which we are known. We fight against anonymity at the grocer's, the dry-cleaner's, the newsstand, the coffee shop—and are often thwarted by the supermarket, the discount pharmacy, the fast-food counter.

The more anonymous we are in public, the more we forget our small towns at work and home, among family and friends. But our communities are private ones. Indoor ones.

I'm not sure why it's so hard to maintain some sense of community in the city streets. Perhaps it is just arithmetic. At a certain point, numbers make strangers.

But I suspect that it is also because we urban people think of ourselves as transients in our communities. Even the third-generation city people travel light. We don't sink our roots in neighborhoods as deeply as our grandparents did. We don't claim the street turf.

Pascal said, "We do not worry about being respected in the towns through which we pass. But if we are going to remain in one for a certain time, we do worry. How long does this time have to be?"

I don't suppose any visitor cares if he is known in a strange city. But many of us live our whole lives as if we were just passing through.

And if we are all tourists, where are the natives to teach us how to wave?

SEPTEMBER 1982

HEADING NORTH

ANCHORAGE—Our car swings out of the downtown traffic and into the gas station. We are looking for directions out into the snowcapped mountains that surround this city, embellishing and embarrassing it with their elegance.

The young gas station attendant bends down to the window and apologizes. He doesn't know the way to the main highway. He has only been in Alaska four days.

Hours later, we arrive in Talkeetna, halfway between Anchorage and Denali State Park, where climbers assemble before they "assault" Mount McKinley. We who are not into assaults ask where we might find a walk with a view.

The cook at the restaurant also apologizes. Although he is dressed in a Full Alaska—beard, wool shirt, hiking boots— he has only been here three weeks.

Soon, our encounters with new Alaskans have become a running joke. We easily adopt the opening lines of conversation in this state: Where you from? How long you been here?

In eight days we meet Native Americans who have inhabited this territory since time immemorial. But we meet only one nonnative, fourth-generation Alaskan, and a handful who were born here.

We discover that to have lived in Alaska in the 1930s is to be a pioneer. To have lived here since the 1960s is to have memories of the old days. To have lived here a dozen years is to hold seniority. To have lived here six years carries with it the sound of solid citizenry.

This is undeniably a land of immigrants. The license plates proclaim it "The Last Frontier," with its unimaginably vast wilderness, one-sixth the size of all of the United States. But it is also equally the last frontier of American immigration.

The East Coast of America was the stewpot of Europe a century ago. Alaska is the stewpot of the Lower 48 today. To see it in process is to see the optimistic, boasting, apologetic, insular, and intense self-consciousness of a new culture being created out of old ingredients.

This immigration has a peculiarly twentieth-century shape. The first American immigrants came by steerage. Today's Alaskans usually come (and often leave) by DC-10 and B-737.

Centuries of technology and generations of frontier experience are compressed by this time warp. Log cabins and tract houses coexist. People get their salmon from the water and their Pop-Tarts from the supermarket. The bush and the city, the edge of survival and the center of civilization, are separated by impassable terrain and yet connected by tiny planes that buzz the state like mosquitoes.

It is possible, even ordinary, to stand in rugged country at lunchtime and eat dinner in Anchorage, a place author John McPhee unflatteringly discribed as "that part of any city where the city has burst its seams and extruded Colonel Sanders."

But these are not the only contradictions. In some ways, Alaska preselects its immigrants. If America was the land of opportunity for the world, Alaska is today's magnet.

It pulls on the minds of the desperate, and the daring of

what's called here "The Outside." In the Kenai Peninsula, the "refuse" of Oregon's teeming unemployed "shore" camp out and hope for work in the canneries. In cities like Juneau and Anchorage and Fairbanks, young professionals arrive to become vice-presidents and television reporters and community leaders before they are thirty.

It attracts believers as well. The Lower 48 were settled by advocates of every religion and cause. Today Alaska harbors some of the most ardent of our own environmental believers: the protectors, the owners, the exploiters. There is, in modern Oklahoma style, a conflict between those who want to live in the frontier and those who want to "civilize" it, between those who want to keep it and those who want to "use" it.

Battles erupt between those who came to escape the rules of The Outside and those who want to extend them, between those who create planning and those who resent it. In a single rafting trip you can see signs of many philosophies of daily life: campers who pack their refuse with them, and a cabin with rusting trucks in the yard and a sign: SHOOT ON SIGHT.

At times, in arguments and appearances, it seems that these citizens share only one intense experience: winter.

Yet they are creating something. In the Lower 48, all the foreign elements in our stew eventually simmered into something complex but recognizably American.

Here the ingredients are still raw in places. The recipe is neither American nor foreign. There is something distinctly Alaskan in the making.

JUNE 1982

223

IN THE HEARTLAND OF MISSILES

FARGO, North Dakota—The stubble from last year's wheat crop still stretches like an endless, awkward crew cut along the flat Red River Valley. Any day now, the farmers who have sat through this wet spring of 1983 will begin seeding the prairie again.

This is the breadbasket of America and the military zone. Less than a hundred miles north of here is another huge crop planted in the soil of The Peace Garden State: nuclear missiles.

Sooner or later, almost everyone I meet offers me the same odd tidbit from their state's identity. If North Dakota were to secede from the union, they say, it would be the third largest nuclear force in the world. I cannot figure out whether it is said with pride or irony.

Brian Palacek, a nuclear-freeze organizer, who lives over in the state capital of Bismarck, says that North Dakotans suffer from "placeism, a sense of inferiority, like racism or whatever." A native son once described this as the biggest blank rectangle in our national consciousness. A Louisville, Kentucky, newspaper created a storm suggesting that we could solve our economic problems by selling North Dakota.

There is something perverse in this placeism. Lois Trapp, a writer and grandmother whose family owns some of the last bit of virgin prairie in Enderlin—"forty acres that have never felt a plow"—notes that she lives in a state with the power to destroy the world, and "nobody knows where we are."

In some ways North Dakota is like all of America. It's a land-based territory of plowshares and swords, giant combines and huge ICBMs, with resources to feed the world or destroy it. But it's more obvious here.

The North Dakotans, 630,000 of them, are scattered across country that stretches from prairie to badlands. Like the rest of us, they have finally become conscious of the craziness of the arms race. Last fall, this ground zero, this prime target, voted by referendum to send a nuclear-freeze message to Washington. Yet they have learned to live with the missiles in their own backyard. Like the rest of us, they bury their fears.

Driving along Route 94, past exits with names like Kindred and Buffalo and Wheatland and Bonanzaville, Alice Olson, a lawyer who ran for state attorney general in 1980, says that North Dakotans don't feel more vulnerable in their territory than elsewhere. Even those who have been next-door neighbors to concrete bunkers surrounded by fences since the 1960s complain mostly about the problem the missile sites present for weed control.

Over breakfast at the Tower Truck Stop Cafe, Lois Trapp says that "People feel that if anything happens everyone will go." She and others speak with outraged frugality about the days when the government built the ABMs and then immediately negotiated them away.

In Casselton, Bill Sinner, who runs a 3100-acre farm with his partners, a farm with wheat on the land and a computer in the office, says, "We're far enough away that we don't think about them much. It's like everything else in life. You learn to live with it."

Sinner lives "with it" about a hundred miles from the

missiles. But then, I live with it about a mile from a target called MIT.

The legislature that meets in Bismarck, for about three months every other year, is just coming to a close. The other day someone rode a tractor up to the capitol to remind everyone that law time has to give way to planting time.

The legislature that meets in Washington, 1300 miles back East, spent a week debating a mutual and verifiable nuclear freeze. Even if it votes for a freeze, if we negotiate a freeze, we will still be living with nuclear weapons for a long, long time. And we'll live with them pretty much the way they do in North Dakota.

"Most people here," says freeze-advocate Brian Palacek, "think the arms race is insane, and they don't feel that any government, including their own, has been spending any serious time resolving the question."

But as another native mused, it's still hard to relate this global terror to a nuclear force that sits smack in the middle of wheat country. In the land of the third largest nuclear force in the world, she said, "We keep an awful lot buried underground."

APRIL 1983

THE UPROOTED: I

BOSTON—About a year ago [summer 1981], a man lost his job. I wouldn't ordinarily bother to tell you this. Unemployment is by now familiar to all of us. In fact this particular man was one of hundreds who lost their jobs on a single day when a single company in Pennsylvania closed its doors. He wasn't the only one who'd worked there a quarter of a century.

What happened next wasn't unusual either. The man joined the ranks of the new American migrants, people who leave their families in one place to find work in another. Nobody knows how many of these new migrant workers there are in the country, but you can see them, meet them, everywhere.

Some of them, the Okies of the eighties, pack up everything in the back of the car and go. Others, like this man, are the "heroes" of Reaganomics, people who "vote with their feet." Vote for Dallas over Detroit, Anchorage over Oregon, mobility over unemployment, work over home.

So I wouldn't ordinarily tell you this story. But the letter I got in the daily mail from his wife (I'll call her Anne) says more about the deep disruption of a single family by this economy than all the statistics that flow out of Washington.

In careful prose, Anne describes her husband's departure:

"After wearing out a pair of shoes while beating the pavement in the area for months, [my husband] gave up looking around here and began sending résumés out of town. He was lucky, I guess. He found a job in a field that paid just about the same salary he got from the company that went under. But it's a thousand miles away from here."

This was not a decision made lightly or handled easily. "This is a man, understand me, to whom his family—wife and three kids—is the core of his life. This is a man who actually reads report cards before signing them and who isn't even too busy to pick up his seventeen-year-old daughter and pals from a late movie. This is a man who still gathers his two teenage sons into his arms and kisses them. He went because he had no choice."

And Anne stayed, because she had no choice either.

In another era, these two might have been described in trendy terms as a commuting marriage, their separation buffered by airline tickets and long-distance credit cards . . . money. But this is a two-job family with a house, three kids, college tuitions, and now loneliness.

"Our house is up for sale, but so far, no one is interested. The plan is that I will join my husband when I can find a job in the city where he works. I have a job here and I love it. Will I be able to find another good job, what with all the cutbacks and economizing everywhere? Should I stay here until I find another job? Until the house is sold? Does one get used to being without one's husband after a while? Or does the loneliness just turn into depression? I never *used* to mix myself gin and tonics as soon as I got home after work when he was here."

The effects of this one decision ripple out beyond their own personal relationship. There are the kids who have lived in this house-for-sale so they could commute to college. And there is Anne's mother, "who depends on me to be here when she needs someone to talk to about a Social

Security check that didn't come or a pipe that's leaking. Who will she call when I'm gone? Who will get her the twenty-pound bag of birdseed from the supermarket or get her the books from the library when she's sick?"

No, this isn't a sob story. It isn't even a tragedy as tragedies go in this economy. There are real horror stories from the Midwest about the rising rates of child abuse among the unemployed. There are real horror stories about people who can't find work at all. For the moment, Anne and her husband are both employed. Nobody is going hungry.

But stories about people like these—the new uprooted—say something about the state of the country. They say something about times when, once again, men and women can only support families in the "old country" by leaving them behind and moving to a "new country."

They say something about the ultimate "profamily" policy of Reaganomics when security, community, family relationships are wiped out by unemployment. And the stories say something about why thousands of new American migrants have to choose between those two halves of a healthy human being: work and love.

As Anne wrote, "The economy has become, to me, much more than a word that one finds sprinkled about on the pages. . . . It's a force that has disrupted my career, torn up my family, put my kids' college plans in jeopardy, and taken away my home. What's happening to people because of what's happening in Washington is very real. And the hardest part, I think, is that no one really knows who to blame."

JULY 1982

THE UPROOTED: II

BOSTON—Not long ago, I wrote about the new American migrants, the economically uprooted who are once again choosing mobility over unemployment, work over home.

In particular, I told the story of Anne, a woman whose unemployed husband found a job a thousand miles away. Anne was torn between her children, her aging mother, and her job at home, and her husband half a country away.

The mail I got was not unexpected. I received letters from wives (mostly) who had made this sort of move and wives who had chosen not to. I heard from people who were sympathetic with Anne's situation, and people who were not.

But there was one curious theme in my mail. At least a third of my correspondents and one irate caller reminded me that this was not the first generation of Americans who had to vote with their feet. Several told me of grandparents and great-grandparents who had moved west in the last century. Two at least criticized Anne for not having the grit of her foremothers.

This comparison struck me, because I'd just begun Lillian Schlissel's *Women's Diaries of the Westward Journey*. Her book is a record of the hardships and, yes, the grit of women who took the overland trail to Oregon and California in the middle of the nineteenth century.

The women's story is told in the understated words of their own journals. It's a story that had been virtually lost in the frontier history written by and about men. When, recently, women looked in American history textbooks for their own neglected sex they found themselves hidden in classic lines like this: "Pioneers pushed west over the mountains. Their wives and children went along."

But in Schlissel's book, women on the trail were far more than excess baggage riding comfortably in a covered wagon. They were essential partners along this hostile trail. Though one-fifth of them were pregnant at some point in the journey, though most had small children, they did ordinary drudgery under extraordinary conditions. They rolled out dough on the wagon seats, cooked with fires made out of buffalo chips, tended the sick, and marked the graves of their children, their husbands, and each other.

In comparison, our modern moves, made with a trailer truck along an interstate highway, pale. Yet there is a sense in which the wives and mothers of that migration and this migration—perhaps any migration—have much in common emotionally.

You see, at the moment of the original decision, most of our "gritty" foremothers didn't want to go.

The women who went were almost all married. But it was husbands who were captured by the glowing descriptions of the West, wives who were skeptical. Husbands who thought of what could be gained; wives who thought of what would be lost.

As Schlissel describes them: "Riding side by side, sitting in the very same wagons, crossing the continent in response to the call for free land, women did not always see the venture in the clear light of the expectation of success. There were often shadows in their minds, areas of dark reservation and opposition."

For every woman who saw this as an adventure, there were a hundred like Margaret Hereford Wilson, the grandmother of General George S. Patton, who wrote in 1850 to her mother, with typical anguish: "Dr. Wilson has determined to go to California. I am going with him as there is no other alternative. . . . Oh my dear Mother . . . I thought that I felt bad when I wrote you . . . from Independence, but it was nothing like this."

Schlissel suggests that for men breaking away and moving, the frontier was a pursuit of masculinity, "an expression of testing and reaching." The male pioneers were chasing what our life-cycle plotters today like to call "The Dream."

But women saw themselves as caretakers, keepers of homes, keepers of relationships. For them the separation from parents, home, friends, and environment was far more threatening. In fact, they measured their accomplishment on the trail in terms of their ability to keep the family together.

Unlike Margaret Wilson, wives today have different options and responsiblities. More women now choose to test themselves against some frontier; more men nurture their roots. Yet it is still more common for men to embrace moves and women to dread them.

In this new season of migration, when the economy acts like a centrifuge, it is equally challenging to keep a family together, especially when jobs and generations are a thousand miles apart. No matter what my letter-writers say, I suspect that our foremothers in the caravans of covered wagons would understand.

AUGUST 1982

MOVING DAY

BOSTON—It is moving day. In honor of the occasion the temperature has risen to 90 degrees. Fine weather for moving, a good purging number.

By four o'clock, I am standing in the middle of what was once my living room. The room is empty of living now. I am alone except for the fine vintage dirt that was hidden behind an old Victorian chest for nine years.

I am too tired for any more nostalgia. That too has been purged by the heat. Still, there is something stunning about the speed with which three men can suck all the living out of rooms and into a truck.

There ought to be a ceremony for moving day. There ought to be some ritual more formal than the one that faces me now: a mover holding an old Playskool giraffe, relic of a child's childhood, and asking, "Is this going too?"

The list that I'll sign in a moment itemizes in exquisite detail every Thing that was collected for this space. One by one, Things were placed here. Walls, floors, cupboards were filled. Now, the structure is all that remains, as if left behind by a hungry vacuum cleaner.

Soon we will be filling rooms a mile away. They were emptied by a woman shedding fifty years of habit and habitation for an apartment. Our old house in turn will accept new belongings, new belongers. So will the old house of the people who are buying ours. There is a chain of homes being emptied and filled along this lineage.

The week before, on the other side of the country, in San Francisco, my great-aunt Polly died. She had a passion for collecting, this tiny woman who kept track of all of us. The things that she had gathered around her over nearly nine decades are also being packed: china that was carefully selected, furniture chosen deliberately, jewelry with its own history, expression of her own taste. These Things will be divided.

I have today a sense of some universal pulsation. Homes emptied and filled, Things collected and divided. Each little universe, expanding and contracting and expanding. My great-aunt was the curator of her collection and her clan. Without a center, people cannot hold forever. Universal laws apply to families, too. Some will inevitably be drawn to other galaxies. Which will in turn expand.

Once, at an antique show, I bought a nineteenth-century photo album that still had family pictures in it. Someone had carefully pasted in all the photographs of people who were important to her or him. What had happened to that family? Were there no heirs, no one interested in these photographs?

I emptied that small house of its people and replaced it with my own. This album, too, is in transit today, between homes.

There's something like this in the way we live our lives. My great-aunt accumulated platters of blue Meissen china, but also memories. We all do that. Our lives are museums of private experiences. Some we give a prominent place in our display cases, some we put away in crates, some we try to forget.

But we each have catalogs full of events, impressions, ideas. We acquire them over time, becoming more complex, elaborated, crowded.

234

We distribute some of these things before we die. We disseminate an idea, contribute a gesture, an attitude, a memory. We also leave behind empty space.

The room that I am standing in, the room which once was a living room, echoes today. It seems smaller, not larger, in our absence, already contracting.

Tomorrow, between owners, it will be cleansed. Next week this house will begin again. So will we. Our minds are already expanding the new house. And yet I have the sense of cycles, always cycles.

The mover hands me the itemized list. I sign it. It's hot in this house and beginning to pour outside. Time to leave.

JULY 1982

A LONG, SLOW THAW

BOSTON—In my backyard, the struggle between winter and spring is coming to a close. Even the flowers, stopped in their tracks by an April blizzard, have begun their delayed adolescence.

One tulip, trapped under a pine branch brought down by the wind, has found a detour to the surface. It will, I suspect, survive. Another tulip, open before the storm, was badly shaken by its eagerness and winter's excess. It will also survive.

But in the shady corner of this New England garden, a patch of snow still hangs on. It is covered now with the ugly licorice frosting of urban life. It sits there as a visible remnant of the stormy past.

From my kitchen window, I measure the shrinking snow patch each morning. I find myself checking up on this departing bit of winter the way others check on the arriving spring. I still muddle in some absurd state of preparedness, ready for yet another relapse, prepared for the worst, cautiously moving into a new season with one eye on the last.

I leave the house these mornings wearing just a suit. But in sync with the mixed messages of my yard, I carry my coat. The snow is my patch of caution. The coat is my protection. I drag it along with me into spring.

The garden scene has become my miniature of all the awkward ways things change, in nature and in human nature.

During the thaws of my childhood winters I was the first on the block to put on summer clothes. I accepted the spring without suspicion, without withholding commitment.

Today my daughter still sheds snow jackets at the first sign of warmth, with easy optimism. But I now carry a coat in the car, read signs in the snow, and wonder whether it comes with the age territory. Do we get more cautious, are we overprepared for the worst, as we grow older?

Few of my friends make speedy transitions anymore. They seemed slowed down by their histories. They even enter good times cautiously.

I have a friend who survived a predictable weather pattern of midlife: a cold marriage, followed by a stormy divorce, and an unsettled single life. Finally she moved, by glacial increments, into a new relationship. Her days with this man are more than comfortable.

Yet there is still a prevailing wind from her past. Her memories are also expectations. When we talk, she sounds almost superstitious. If she takes off the snow tire, makes a commitment to this new life, she tells me, another storm may take her by surprise. Above all else, my friend does not want surprises.

A man I know, a father, has been through a season of trouble with his daughter. For years he couldn't talk to her without receiving icy sarcasm. The atmosphere of their home was heavy with her hostility, anger, disapproval.

Now the girl is open, but the father is careful. When they meet, he is still braced against the chill of disappointment. He keeps his expectations low and his dukes high. During all the years he wished that she would soften toward him, he never knew how hard it would be to believe in it.

There are others I know who carry symbols, memories, patches from the past—even when times change. Others who find transitions slower and trickier that they used to. One brings an old illness with her into good health; she cannot yet say she is cured. Another goes to work at a new job taking with him the anxieties of his unemployed months. A third carries his childhood on his shoulders, like a chip.

I don't know if it is universal. But for many of us, disappointments accumulate like snowflakes, each different, until they settle into a cold mass in the dark corner of our lives.

The harder the season, the longer it takes to melt.

Yet it does, eventually. Eventually we feel safe enough to store the storm gear. Sooner or later, if it's warm enough, even skepticism evaporates.

My yard has almost finished its transition. By tomorrow, the snow patch will have become mud. Within a week, I'll leave my coat at home. And by next week at the latest, this most tenacious winter will be over. I am sure of that. Almost sure of that.

APRIL 1982

LENINGRAD—It is a raw April day and the war is all around. I have driven a half hour out of the city into a landscape painted from a monochromatic palette of gray and beige.

To my left, a tall grove of white birch trees hovers over lines of gray tombstones. In front of me, huge rectangular mounds of earth stretch out in rows, only identified by a discreet granite marker with a number: 1942, 1943. In each mound are buried 10,000 people.

In all, there are 460,000 Soviet dead in this vast, haunting place, the Piskariovskoye Memorial Cemetery. They are men and women and children killed during the Nazis' 900-day siege of Leningrad, killed during what the Soviets call the Great Patriotic War. As my guide tells me in morbid one-upsmanship, there are more Russians buried in this one place than the total number of Americans lost in the war.

For the past week, I have watched this country preparing to celebrate May 9, the fortieth anniversary of victory. It is not being commemorated coolly as some distant historic event here, but emotionally, with all the immediacy of a recent and nearly fatal wound. Every night, on television, there is another war movie. Every morning, the newspapers carry another story: Today it is the tale of a woman who lost nine sons.

The theme of war is as somber and relentless as the Russian music broadcast from the loudspeaker over the cemetery. It is so heavy, so constant, that I am tempted to dismiss the war as a relic resuscitated for holidays, waved in front of the people for current needs rather than past. The Great Patriotic War, after all, forged a nation out of its diverse nationalities. The war still impresses Soviets with their vulnerable place on the European map. The war still subliminally persuades many that sacrifices have to be made for defense.

But here, before me, is another reality. A small sample of death. Twenty million Soviet people died—one out of every four citizens. The figure translates into spouses, parents, and now grandparents. Of all the men born in 1922 and sent to the front, only three percent survived. The figure translates into a generation of twenty-year-old widows, now sixty-year-old widows.

Among the older people, these memories are indeed vivid. Just this morning, Vasilisa Kulik Emezova, a warm, engaging Leningrad grandmother who lived through the siege, talked to me in the rhythmic cadences of a practiced storyteller about the winter of 1942. For seven months, she remembers, people lived on a ration of 125 grams of bread a day. Young girls brought food rations to people too weak to get their own. Some of these girls brought back the live babies they found in the arms of their dead parents.

The middle-aged Soviets, postwar born, talk about what it was like to grow up with shortages of everything, especially fathers. Even the teenagers who confess—rolling their eyes to the heavens—that they are turned off by war movies and have overdosed on this spring's portion of history pay their respects. As a seventeen-year-old high school student said: "I don't like to talk about it with my grandparents. But it's important to remember. To forget means to forgive."

It's an article of faith with the Soviet people that Americans don't really understand war because it hasn't touched American soil for so long. Even a young Jewish scientist and refusenik whose own parents fought on the front echoed the common refrain: "Americans do not understand what Russia went through in the war."

It is also a successful prop of propaganda that convinces the Soviet people that the experience of war has made them more diligent in pursuit of peace. As a professional America-watcher at the U.S.A. Institute in Moscow tells me pointedly, "One of the main dangers in the world is that you lack firsthand experience with war." Ironically, this man was born in 1947.

In the last week, Arthur Hartman, the U.S. ambassador to the Soviet Union, tried to counter some of this feeling. In a letter published here to commemorate the meeting of Soviet and American soldiers on the Elbe, he wrote: "Our sacrifices remain as real and as vivid to us as those of the Soviet Union are to its people. We hold them no less sacred. And we learned no less from them." But his message was erased by reports of Reagan's plan to visit Bitburg. In or out of government, the Soviets I met found that trip to lay a wreath in a Nazi cemetery incredible, insensitive, even sacrilegious.

Walking down the pathway between these common graves, counting by the tens, the tens of thousands, I am struck by how far the two powers have traveled from the Elbe, from the time when war made us allies. What a cemetery this would have been for a presidential visit—a place to side with victims, not aggressors. It's the victims who inhabit these grounds now, hundreds of thousands of them.

And on this damp and dismal day, at the nadir of relations between my country and this one, those great humps of common graves seem less like a memorial to the distant past and more like a warning about the future.

MAY 1985

ALL THIS HAPPINESS IS KILLING ME

MOSCOW—One of the many surprises in this massive, lumbering capital city is the palpable energy and ingenuity of the people who live here. The formal Soviet system may grumble at change and muffle initiative in blankets of bureaucracy, but there is an informal system at work, one as chaotic and irrepressible as human nature.

The spirit of free enterprise is thriving and not merely in the semi-official peasant market where private farmers sell their hothouse tomatoes this week for five dollars a pound. It is part of the psyche of the Muscovites, a people with rising expectations and Western tastes in a Second-World marketplace.

In seven days on these streets, I have seen some of the most passionate shoppers that a mall-weary American could imagine. It is rare for a Muscovite to pass one of the stands set up on street corners or in doorways without checking the contents. When a line forms at a shop, there is a universal urge to find out what's for sale. Even my translator, walking our rounds of formal appointments, veers automatically, into a shoe store that is expecting a shipment, and then, catching herself, backs out in embarrassment. Nearly every private conversation with an urban Russian turns to prices. How much does a shirt cost in America? A good coat? A tape recorder?

The stores are not empty of goods. The state supermarkets have enough staples to satisfy hunger, if not relieve boredom. A constant, defensive refrain from a Soviet companion is, "We have that too; we have that too." The Soviet Union makes almost anything made in the rest of the world, but in quantities that tease the imagination and whet the appetite. As an American friend here reminds me, "They make ten thousand toasters a year."

To my Western eye, an extraordinary amount of time and interest is invested in getting hold of something scarce and desirable. I am regaled with boisterous stories about the search for food for a party, a good pair of boots for the winter, tickets to the theater. Americans may work to acquire the money to buy these items, but in Moscow it is equally important to have contacts, to develop a relationship with the butcher, to exchange and share with friends, to know someone with access to a Beryushka store where goods are sold for foreign currency only.

The enormous vitality of this second system, this private sector, contradicts the Western stereotype of Soviet citizens as dependent and passive. The state may regulate production, distribute housing, and control wages, but in the reality of everyday existence, the struggle to enrich life is met with imagination, flexibility, and a passion largely lacking in public life.

Indeed, if there is a collective spirit in Moscow, it is not in the government but in the effort to get something done despite, around, over, under the government. It is the difficulties, the daily hassles, that throw people together— families, neighbors, friends—into webs of interdependence.

Even as a visitor, I catch glimpses of this. I try to change my hotel reservations and encounter a barrier of new rules. To change a reservation, I must pay for the whole stay all over again. This is crazy, I tell the clerk, using my most useful Russian phrase. We smile at each other, she hesitates, cuts through the reddest of tape and suddenly, unofficially, it's done. One way to move the immovable is to appeal directly for the commodity in great demand in this city: help.

At the same time, I begin to sense and share the Muscovites' pleasure in personal victories. A woman tells me in great and ironic detail about her month-long campaign to get the right travel papers. A success story. The third item we try to order from a restaurant menu is actually available. I applaud. I dredge up a telephone number in this city without directory assistance, where telephone books are at a premium, and I cheer.

But it's also clear to this outsider that much too much creative energy goes into these victories: beating a bureaucratic obstacle, chasing a shortage. The energy siphoned off from work or public life is as obvious as the sight of government workers standing in grocery lines at three o'clock in the afternoon. I don't envy the new leader who wants to change these systems in the cause of productivity.

Finally, I begin to understand the joke that was told to me my second day in Moscow. It's about a man who wants to leave the Soviet Union because he is too happy. Why, a friend asks, would you leave if you are happy? "Well," he explains, "if I go to the store for good meat and I find it, I'm so happy. If my television breaks and I get it fixed, I'm so happy. If I find a shirt in my size and it even fits me, I'm so happy. All this happiness is killing me."

MAY 1985

CAVES, GRATES, AND MISCONCEPTIONS

MOSCOW—When a group of American congressmen left here some weeks ago, there was a final barbed exchange of invitations between Representative Robert Michael and Mikhail Gorbachev. The new Soviet leader invited the congressmen to come back for a longer visit so they could see "we don't all live in caves." The congressman from Illinois invited Gorbachev to the Unites States so he could see "we don't all sleep on grates."

Since I have been here, I have thought about these caves and grates. The Soviets, especially official Soviets, are highly sensitive to their country's Western portrait. One, a professional America-watcher, tells me resentfully, "The Soviet Union is seen in your country as a very primitive place where people are under constant surveillance." It is the word "primitive" that wounds him and others.

At the same time, the party-line picture of America is foreign to my eyes. If Americans see a Soviet Union full of dissidents, the Soviet people see an America full of derelicts and demonstrators.

The newspapers here run endless photos of the homeless and the protestors. A recent *Literary Gazette* carried a picture of a derelict with the caption, "Everyday Life in the Free World." The youth paper, *Komsomol Pravda*, featured a photograph of American police in tear gas masks captioned, "Residents of Crossroads, Ky., treated like insects."

The cartoons in the daily paper *Pravda* are as subtle as the one that portrayed "America's Peace Plan for Nicaragua" with a huge foot coming down on the country. Even the current humor magazine, *Krokodil*, had a cartoon entitled "Democracy in All Its Arms," that showed a towering male figure outfitted with syringes "for heretics," brass knuckles "for colored people," and machine guns for "the fighters for human rights."

Despite this portrait, the same America-watcher complains that the Soviets have "an idealistic view of American technological prowess. They have myths about American prosperity. They don't know enough about your severe problems." It is an admission of public cynicism about the Soviet press.

In fact, there is little firsthand knowledge of any kind about the United States among the unofficial people I visit. Very few have been allowed to travel to the West, although travel ranks high on the wish list. Few have read the Western press, although Hemingway and Updike may have more Soviet than American fans and *Gone with the Wind* is a high school hit.

This mix of ignorance, propaganda, and skepticism of propaganda produces a complicated impression of America. Some of the most educated people I have met express simultaneously an exaggerated idea of American unemployment and envy of American prosperity. There are also subtle misconceptions that come to the surface in an odd phrase, an assumption, or a question.

In a school visit, a fifteen-year-old student explains to me that, "In America everything is done for the sake of business." I hear a report from a geography lesson: "California is a place with a lot of rich people where they build missiles." Five or six times I am told with absolute certainty that "American families are not close like our families." Once, after a long afternoon with a sophisticated, thoughtful teacher, I am startled to hear her ask about communism in America, saying, "We know it's the second largest Communist Party in the world."

But the widest gap between image and self-image emerges one night in a home in Leningrad. My hosts, Lydia and Alexei, are gracious but uneasy, and halfway through a supper of dumplings and cake, I suspect that I am the first American this young family has ever entertained. When the conversation turns to world affairs, the doctor expresses her utter conviction that the Soviet Union is peace-loving and America is threatening. When I tell her that many Americans believe the reverse, she is sincerely startled. If it is so, she says quietly but firmly, it's because of your propaganda. As I leave, she gives me a copy of John Steinbeck's *Grapes of Wrath* and I have the distinct impression that she believes it is banned in America.

More than once in these two weeks, I have been tempted to shake my head in disbelief at Soviet descriptions of America. But each time, I think about the exchange between Gorbachev and Michael, about our own narrow vision.

Some of it is as blatant as the headline in a British paper asserted: "Soviet Union Keeps the Worker in Chains." Usually it is more subtle. An ebullient Leningrad sociologist, Vladimir Lisovski, for example, tells me pointedly of his trip to America, and his account echoes with my own experiences. As Lisovski left the New Jersey family he was visiting, he said to them, "You know, I am a communist." They said, "No, no, you are too jovial, too nice," and he repeated it until at last, impishly and provocatively, he said to them, "What do I have to do to make you believe me? Put a knife between my teeth?"

I suspect there are as many misconceptions as miles between the land of caves and the country of grates.

MAY 1985

THE SOVIET SUPERWOMAN

MOSCOW—Eventually it comes up in any conversation with Soviet women. They don't call it the Superwoman Syndrome here. It is simply the Problem of Women: the double burden of work and family.

The first time the subject arises is in an official meeting with the Soviet Women's Committee: "There are some traditions which are dying very slowly," says Xenia Proskurnikova, the first vice-president, "especially the idea that housework is only a woman's occupation." When I ask if any of the prominent women around the table has a husband who shares the housework equally, there is an awkward, smiling silence.

The next time is in a private gathering when a young university professor says: "We have two problems, queues [the shopping lines] and men. I think we will solve the problem of queues before we solve the problem of men." A third time is in an interview with sociologists who add another familiar dimension to the problem: the inflexibility of the work world.

In some ways it is remarkably easy to talk here about the Problem of Women. The dialogue cuts through politics and rhetoric, to everyday dilemmas familiar to women in both the U.S. and Soviet cultures. In another way it is unsettling, precisely because the problem is universal, and unresolved. Neither of these two vastly different systems has figured out a way to balance the demands of work and family; neither has distributed the private work load fairly between men and women.

More than half the workers in the Soviet Union are women. More than 90 percent of adult women are either workers or students. Nevertheless, romanticism and chauvinism run deep.

The same people who talk practically about women as comrades turn sentimental talking about motherhood. Zoya Krylova, the enthusiastic forty-year-old editor of *Working Woman*, is typical of this synchronized cultural swimming. Her magazine serves as a gutsy advocate for the rights of its 16 million female readers at the workplace.

Yet, she says, "We are also trying to teach a woman to stay a woman in the family. Women are the heart of the family and must be warmer to create the atmosphere of warmth and love." In the contest she runs, the prize for the best idea to improve women's workplace is a glass Cinderella slipper.

The research on young women shows, not surprisingly, that they want a marriage in which husband and wife are equals, but the reality is, also not surprisingly, different. The Soviet versions of "the new man" are few and nurtured hopefully by women. When one such man wrote into the paper about how his co-workers heckled him for sharing duties with his wife, 5,000 women wrote in his support.

But many men, perhaps most, simply resist taking on "women's work." Some of the most contemporary husbands speak with the edge of smugness in the voice of this thirty-year-old husband: "Woman have learned it's so hard to make a career at the office and so nerve-wracking that they don't really want it." His wife translated this, dissenting all the way. A more moderate, chivalrous chauvinism was echoed by sociologist Vladimir Lisovski: "First of all a man should be more responsible for his family. But with all due respect to the emancipation of women, I'm convinced men should be the head of the family."

A number of women complain in turn that since the postwar years, when Russian men were an endangered species, the men have been pampered beyond redemption. As one twenty-year-old student said in words much harsher than her gentle voice, "I want to say that the boys of my age are so spoiled by their mothers that they never help in the family life." An older, divorced journalist said, "I had the choice of doing all the work without complaint, or fighting all the time, or getting divorced." The Soviet Union has a divorce rate that matches our own, and 70 percent of divorces are initiated by women. More than a few of these marriages falter on these "choices."

Of course, the Problem of Women is not without its problem solvers. In the big cities now, some workplaces have food concessions to cut down on shopping. The government is increasing child care as the web of grandmothers breaks down. In a few schools, boys are being taught to cook along with girls.

But the biggest policy push is not directed at men or institutions, but at the clock. The latest plans call for more flexible work hours for mothers; the latest hopes are for more part-time work. Eugenia Zubareva, who runs the social welfare system for the city of Leningrad, says that if Mikhail Gorbachev came to her office, "I would ask him to make women less engaged at work so they could spend more time with their children." It is a sentiment that I hear echoed again and again.

It is hard to compare the lives of Soviet and American women. The Soviet officials boast of paid maternity leave and child care centers; the Americans boast of supermarkets, cars, and washing machines.

But in any circle of working mothers, the word *time*

resonates across cultures. Women have been in the work force a generation longer here and the "problem" is just as acute. It is basically women who are spreading their energy thinly across all needs. Maybe this is what happens anywhere that balancing work and family is still called "the Problem of Women."

MAY 1985

SWIMMING AGAINST THE TIDE OF CHIC

BOSTON—Dear Sir: Allow me to respond to your recent letter asking why I go to the Maine shore every summer despite the fact that "everyone knows that you can't swim there."

I am unaware, sir, of the exact penalty for slandering an entire state. As a spiritual Down Easter, I am inclined to take insults with a taciturn style. But you should be aware that the next L. L. Bean catalog to darken your doorstep may be booby-trapped.

The very idea that the Maine water is too cold for an Australian to crawl in is a malicious rumor that was begun by a man selling stock in the Gulf Stream and scholarships to the UCLA pool. If it's impossible to swim in Maine, what precisely do you think all the seals are doing there?

It is true that until recently few Maine fishermen learned to swim. You are quite correct in assuming that this was because a man who fell overboard during the winter was suitable only as fodder for Mrs. Paul's frozen fish sticks.

But that has nothing to do with the summer. People in Maine don't even put in their antifreeze until September. By June, you can see naked forearms along Penobscot Bay.

What I infer from your letter (which carried no postmark, but we shall find you anyway) is that you are one of those people who summer in Malibu or Martha's Vineyard. You probably frequent the sort of resort where people pick their lobster out of the mayonnaise instead of the ocean.

Perhaps you go to Fire Island where you can rent a cottage for approximately the same cost as a year at Yale. Perhaps you vacation where they have cable TV and home newspaper delivery and dinner parties that sound like "Washington Week in Review."

Maine, I submit to you, indeed I boast, is different. In the Hamptons, jeans may be stonewashed; in Maine they are simply old. In Southern California, T-shirts come professionally ripped; in Maine it happens naturally.

My point is that you, like so many Americans, have grown softy. We in Maine have remained hardy. So, I say to you, sir, that we may not "bathe" in the ocean as you put it so degenerately, but we absolutely do swim in it. It's just that we do it our way.

How is that? you ask. Over the course of many years, I have come across at least three distinct methods of swimming in Maine which I will now share with you.

The first way is to simply run off the pier and jump into the water. This is a style which has been developed almost exclusively by native children between the ages of seven and twelve. You can spot these children by the strange genetic pattern which has emerged among them over many generations. It is called, in these parts, Purple Lips or Lipus Purpulus.

There is another method more common among adults. It begins about midday with approximately two hours of brush clearing in full sun. If necessary, it can also begin with digging out the cesspool. Thus having absorbed solar energy into the skin's own natural collectors, adults race immediately to the shore, do not stop to wonder why the mussels cling to the rocks, and plunge in. I am told by a reliable source that a particularly good sun collector can stay in the water exactly the same number of minutes as he or she spent hours in the sun.

The third, or tourist method, will show you that even in Maine we understand delicate sensibilities. What you need for this method is a clam flat and an incoming tide. The flat is, of course, exposed to the sun during low tide. As the water comes back it is warmed by the flat. Thus you have a window of vulnerability when the water is both warm enough and deep enough to satisfy the most southern soul. We call this the Mediterranean hour, although it generally lasts about a half hour. It is considered prudent to wade back to shore when both ankles begin to lose all sensation.

This methodology is not something, quite frankly, that I willingly share with people. It is well-known that the gentrification of the shore rises in direct proportion to the temperature of the water.

Those of us who summer in Maine prefer to keep out the sort of tourists who have their jeans faded by Ralph Lauren. Indeed, there are some in Maine who are prepared to emigrate to Nova Scotia when the first platter of pasta primavera crosses the New Hampshire border.

Unless we are severely provoked, as I was by you, we prefer to maintain the myth of unswimmability. What you must understand, sir, is that nobody goes to Maine to be in the swim of things.

AUGUST 1984

Part 7

OF GENDER AND OTHER GAPS

I DREAMED I WAS LIBERATED
IN MY MAIDENFORM BRA

BOSTON—It's not that I'd never seen her before.

Years ago, she'd been photographed outside of her apartment building, dressed in a fur coat and bra and panties. Since then she'd been found in similar attire in the theater and hotel lobbies. Usually, of course, you get used to this sort of thing if you live in a city long enough.

But it was a shock to see her in a hospital room. There she was, hair tied back primly, medical chart in her left hand, pen in her right hand, long white jacket over her shoulders, exposing her lacy magenta bra and panties. What was she doing dressed like that in the hospital?

Was it possible? Why, yes! Stop the presses! The Maidenform Woman Had Become a Doctor! According to the caption under this photograph, she was "making the rounds in her elegant Delectables."

At some point when I wasn't looking, everybody's favorite exhibitionist must have actually gone to medical school. I suppose that I had underestimated her intelligence—this happens so often with attractive women. I always thought she was a candidate for a cold, not a medical degree. I can only imagine the difficulties she had getting accepted, what with her portfolio and all.

But now any number of magazines are featuring her personal success story. On their pages, the Maidenform

Woman is willingly displayii.g her new bedside manner in living color.

Poised, concerned, even prim, young Dr. Maidenform is photographed looking down compassionately at her bedridden patient. We don't know exactly what the patient thinks of all this. Fortunately for her, his leg is in traction and he can't move.

The other doctors in the ad seem quite unconcerned about her outfit. Dr. Maidenform seems to have made it in a world that is entirely nonsexist. They aren't even glancing in the direction of her nonairbrushed belly button!

Quite frankly, I must admit that the Maidenform Woman cured me of a disease. She cured me of creeping complacency.

Until I saw her, I had become virtually numb to the advertising image of that handy creature, "The New Woman." We are now out of the era of housewife-as-airhead. We've even come a long way from the era of coming a long way, baby.

We are plunging into the "successful woman as sex object" syndrome. The more real women break out of the mold, the more advertisers force them back in. We are now told that, for all the talk, the New Woman is just the Total Woman in updated gear.

Under the careful dress-for-success suit of an MBA is a woman buying Office Legs for sex appeal. Around the briefcase of a lawyer is a hand shining with high-color nail gloss. Take away the lab coat, the stethoscope, and syringe, and the doctor is just another set of "elegant Delectables."

The point in all this isn't especially subtle. As Jean Kilbourne, who has long studied media images of women, said, "It's out of the question that they would ever show a male doctor like that. She is aloof but available. Underneath she is still a sex object."

Kilbourne's favorite entry in this category is a perfume

ad that shows the successful woman mixing business with, uh, pleasure. In the first frame we see the busy executive at a business lunch with three men. In the second frame, we see her under the covers with one.

Advertisers have a big investment in this new-old image. I'm not talking about the professional woman market. There are hardly enough women doctors to keep the magenta lace factory in business. But there are now an increasing number of women who see professionals as glamorous and want to identify with them.

The advertisers are betting that these women want, as the Maidenform ad puts it, "just what the doctor ordered." So the doctor is ordered to strip, literally, her professional cover. She is revealed in the flesh, to be—yes, indeed— just another woman insecure about her femininity, just another woman in search of sex appeal, just another woman who needs "silky satin tricot with antique lace scalloping."

Pretty soon, I suppose, she will need it in the Senate, in the Supreme Court, even in the Oval Office. The Maiden- form Woman. You never know where she'll turn up.

OCTOBER 1982

FEMINIST FATIGUE

BOSTON—The professor was telling a story. It was a story about the Third World, a library, and *Playboy* magazine

Years ago, this man had tried to find out why *Playboy* was the most popular item on the bookshelves on the university of the African country where he lived. It was not, he discovered, because the students were ogling the centerfold. What they lusted after were the ads for stereos and Scotch and sports cars.

The professor finished by explaining to his dinner audience that in the Third World, the symbols of status were Scotch, stereos, sports cars, and only then women.

The women in the audience, First World women, looked at each other and at their men across the tables littered with dessert plates and coffee cups. Eyebrows were subtly lifted, eyes politely dilated with messages to each other.

A list of questions for the speaker formed in at least one women's mind: (1) Were "they," the inhabitants of this professor's Third World, only men? (2) Were the women in that country, that university, in his mind, just objects which the "people" might want? (3) Did the professor hear what he was saying? (4) Did she, dear gawd, have to raise these questions again? Still?

The woman sighed, not in anger but in exhaustion. The innocence of this professor's remarks was untouched by self-consciousness. Ten years of reminders by women that they want to be counted had glanced off him.

Suddenly this woman knew she too was suffering from what a friend had called "feminist fatigue." There had been a lot of outbreaks recently. Hers was just the most recent case.

Feminist fatigue is a special kind of weariness: weariness at the persistence of old attitudes, and weariness at the idea of explaining it all again.

Recently, it had struck two women planning a debate about the nuclear-freeze issue. The women had entered a hotel elevator to find the three men inside, joking and jostling with each other to "make room for these girls." The two who had been "girls" at thirty were now apparently "girls" at forty.

Another case report came from a friend who had spent ten years in one city on the cutting edge of change—first woman here, first woman there. She had recently been promoted to a new town and a new job. After a month, she realized with a thud that it was like moving back to Box Two.

They all had acute attacks of feminist fatigue. Caught in numerous replays of the 1950s mentality, they heard their own responses like songs of the 1970s. It was as if someone kept putting quarters in a rusty jukebox demanding that they play once again from the top a feminist standby like, "I'm not a girl, pal, I'm a woman."

The victims of this recurring disease were women who had been into anger and had come out the other side. They had had their consciousnesses raised to electric sensitivity and then modulated with a sense of humor and a sense of complexity.

They were women who wanted to move on and yet were confronted with people pushing them back. Sometimes they felt caught in an elaborate game of chutes and ladders, and wondered if they had the energy to climb the same paths again and again.

The woman in the audience at this dinner had recently been to Betty Friedan's class at the Kennedy School of Government. Friedan was teaching "The Second Stage" of the women's movement. This was a more mellow place where feminism folds into humanism, where men and women together create their own shared society. It was a vision driven by Friedan's own desire to move on, not to be everlastingly frozen into a first stage of confrontation.

But the same men and women evolving into this second stage also live in a world where they must explain why women are different from sports cars, why women are different from girls.

Yes, there's been enormous change in ten or fifteen years.

259

But today it's less a matter of two stages, one replacing the other, than of two cultures, existing side by side.

One culture has been enormously affected by this change, grown out of rhetoric and into easy living with the new ideas and ideals. The other culture remains powerful and pristine in its old ways. One culture understands. The other demands tired explanations or ancient passivity.

The constant commute between these two cultures could make anyone come down with a case of feminist fatigue.

MARCH 1982

DRESS FOR MATERNAL SUCCESS

BOSTON—From time to time, there's an ad in *The New Yorker* for a woman's three-piece suit. What distinguishes this offering from the rest of the dress-for-success couture is that this is a three-piece maternity suit.

Every time I see this ad, I am convinced that the costume is pregnant with meaning. It suggests that even when workingwomen are in the family way, they are supposed to dress in the male way. Any woman who wants to be seen professionally had better fit into the traditional business mold.

I thought of the Woman in the Gray Flannel Suit when a U.S. District Court struck down a California law that granted women the right to return to their own or a similar job after maternity leave. The court said that the legislation was illegal because it offered special treatment to women.

Federal law classifies pregnancy as a disability. Since California companies were not forced to reinstate other disabled workers, they didn't have to reinstate women disabled by pregnancy. Women were to be treated equally. Equally shabbily.

In some ways, this decision sounded absurd as well as harsh. Child-bearing is unique. Fitting pre- and postpartum women into rules made for men is like outfitting them in three-piece suits.

Now this California decision has given new focus to the old debate within the women's rights movement. Is there a way to get equality in the work force AND special treatment for pregnancy? Do women want the same rights as men? Do we want more? More for ourselves or for both sexes?

The argument between equal and special treatment has gone on for a century. In the 1920s, women and men worked long hours in hazardous conditions, but women workers won protective legislation partially on the grounds that they were mothers. Later, "specialists" at the Women's Bureau recommended that women stay out of work from six weeks before delivery to two months after.

These policymakers had the best of intentions. Legislatures of the 1920s would never have voted shorter hours for all workers, so they got what they could. It wasn't until the 1960s that women complained of being protected out of their jobs and paychecks.

In the seventies, the advocates of "equal rights" took over. Title VII gave women the same employment rights as men. Then, the Pregnancy Discrimination Act classified pregnancy as a disability so that pregnant women could be treated as well as men disabled by, say, back trouble.

But as the California ruling suggests, equal treatment isn't always good enough. In the 1980s, 43 percent of the mothers with children under the age of twelve months are in the work force. As Georgetown law professor Wendy Williams says, "Most of us are in the work place and still carrying the major burden at home and we are overburdened. The work place is not accommodating to the needs of women. At the point at which we feel strung out, we're likely to say, 'Damn it, something has to be done here and my special needs have to be met.'"

The renewed cry for special treatment that comes out of this frustration is a very genuine one. Surely a woman who leaves work to have a child should, by any standard of fairness, be entitled to regain her old job. Many women are encouraged by their companies to return. At least four states—Colorado, Montana, Connecticut, Hawaii—have laws similar to the one shot down in California which enforce this job security.

But, as Williams warns, the problem is that women haven't yet found a way to be treated "equally" and "specially." Special treatment comes with strings attached. Historically, it comes with lower wages, employer skepticism, and the resentment of co-workers.

The security needs of pregnant workers are crucial. But before retreating to the bad old days, we ought to at least give "equality" a fair shot.

There is a more idealistic if more difficult solution to the conflict. By establishing women as "normal workers," we can extend the law to men as our equals. Why shouldn't any worker who has been disabled for four months be entitled to return to his or her job? Why shouldn't fathers also be entitled to benefits after parental leave?

The economic climate is not friendly to such notions, but it's premature to give up on this goal. Parental-leave legislation is being discussed in Congress right now. New options and appeals are being considered in California.

Instead of settling for equally shabby or dangerously

preferential treatment, we can embrace the ideal of equally decent treatment. We don't have to dip into the ready-to-wear notions of the past. Nor do women have to camouflage their difference in three-piece maternity suits. We can still cut our own cloth.

APRIL 1984

EULOGY FOR AN AMENDMENT

BOSTON—Allow me a moment for mourning. I promise I won't abuse it. It is, after all, unsophisticated to grieve for a piece of legislation. Politics is politics. You win some, you lose some.

But this time we lost the Equal Rights Amendment and it feels lousy.

The defeat was no surprise. By the time the grim bulletins came in from Raleigh, Tallahassee, Springfield (Illinois), we knew it was all over. Some of us felt like members of a family who used up their emotional energy tending the sick. We greeted the end dry-eyed, a bit tired, even numb.

Still there is a need to mourn. So, spare me for now the official lines of optimism.

Next week, next month, or next year, is time enough for perspective, the long view, the historical glance. Then I'll remember that it took three generations to pass suffrage. It will take a third generation to pass ERA. Nothing can kill an idea. It will start again.

Next week, next month, or next year is time enough to

analyze what went wrong. Then I'll play the games. Was it ERA strategy or right-wing opposition? Were women their own enemy, or men? Were the ERA supporters too controversial or not confrontational enough? Was it the draft, the "family"? Were we just weak on votes or also on consensus?

Next week, next month, or next year is also time enough to tally up the good that can come with defeat. Then we can all chart how innocence has been replaced by savvy. The sanguine have become the cynical.

We can make optimistic comparisons. In 1920, when the Nineteenth Amendment was passed, those who believed in women's rights went home with the illusion of victory. As the Twenty-seventh Amendment goes down [1982], those who believe in women's rights are fresh out of illusions. Women who have stood in the chambers watching their rights treated callously will take that memory to the ballot box

But not yet. For today, please, a moment for mourning.

My country has refused to promise that "equality of rights under the law shall not be denied or abridged by the United States or any state on account of sex."

Today, those of us who expended energy and idealism in the notion of equal rights are the losers. Those of us who believed the system would work for women are the losers. Those of us who just assumed that something as simple as this amendment would pass are losers. So are those who underestimated the enemies, and the enmity.

The angry won: people who linked the ERA with every evil from unisex toilets to homosexual marriages. The scared won: people looking for a scapegoat for the "breakdown of the family," the changing expectations for women. The politicians-as-usual won: people who traded our rights away as if they were baseball cards.

And so did those who simply want to keep, or put, women down. The antiwoman sentiment was always there

264

in this debate, raw and overt, ringing with biblical incantations about submissiveness. It was also there, civilized and sedate, covered by a veneer of protective language and states' rights litanies from people who were for the E and the R but not the A.

No, I will not bury my heart in Tallahassee or Springfield or Raleigh. The defeat won't stop this women's movement, this movement of women, any more than legislation could stop the continental drift. Someday our children-historians will look on this campaign as a time when fear got the better of our ideals and lynched our rights.

But it will take, at least, another ten years to pass the ERA. I will be fifty-one, my daughter will be twenty-four. Another generation of women will have grown up without their rights guaranteed by the Constitution. Another generation will have expended their energy on basics. Another generation will have felt discrimination.

The ERA was no guarantee of Utopia, but it promised something: progress. For the moment, the bad guys have won. It's a moment worth mourning.

Back in 1952 when he lost the election, Adlai Stevenson remembered a story about a little boy who stubbed his toe in the dark: "He said he was too old to cry but that it hurt too much to laugh." That just about sums it up.

JUNE 1982

BATHING SUITS AND MORTARBOARDS

BOSTON—It looks as if the lawyers at King & Spalding had better skip the bathing-suit contest this summer [1984]. Last summer at their outing, a third-year law student and summer intern won a prize for "the body we'd like to see more of."

Now the giant Atlanta law firm had better watch its Ps, its Qs and its image. The Supreme Court ruled unanimously last week that a former female associate, Elizabeth Hishon, has the right to sue King & Spalding for sex discrimination in denying her a partnership. Under the circumstances, another bathing-suit contest might make the men look bad.

The decision itself merits a sigh of relief more than a round of applause. The law firm had argued that they were exempt from Title VII of the Civil Rights Act of 1964, which outlaws discrimination against employees. Partners, they said, are different from employees. If the Supreme Court had agreed, any law firm, accounting firm, investment firm, or partnership could have hung a sign on the door that read NO BLACKS, NO JEWS, NO WOMEN NEED APPLY.

The reassurance that upper-level jobs like these are not entirely exempt from the law comes just in time. At the moment there are two places in the economy where women are stuck. One is at the bottom, in that feminized zone called poverty, in jobs marked dead end. The other is at that more rarefied professional plateau where Hishon found herself, right below the top.

In the past decade, women have gained at least token access into even the stuffiest of professional or corporate establishments. They are in all the jobs that qualify them for admission to yuppiedom.

In the legal profession, there has been a striking rise in the number of women. About 37 percent of law students are female. One out of every six lawyers is female. Sixty percent of these women are still under thirty-five. Like the young MBAs, accountants, and executives, these lawyers form an impressive wedge.

But there are still few women in any profession who have percolated up to the top. Only 5 percent of the partnerships in law firms are held by women. At King & Spalding, only 2 women have joined the 48 male partners since the Hishon suit was filed in 1979. Some investment firms are still entirely white and male. Even the gargantuan accounting firm Arthur Andersen has just 14 women among its 700 partners.

The next few years are going to be the crunch years, as this ambitious group of professional women try to make the final cut. The barriers they face are going to be subtle, and frustrating.

The decisions to admit people into the inner circle of success are highly subjective. When two or ten people, all technically qualified, compete for the same post, the choices are often emotional, and impressionistic.

In Hishon's case there were no complaints about her work but, rather, a general feeling that "she just didn't fit in." As another woman who'd been at the firm said, "If you can't discuss the University of Virginia–University of North Carolina basketball game, you're an outcast."

It's hard for anyone just passed up for tenure or partnership or promotion to know whether she lost out or was kept out. It's even harder to convince a court.

Hishon rescued the right of women in high-echelon jobs to sue under Title VII, but it's not clear whether she or others will be able to win such suits. Unless there is a "smoking gun"—absolute proof that she wasn't made partner because of her sex—the firm can claim some other and legal reason why she didn't make the grade.

In general, the courts have a double standard for lower- and upper-level jobs. In blue-collar jobs the courts looked at the results of employment policies. If the policy had a disparate effect on blacks or women, courts usually ruled it was illegal unless the employer could justify it by "business necessity." But policies that keep blacks or women out of the most important posts were justified as necessary.

Harvard Law School professor Elizabeth Bartholet, who teaches employment-rights litigation, says that judges are just too close to the problems of elite decision makers. "It's easy for judges to look objectively at the lower-level blue-collar factory. But they identify too strongly with the upper-level elite who are hiring people." Especially hiring lawyers.

At the moment, an impressive group of women is in position to move into top professional slots. Many of them made this lineup because the courts opened graduate schools and entry-level jobs. Now they face the most subjective screening.

If the courts treat upper-level jobs the way they treat lower-level jobs, women will win. But if they don't, somebody better hand out bathing suits along with mortarboards.

MAY 1984

MOTHERS, DAUGHTERS, AND THE DRAFT

BOSTON—The verdict is a bad one. I know that even as it first comes in over the wire.

The Supreme Court has ruled that the Congress can draft men only.

The Court has ruled that it is constitutional for the government to pass over the houses where our daughters dwell and pluck our sons off to war.

As I read about it, my mind instantly turns to the file of arguments against this verdict, why it is wrong for men, wrong for women. The Congress has treated men as expendable, women as inferior. The Court had upheld its right to do so.

I run through the file quickly, almost ritualistically. And yet, in all honesty, I find it hard to feel this decision, really feel it, as a "devastating blow" to women. Perhaps I am no longer willing to see women drafted into equal responsibilities without equal rights. Perhaps I am tired of being unilaterally fair. Perhaps I am just terrified of war.

But I feel, momentarily, relieved.

I talk to Ellie Smeal, the head of the National Organization for Women (NOW) and opponent of an all-male draft, and she is not surprised at this emotion. "I think people don't want anybody to be drafted unless there is some compelling reason," she said. "We are coming to the conclusion that war is not a rational foreign policy. We know we can't win a war now.

"It's not a question of being unpatriotic. If we knew the Nazis were coming through Europe I think we would fight again. But now we're afraid our kids will be fighting for some damn oil well. So I think we breathe a sigh of relief that at least we can save our daughters."

I share my sense, too, with Dr. Helen Caldicott, a leader of the antinuclear war movement. She knows this feeling, but for another reason. She says simply, "I am thoroughly against women becoming soldiers. It goes against everything we stand for as sisters, as nurturers. Women are the civilizers. To join the draft is to join the killers."

Yet both of these women, coming from different places, different platforms, also sense how illusory the relief is. If there is a war, women may not be equal soldiers. But they will be equal victims.

If there is a war in the 1980s, it will not be fought in trenches but in computer centers, not with bayonets but with nuclear bombs. There is no way to protect our daughters, or ourselves, from that.

So I turn away from thinking about the impact of this decision on women, and think about its impact on peace.

Ellie Smeal—who makes no claims of women's innate peaceful nature, to intuition, to moral superiority— acknowledges that the women's movement has always been a peace movement. She is part of that. NOW is part of that.

"There is a twenty percent difference between men and women in terms of peace advocacy," she says, citing poll data. But Smeal believes that the women's peace movements of the past were ineffective because women were never going to be called on to fight.

"Part of the way they have diminished our effect is by keeping us on the sidelines," Smeal adds. "They continue to perpetuate the myth that we have no stake. Now they have taken away our voice of protest. We can't even say, 'Hell, no, we won't go.'"

But Dr. Caldicott believes that the women's peace movement failed for a different reason: "We won the vote sixty years ago and did nothing with it. We can't blame men that we haven't used our power. It's really our fault."

Despite this ruling, Dr. Caldicott says, things are different now. The woman who talks with terrifying eloquence about doomsday believes that, "We have learned to be powerful. We know that the men running the world embody only the killing principle. There's an urgency now that has never before occurred."

In this climate, my relief does not even last the afternoon. There is too little room for it in the midst of so much anxiety about the new militarism, the spread of nuclear bombs.

It is clear that in the courtroom, women lost one vigorous voice for peace, the sound of a might-be soldier. Now it is more crucial than ever to increase the decibel level of the might-be victim.

JUNE 1981

LEARNING TO SPEAK DEFENSE

WASHINGTON—If you were to project a mental slide of the place of men and women in the arms debate, it would show men on the inside planning, and women on the outside protesting. The men would be captioned "national leaders," while the women would be captioned "mothers."

The portrait isn't entirely accurate, of course, but it will do as a negative for the gender-gap photography. By now we know that men and women are furthest apart in their attitude toward the military. We know that the ranks of most peace movements are filled by women.

It is common and comfortable for activists, for analysts, and for polltakers to attribute women's great military skepticism to their role as nurturers, as earth mothers. Women themselves have often claimed moral superiority as the world's peacemakers.

From Greenham Common in England to the Pentagon steps, there are women who say that all we really need to know about the arms race is that nuclear bombs are bad for children. They keep arm's length from the military charts, and think of defense statistics like football statistics, numbers for the games men play.

But it is no longer enough for women to rest their case on morality. It isn't enough to demonstrate in the Pentagon entryways while arms are designed inside. It is clearly time to learn the rules of the game and to enlarge the image of peace movement people from earth mothers to informed citizens.

This was evident, when 300 women came to Washington for a total-immersion course in the Economics of National Security. The Third Annual Women's Leadership Conference held by the Committee for National Security attracted mayors, state legislators, academics, bureaucrats, religious women, and a host of activists from across the country.

Most of them came simply to learn. They empathized with Sheila Tobias who said that, "Three years ago, I didn't know an M-1 from an M-16 [a tank from a rifle]. I was a defense avoider, a weapons avoider." Tobias, who authored a book on mass anxiety and coauthored a highly readable book on national security, urged women to believe that they could grasp the language of defense the way they once learned French.

For defense beginners she suggested the value of simply memorizing foreign phrases like these: "The Defense Department spends a billion dollars every working day; ten million dollars every five minutes." But she also had some encouragement never given to a French beginner: "The more you know, the more you know that they don't know everything."

These total-immersion students studied the defense budget, complete with administration charts and antiadministration skepticism. The statistics that form and inform the debate over national security were calculated and dissected.

At the same time, leaders like Randall Forsberg, a former English teacher who founded the nuclear-freeze movement, showed how to keep the perspective of the outsider while learning the grammar of the insider. She cautioned the women not to be trapped into the traditional debate over the cost of personnel versus hardware. She said to ask the most basic questions of foreign policy: What portion of our military budget is being used for what is literally national defense?

By the last day of the conference, even a low-intermediate student in defense economy could grasp the outlandish nature of statistics that "prove" the Russians are outspending us in a frenzied military buildup. "My Lord," said one woman in the hall after the session, "it's just guesswork."

For most Americans, such revelations are rare. The sheer difficulty of understanding defense-speak, of communicating with the statisticians and technicians, keeps most of us out of the discussion.

Winston Churchill once said that "the experts should be on tap, not on top." In a democracy, citizens are supposed to be the decision makers, on top. Many women, either as mother superiors or as defense phobics, have been excluded to talk about that anymore. It had become a cliché, a stereotype to shatter.

It isn't just a question of genders and gaps, of motherhood and morality. It isn't a question of men versus women, but of citizens who do and don't participate. At the core, the arms debate isn't a matter of statistics but of values and choices. That's a language anybody can learn.

JUNE 1984

A WHOLE NEW BALL GAME

BOSTON—The Karen O'Connor story began on a basketball court in Illinois and ended in the Supreme Court in Washington.

It began looking like a simple enough tale about boys and girls and basketball, and ended looking like a case study in mental gymnastics.

The star of this legal sporting event was four feet eleven inches tall and eleven years old when she wanted to try out for the boys' team at school instead of the girls' team. Karen's reasons were the obvious ones: The boys' team was better and she was good enough to make it.

But the school kept her out of tryouts, and off the team, because she was a girl.

The way Karen and her parents figured it, this was an out-and-out case of discrimination, just the sort of thing banned by the Fourteenth Amendment. And so they sued.

The school, on the other hand, figured it differently. They

said that single-sex teams didn't discriminate: they gave girls a separate but equal chance to participate in sports, just the sort of thing encouraged by Title IX. And so they defended.

Well, the case dribbled up the legal system. Karen's offense won in the lower court. The school's defense won on appeal. Finally last week, the Supreme Court left intact the court of appeals ruling. For the moment, at least, single-sex teams are both legal and constitutional.

But what is most intriguing to me isn't written on the scoreboard. It's the way this case walked the balance beam of equal opportunity.

On one side we had Karen, who wanted to be treated as an individual. She wanted her talents judged against all comers, male or female. That is, unquestionably, one definition of equal opportunity.

On the other side we had the school officials, who wanted all girls to have an equal chance with all boys, an equal chance to play team ball and learn sports skills. That is another definition of equal opportunity.

These two notions don't necessarily conflict. But in real life, they can.

If the Supreme Court had ruled that all team sports had to be integrated at every school level, the end result might have been technically "fair," but disastrous. The best players would have won the varsity letters, the chance to play team sports, the chance to play at all. But at this point in history, those players would have been overwhelmingly male.

A few talented girls like Karen might have benefited from this "opportunity," but the majority would have ended up on the sidelines. Even the traditional girls' sports could have been taken over by boys.

As Jennifer Nupp, head of Sprint, the sports project for the Women's Equity Action League, puts it, "Letting in one girl here or there, doesn't really help the overall picture of women in sports." Equal opportunity for the individual can even retard equal opportunity for the group.

If I were choosing a model for women in sports, it wouldn't be the match between Billie Jean King and Bobby Riggs. It would be the gradual and permanent development of women's team tennis into an exciting and competitive sport of its own.

In that same vein, Title IX has generally been implemented in a way that provides women with separate but equal (or less unequal) equipment, money, coaching, teamwork in sports like basketball.

But there is still this quandary: Siphoning off the stars, the Karens, into boys' teams hurts the goal of building better girls' teams. But preventing the stars, the Karens, from playing on boys' teams hurts their own personal goals.

The conflict between the Fourteenth Amendment and Title IX in sports, between methods to achieve equal opportunities for an individual or for a group, is likely to be raised again. It's a real one. But I don't think it will last forever.

At the moment Karen herself is playing on a coed community team and a girls' school team. But as girls are encouraged to play sports, the Karens won't be such exceptions. The teams may integrate more completely at her age, or the skills of the average girl may sharpen enough to challenge the best.

Karen was just caught in the gap. She took a free throw at the Supreme Court and she missed. Her aim was good, but her timing was off.

DECEMBER 1981

A MENTOR CALLED LUCK

BOSTON—The three women on the panel described their work histories in a nice orderly sequence—jobs, titles, dates.

They appeared to be the very model of proper career women, the well-organized success stories of five-year plans and life-management courses. Their autobiographies would have impressed any personnel manager or editor of *Who's Who*. Surely they impressed the college audience.

Yet later, when they talked alone, different words crept into their résumés. The first woman sheepishly confessed to "luck," the second woman admitted "chance," the third talked about "accident."

Not one of these women had tipped her hat to luck in her public job description. After all, they were enlightened women. They had all read the research.

Hadn't it been proved that most women attributed their success to luck while most men attributed it to their own effort, skills, talents? They knew that trap and wanted to avoid it, and so, had expunged luck from their curriculum vitae. At least, said one of the women, the younger generation could be spared their self-doubt.

It was the first of two conversations that I heard about luck. The next one occurred when a woman who had started out in English criticism and ended up in political research confessed she, too, felt awkward explaining the role of accident in her peculiar progression. One wasn't supposed

supposed to talk about that anymore. It had become a cliché, a stereotype to shatter.

But this time, it occurred to me that I wasn't sure anymore. I wonder if "planning" isn't just as much of a cliché and "control" as much of a stereotype to shatter. I wonder which point of view is more realistic?

I know that when assorted studies about the differences between men and women filter into our popular language we usually begin by seeing men as the norm and women abnormal. If the topic is success and more men are successful, then we begin by worrying about the female success psyche. We assume that women need to change.

But if more men believe they made their own way deliberately, purposely, skillfully, is it because these men plan better or because they rationalize better? Is it because of their skills or egotism? Were their lives more in their control or are they more reluctant to admit a lack of control?

And if more women see fate, luck, accident as a central force in their work lives is it because they are passive, slow to see and reluctant to admit their own skills? Or is it because they are quick to see and comfortable to admit the reality of chance?

The answers depend less on our perception of men and women than on our perception of the truth. It depends on how we determine the tricky equation of luck and skill in a life.

I know there are many things we can't do without acquiring the skills, making the plans. We cannot, blessedly, do brain surgery without medical training. Few people "luck" into medical school.

But there are many things we can't do with planning. We cannot chart a course from English critic to political researcher. We cannot figure out how our interests will change and skills grow. We don't know when chances will come, including the chance to throw over all our previous plans.

It is always easier to plot our lives backward and discover a straight line than to plot them forward on that line. To make a life, we need a peculiar combination of energy and persistence, skills that make readiness, and a lot of luck.

I don't say this as any kind of revelation but because luck has gotten this bad rap. Those who acknowledge luck as a mentor are tempted to believe that their experience has no meaning for others. It was just luck after all. Women in particular are tempted to hide the happenstance behind a timetable.

But we're dealing with a younger generation full of anxieties about the future, a generation longing to be told the one true path. Maybe what they really need is people who will give them firsthand accounts of chance. Maybe they need our experience and our wishes for good luck.

MARCH 1983

FANTASY OF THE FIRST FEMALE PRESIDENT

BOSTON—From California to Minnesota, the first candidates have begun to sprout like crocuses in this early and chilly season [February 1983] of the 1984 presidential race. It's only a matter of time now before we notice that, once again, all the early bloomers are men.

Soon someone will raise the perennial question. What about the possibility of a First Woman in the White House instead of a First Lady?

So today, as a service for those who like to leaf through

political catalogs a bit early, I'll pass on the description of the first female who may be raised to the Oval Office.

This profile comes originally from Elizabeth Janeway, intellectual doyenne of feminism, author of *Man's World, Woman's Place* and *Powers of the Weak*. A landscape analyst of no mean skills, Janeway offered up her best-guess vision at a conference in New York in December 1982.

Janeway did not name names. She chose rather to name characteristics, species, the shape of bulb, if you will, from which the Number One Woman would emerge in the next generation.

To begin with, the first woman president, suggested Janeway, would be elevated by fate (always a female in Western mythology) from the ranks of vice president. She will have been given a place on the ticket, as vice presidents before her, for "balance." The male-controlled convention that nominates her will be thinking largely of geography, or ideology, although there may be some visceral understanding that women also provide an attractive "balance."

As for the personal details of our First Woman, explains Janeway, she will almost certainly be married, with a "healthy, non-henpecked husband . . . neither a wimp, nor a hanger-on . . . ," probably a lawyer. Children? "A couple of post-adolescent children, out of college or finishing well, with good reputations and an average amount of success would be an asset, though no children at all, who could go wrong and get into trouble, would be a safeguard."

Our First Woman will also have stamina, an impressive political background, and, because she's had to break stereotypes about female docility, she may be a touch pigheaded.

So much for the easy stuff. What will she be like politically? Swallow hard. According to this analysis, the First Woman will be a conservative Republican who believes in the status quo.

As Janeway noted wryly, "She will certainly say, in her acceptance speech, that she looks upon her nomination as an opportunity to represent the whole party electorate, not just women. If asked, she will firmly dissociate herself from feminism about which, in fact, she will be thoroughly, purposefully, ignorant."

This portrait is enough to make most of the people in favor of a woman president, including Elizabeth Janeway, groan. It is, of course, just a guess, but you don't have to be a subject of Maggie Thatcher to see its possibilities. It's no accident that both women in the United States Senate and the sole woman on the Supreme Court are conservative Republicans. A substantial portion of the most successful women in this country has risen on the tide of feminism only to declare that they are not "women's libbers."

The path of social change to the Oval Office or the Corporate Office is often a curious one. The advance troop of any protest group is made up of demanding, aggressive people. They sue governments, petition bosses, raise consciousness, upset order, and, despite all the paths they break, rarely win their way to the top.

The power structure turns instead, and with relief, to people who will fit in, who will minimize change, and make it less threatening. They choose the women who look and sound like they do, except that their three-piece suits come with skirts. As Janeway puts it, they look for the woman who "does not threaten innovation except by her presence."

Does all this mean that the first woman president will be a dud as far as women are concerned? Not entirely. As Janeway concluded, "I won't vote for her, but I will welcome her presence. . . . A woman in an office that no woman has held before breaks down barriers and makes the impossible possible, if not likely."

This candidate is just a composite, a species of first

woman president, and not a first choice in my catalog of candidates. But even her existence, in this saga of long-term change, says something about a climate that is slowly, yet perceptibly, warming.

FEBRUARY 1983

ROLE OF THE FIRST FEMALE VICE PRESIDENT

SAN FRANCISCO—If you need a label to describe the role of Gerry Ferraro at the Democratic Convention in 1984, don't look up the history of the words "running mate." Before those words were ever used in politics, a "running mate" was the second horse in a racing stable. It was the pacer, the horse who ran but never, ever beat the stable's number one contender.

The candidate from Queens is anything but a running mate. In the first flush of "newness" there is more genuine enthusiasm for Gerry Ferraro than for Fritz Mondale. Back in Minnesota, the former vice president said, "This is an exciting choice." Here in San Francisco there is more excitement about the choice than the chooser. The would-be future vice president is winning the popularity contest by a furlong.

The most common sentiment on the floor is seen in the green-and-white sticker that reads WOMAN VP NOW. The fastest-selling button on the street carries a portrait of Ferraro. The loudest cheers at the rallies greet Ferraro. At one Mondale press conference the questions were directed to the man but the eyes were on the woman.

Much of this attention is absolutely predictable curiosity. It is hard to exaggerate the stunning visceral effect of the first woman on a major national ticket. Every time Ferraro moves in this first campaign circuit, there's another "first."

For the first time, a candidate for vice president of the United States answers a question about abortion with the words: "If I were pregnant..." For the first time, a candidate talks about women's rights and calls them "our rights." For the first time, the political spouse is a husband. For the first time, the professional costume is not a pinstripe suit with pants but a white jacket with a skirt, or even a dress.

The number one man seems unflustered by the spotlight on his second fiddle. On the flight to San Francisco, when asked whether he was worried about being upstaged by Ferraro, he joked, "I'm assigning her to another plane." At the first meeting with women delegates he said wryly, "When I was vice president, I spent four years introducing the president. Now here I am about to be president of the United States and I am going to spend the next four days introducing the vice president."

His ease and obvious pleasure with Ferraro's stardom prompted a prominent Democrat here to say, "You gotta give Mondale credit. We should all be wearing our old T-shirts that read: A MAN OF QUALITY ISN'T THREATENED BY A WOMAN OF EQUALITY."

In part, what we are watching here is another first, the very public evolution of an entirely new political relationship. Mondale and Ferraro are not a political "couple." Ferraro bristles at phrases like these. But they are a team in a country that is still getting used to male-female teamwork.

Sometimes awkwardly, they are beginning to forge a new set of roles and a new body language. And they are doing it in front of the cameras and the country's eyes.

At more than one meeting Mondale and Ferraro have

each greeted supporters, hugging his or her way down aisles, and then have stood a professional pace from each other on the platform. By intent or intuition, the two candidates have barely touched since the announcement. Ferraro doesn't look up at Mondale when he's speaking, in the requisite pose for wives. She looks directly into the audience.

There is a certain consciousness, even self-consciousness, in all of this. The fact is that Ferraro is not, and cannot be, a "woman of equality" in this political team. If the Democratic ticket is a partnership, the vice president is the junior partner. The success of the venture requires that the first woman look strong. Strong and tough are words being prefixed to her name by the Democrats. At the same time, she can't be overpowering. As for the senior partner, Mondale has to carry authority without looking overbearing.

For the moment, the moment of beginning, the sum is greater than its parts. She plays Italian to his Norwegian. She plays daring to his cautious. She is camera-warm and he is camera-cold. They look good together. But like any new relationship, this is one that needs time and tact.

In the long run, from here to November, Mondale and Ferraro will spend little time in the same room, the same plane, the same city. But they will occupy the same piece of turf called a ticket.

The test for Ferraro will be to keep the current excitement high, but also to transfer that wattage back to Mondale. After all, running mates aren't trained to win alone.

JULY 1984

SUMMING UP THE FERRARO CAMPAIGN

BOSTON—It was less than four months since that day in Minnesota [July 1984] when a congresswoman from Queens was introduced to America. "Thank you, Vice President Mondale," she said, and paused. "Vice President. It has such a nice ring to it."

It was less than seventeen weeks since Mondale injected that lackluster campaign with a booster shot of energy named Geraldine Ferraro. "American history," she said that day, "is about doors being opened."

It was exactly 116 days from that July 12 high to the election-night low when all the polls came true and Geraldine Ferraro did not become the first woman vice president of the United States.

From the beginning, Ferraro was running two campaigns and she knew that better than anyone. She was running as the Democratic nominee and running as a woman. "I want to come out of this campaign a winner, I want to be vice president," she said in North Carolina on one of her innumerable campaign stops. And if she didn't get that job? "I want it to be said, 'She was a professional.'"

In the next weeks a great deal will be written about the Ferraro factor. Was it a political plus, a minus, a wash? What happened to the female surge, the male backlash, the vice-presidential drawing card? Are women better off than they were four months ago?

For people who judge things by statistics, the results are bound to be mixed. There was an eight-point gender gap. But women didn't stop the flow of blood out of the Democratic party from becoming a geyser. Ferraro didn't do the impossible: She didn't make Fritz Mondale president.

The analysis is more mixed. Surely, the financial investigations rubbed glitter off this new star. But there were other mistakes. The Mondale camp never played to the women's vote until the very end. The strategy laid out July 4 when women leaders talked to the candidate about the political possibilities of a woman on the ticket remained dormant. It was as if the Mondale people expected Ferraro to win women's votes on mysticism.

From the beginning the Republicans went after the women's vote with ads and a campaign that stressed economic gains, not equal rights. In contrast, Ferraro made her final full-tilt emotional pitch for the women's vote just four days before the election.

But not all victories come down to numbers. Ferraro did win that second race—the race for women. She won it among those who rooted for her even if they didn't vote for her. She won it among the skeptical and the sexist who came to admire her. She won it among those who never thought they'd live to see a woman on the ticket.

In many ways this race was a qualifying test. Ferraro was given oral exams by reporters and pols and the public. The first woman, the outsider, was tested for admission to the highest ranks of the profession. She also was put through tests of nerve, answering questions about family finances, debating toughness and leadership with George Bush. At times, it seemed that there were millions of graders poised, waiting for the first break of emotion—a single tear, flash of anger, "hysteria"—to flunk her. She passed, not just with the 16 percent of voters who said a woman on the ticket was a plus, but with the 55 percent who said sex made no difference.

I don't know how Ferraro will assess these four months in the long morning after. When the cameras have moved on to other subjects, John Zaccaro, her husband, will still be facing lawyers. She will have to weigh the hurt of that mean-spirited, gratuitous *New York Post* story on her parents' forty-year-old gaming charges. It was not painless to be targeted by the church Ferraro had grown up in. On election eve she said, "It hasn't always been easy, but it's been worth it for all of us."

I hope that's true for her. I am sure it's true for "all of us." Are we better off than we were four months ago? Ask the women at the rallies who reached out to her. Ask the mothers and fathers who held their daughters up just to see her. Ask Carrie Giardino, a fourth-grader who ran for school president in South Yarmouth, Massachusetts, on a Ferraro ticket—"If that Italian woman can do the job . . . so can this one!"—and won.

In blistering defeat, this candidate told a room of supporters: "Campaigns, even if you lose them, do serve a purpose. . . . We made a difference." Geraldine Ferraro, first woman, family woman, politician, ran with grit and grace, humor and intelligence. She made history. "Not bad," as she would put it, "for a housewife from Queens, huh?"

NOVEMBER 1984

THE SKIRMISH OF THE SEXES

BOSTON—About halfway through *Tootsie*, when Dustin Hoffman stops to contemplate the woman he is portraying, he says, "I think Dorothy is smarter than I am."

It's an appropriate midline to this movie. *Tootsie* is not just another zany tale of a man dressed up as a woman. Dustin Hoffman, an unemployed and unemployable actor named Michael Dorsey, finds work in a soap opera as an actress named Dorothy Michaels.

But he does more than step into a woman's shoes; he slips into a woman's mind-set and life. In the process he turns from something of a cad, even a pig, to someone who listens and cares.

Indeed, the central conceit of the movie is that Michael Dorsey is not only smarter when he is playing Dorothy Michaels, he is, well, nicer. More to the point, the conceit is that women are smarter, women are nicer.

I wasn't surprised to find this theme in such a wonderfully funny, even touching, movie. In some ways I think it has been the theme for some time. We seem to have seesawed in some peculiar competition of the sexes from seeing men as superior, to seeing women as superior.

We have been deluged with studies of gender gaps by political pollsters and social scientists suggesting that women are more moral, more caring. We used to ask, Why can't a woman be more like a man? Now we ask, Why can't a man be more like a woman?

Tootsie, billed as the relationship movie of the year, is about a man who does become more like a woman. As such it works delightfully. But I think there is something else going on in the film and maybe in real life. If *Tootsie* pushes the idea that men are nicer in their personal lives when they are acting like women, it also sells another subliminal notion: Women are more successful in public life when they are really men.

Dorothy Michaels lands a role in the television soap opera, and becomes a heroine and a battler for women's rights. In fact, it is a man, finally, who is the strongest woman, the one feminist on the set.

He becomes the female role model, the female mentor, the one who sticks up for "her" rights. He cuts through sexual harassment, rewrites a script on wife abuse, confronts the male chauvinist director. He never once worries what he has done to provoke their behavior. He is never once called a bitch or a women's libber or "one of them."

"I know, I know, this is just a movie and lately there's been a modest trend among moviemakers to give a leading man a "woman's problem." In *Kramer vs. Kramer*, Dustin Hoffman portrayed the single parent in a world that doesn't help us balance work and family. In *Author, Author*, Al Pacino had eight kids and a Broadway deadline. In this movie, Hoffman is called "Tootsie" and pursued around the set.

It's as if the stories that center around women's issues—*Diary of a Mad Housewife*, *An Unmarried Woman*, *Nine to Five*—become feminist tracts, labeled "preachy" when they star real live women. It's as if movie producers, and maybe audiences, are most able to accept these problems as "legitimate" if they happen to a man.

In real life, no one calls Dustin Hoffman or Alan Alda strident. In real life, women's issues acquire an enhanced legitimacy when they are portrayed by men, pressed by men, taken seriously by men.

On the screen, Michael Dorsey came away with something from his life as a woman: sensitivity, people smarts. But he also, and less consciously, had brought something to his life as Dorothy Michaels: an unambiguous instinct to fight against being put down, and kept down.

These are in some ways traditional values. If sensitivity has been a female strength, fighting for yourself has been a male strength. In a time when the differences between the sexes are being seen as competition—who is bigger, better, smarter, nicer—there was a trade-off worth noting.

At the very end of this movie, Jessica Lange says to Dustin Hoffman, "I miss Dorothy." He says, "So do I." What does she miss? Dorothy's strength? What does he miss? Dorothy's understanding? It's all these missing pieces that are floating in the gender gap.

JANUARY 1983

AMBITION

BOSTON—"Do you think I'm losing my ambition?"

The question filled the air between these two old friends. Unexpected and earnest, it erupted from some fissure in the smooth surface of their conversation.

The woman who asked it had been visiting from New

York and together they were renewing friendship and reviewing lives.

The woman, a lawyer, had remarried a year ago and nested again in some new high-rise aviary. The pots and pans that had been used to warm food for the years of her divorce were stir-frying and clarifying once again.

The evenings she has used preparing for the days now had a life of their own. Once, she said, she spent Saturdays preparing for Mondays; and on Wednesdays she found herself thinking about Saturdays.

The woman from Boston took all this in. A journalist, she had always been awed, and a bit unsettled, by the other woman's efficiency. The lawyer had been accomplished at arrangements. She cleared her life of details, and then filled it with work.

But at times, the people in her life had also been treated like details. There had been evenings in their long relationship when the journalist had thought their meeting was another accomplishment, rather than enjoyment. Evenings when she wondered if friendship was something else to be crossed off the lawyer's list.

It was a pleasure to see the easing of this efficiency, to see the overthrow of this domineering work. It was a pleasure to see the texture of a life reemerging from under the lines of a schedule book. But when she shared this pleasure across the table, the lawyer responded as if she had been found guilty by her own evidence: "Do you think I'm losing my ambition?"

Along with the glowing report of her new life, the lawyer had, you see, readied evidence on the other side. She had built a case against herself.

Since her second marriage, her hours were down from twelve to nine. She had refused a case that would have meant weeks of travel. The goal of becoming a partner in the firm seemed less crucial.

Do you think, she asked, with only a touch of humor, that my get up and go got up and went?

The journalist looked back in amusement. Her friend had been rescued from the intensive-care unit of workaholics. After all, she was not spending her days worrying about slipcovers. But now she was worrying about loss of ambition. Somehow it was typical of the lawyer to look at life as an either/or, pro/con, gain/loss proposition.

The two talked about it some more. The lawyer had been divorced for a decade. Work had been her taskmaster, her goaltender, her security. She had excess energy from her personal life; she gave it at the office.

Then slowly, purposefully, she had redistributed her life, taking a portion back home again. But over her new sense of well-being hovered a small cloud of disloyalty and guilt. Was she breaking a prior commitment? Losing ambition?

The lawyer sat there half-expecting a verdict. The journalist didn't deliver. This was a difference between them. The lawyer saw life as a case being built; the journalist saw it as a story being written. The lawyer expected conclusions; the journalist expected contours.

Finally the journalist told her friend that she just couldn't see it as a matter of warring principles. It was a question of proportion. The woman from New York was recreating a life. She was belatedly experiencing the competition, the demands and attractions of ambition and dailiness, of struggle and satisfaction, of the desire to wrestle with the world and the desire to live within it. This was not something that she would win or lose. It was not something she would ever, finally, resolve.

If she were lucky, the lawyer would do what most of us do: tinker with the proportions of our restlessness and peace, from one day to the next, from one year to the next, paying attention to our symptoms, constantly changing our own private formulas.

Had she lost her ambitions? Redefined it? Neither of them could judge that fairly. But the journalist had found something remarkable in her old friend. A new complexity, a liveliness, a creative confusion had emerged out of the old certainties. That was something she would never lose.

JANUARY 1982

PEACE ISN'T JUST FOR MOTHER'S DAY

BOSTON—There is an announcement on my desk for Mother's Day. It comes with a brown-and-white bumper sticker for my car that reads: MILLIONS OF MOMS CARE . . . PREVENT NUCLEAR WAR.

The messages were sent to me, as a mother of one and daughter of another, from the Women's Action for Nuclear Disarmament. The press release tells me that they have planned antiwar events in fourteen states to commemorate this Mother's Day with rallies and speeches and white "mums."

The point, I am told, is to revive Julia Ward Howe's idea. Back in 1872, long before Anna Jarvis made this a national celebration of maternity, Howe called for a Mother's Day for peace.

This remarkable lady, author of the "Battle Hymn of the Republic," had also seen the devastation of the Franco-Prussian War. She wanted mothers to organize "to prevent the waste of human life of which they alone bear and know the cost." Her modern heirs can envision the devastation of a nuclear war. They want mothers to organize because, as the coordinator said, "The ultimate mothering issue is the prevention of nuclear war.'

Between these two Mother's Days, these two generations of women, stand 111 years and one shared idea: the idea that there is some special quality which makes mothers "naturally" more invested in peace—in the future of their children. Helen Caldicott, for one, calls the antinuclear impulse a mother's "instinct."

Yet, I wonder if Americans assign mothers the role of peacemongers to the exclusion of others. I wonder how peace became our issue, our specialty, and our minority platform.

In real life, mothers have had very little "maternal" influence on a bellicose century. Even Mother's Day was often an occasion for manipulating this female peace constituency.

In the carnage of World War I, Congress wrote special tributes to Mother's Days because women felt "most deeply the pangs of war." On Mother's Days that fell in wartime, we were praised and handed gold stars for sacrificing our children. On Mother's Days that fell in peacetime, we were promised "never again."

Our most recent history is filled with the protests of mothers: Mothers Against the War, Another Mother Strikes for Peace, Gold Star Mothers Against the War, and now my own bumper sticker: MILLIONS OF MOMS CARE. At times it seems as if only mothers are expected to care about the future.

I don't dispute for a minute a prejudice for peace among women. We have read it over decades of polls registering opinions about the Vietnam War, the neutron bomb, Reagan's foreign policy.

There are risks in single-sex disarmament, when peace is thought of predominantly as a mothers' issue. There is the risk that women may simply stake out a higher moral ground—NO NUKES—and refuse to engage in questions like "how?" There is the risk that mothers, claiming some superior sensibility, psychologically exclude their allies, whether these are bishops or statesmen or fathers. Finally, there is a greater risk: that society, having assigned mothers the role of peacemongers, will go about the business of the arms race.

We've seen evidence for that kind of ideological sex-segregation. In the history of the nineteenth century, women were given the job of upholding the traditional kinder virtues of a benign domestic world, while men forged into a ruthless industrial world. Women were to create the haven of family. Men were to create the heartless world.

Today, I carry two pictures in my own mind. One shows 30,000 women forming a nine-mile ring around Greenham Common at an antinuclear rally in England. The other shows gray-suited men at the START talks in Geneva. The women are on the outside, protesting. The men are on the inside, making policy.

Am I opposed to Mother's Day rallies? Pin the white "mum" on my lapel. But on some Mother's Day, we must move beyond thinking of mothers as the private manufacturers of the next generation, the women who have the vested interest in life, the future peace.

What we are talking about is survival. And, surely, all men and women have that "instinct."

MAY 1983

THE LAW ENFORCER AND
THE BATTERED WIFE

BOSTON—In 1984, Charlotte Fedders wrote a letter to the president. She never posted it, but her sister did. In it, the forty-one-year-old mother of five said, "I am a victim of wife abuse. For over 16 years of marriage my husband periodically beat me.... I have had a broken eardrum, wrenched neck, several black eyes, many, many bruises. Once he even beat me around the abdomen when I was pregnant.

"I do not understand ... how a man can enforce one set of laws and abuse another."

The man she was writing about, her husband of eighteen years, was John M. Fedders, the enforcement chief for the Securities and Exchange Commission. Until his resignation on February 26, 1985, Fedders was the top cop of corporate America, a man in charge of two hundred lawyers, accountants, and administrators, a man who oversaw hundreds of cases of corporate ethics.

The private life of this man, this woman, and their sorry marriage came to public life this week on the front pages of the *Wall Street Journal* and in the divorce proceedings of a courtroom in Montgomery County, Maryland.

It is now public knowledge that John Fedders had at least seven "highly regrettable episodes" of violence against his wife. He admits to that. It's public knowledge that he abused her verbally. We know that he didn't allow shoes worn in their carpeted house. We know that she laid out his clothes in the morning, and picked them up in the evening where they were dropped. We know that he grew up calling his strict parents by the joint name "General Patton." We know that she stopped being a victim.

In that sad context, Charlotte Fedders' question to the White House had a curious psychological edge to it. How, indeed, can the same man enforce one set of laws and abuse another? First, I suppose, the man has to see himself as the law.

If Fedders' profile fits that of wife beater, he was family lawmaker and enforcer rolled into one. As he once said, "Everything in my life is discipline, organization, and structure." Human relationships, though, are messy and there are many who try to control them with force.

But this is more than just another piece of high-powered gossip. The controversy over Fedders' resignation is part of a larger ethical dilemma. How and when does a person's private life disqualify him for public life?

Fedders had other troubles. He was subject to an inquiry in a grand-jury investigation of a client. He lived a corporate lawyer's life-style on a bureaucrat's paycheck and a bank loan. But it was the accusation and confession of family violence that threatened his reputation and his job.

In the past, such scandals were kept tightly wrapped. In the past, a mere whiff of an "immorality" was professionally lethal. Today, we have more revelations and fewer guidelines. Instead of talking about sin, we talk about the relevance to job performance. Does promiscuity prohibit a run for political office? Is drunkenness a public matter in any high office or only during office hours? Should someone caught smoking marijuana be banned from making policy for air travel or arms control?

In this case, the charge of wife beating is a domestic matter, not a criminal one. Indeed, Fedders won a delay from the divorce court in hope of a reconciliation. Whatever his family troubles, he did his job well. From all reports, as head of the SEC, he was one of the driven and dedicated, a federal tough guy. He's cracked down on insider trading and Swiss bank accounts. Is a domestic battle enough to end this career?

Once, after an ugly personal exchange, a critic told the poet Robert Frost, "Robert, you are a very good poet and a very bad man." Robert Frost went on writing wonderful poems and behaving rottenly to many around him. Do we have to lose a good cop because he is a bad family man?

In the end, I think the Fedders affair hinges on the essence of wife beating: violence. All six feet ten inches of John Fedders beat another person, not once, not twice, but at least seven times. It's violence that separates this case from the others and simplifies it. This is not like those delicate questions of drinking in the office. It's more like the case of a drunk who has already hit and run.

Fedders and his colleagues insist that his personal woes didn't affect his work. I believe that. The same man can perceive and pursue wrongdoing at work and at home with vastly different results. Fedders can hone his hairline distinctions, denying wife beating, admitting violent "episodes." But the public doesn't have to accept these distinctions as valid.

Let me rephrase Charlotte Fedders' question. Should a man who has brutally violated one code of behavior have the power to enforce another? The answer is no.

MARCH 1985

THE FEMINISTS AND THE YUPPIES

BOSTON—I never thought that women my age would spend midlife talking about "the younger generation." After all, historically *we* were The Younger Generation. We were destined by the star of the baby boom to be always at the cutting edge.

Yet this winter, wherever I go, I hear a peculiar echo in the voices of my peers or my cohorts or whatever the demographers call us. I catch them repeating the question once uttered by our parents and grandparents about us: "What has happened to the younger generation?"

The women who seem most disappointed are those who call themselves feminists. Now in their mid-thirties and forties, they matured on the wave of the women's movement. For many change was exhilarating; they were too young to feel betrayed by new ideas. They took pride in the assumption that they would make life better for those who came behind them.

Now they look at students and business associates and colleagues, self-confident women in their twenties who feel little connection with the women's rights movement. They look at those who have few qualms in being described as the postfeminist generation. They look at women who fit at least partially under the abused heading of yuppies. And they wonder about them.

A generation gap has opened between the feminists and

the yuppies. It is, at least on the surface, about politics, but it's also about change. The feminists are conscious of sexism as an aroma over the landscape. The yuppies do not have the same sensitive olfactory nerve. Many have never, or so they will tell you, been discriminated against.

To the feminists, the women's rights movement is as current as the latest slur or lawsuit. To the yuppies, it is a tale from the old days when, once upon a time, women had trouble getting into the schools or jobs they now hold.

The midlife generation of women genuinely worry that the young are pulling the covers of denial back over their heads. They worry that the young are being misled again into the belief that they can cut a private deal for progress, one woman at a time. The younger women listen to the repeated warnings of their elders with the polite distancing patience of children told how grandparents walked ten miles in the snow to school.

In distress, the more liberal midlifers say of the more conservative young: They'll find out. They'll find out when they have children and try to balance work and mothering. They'll find out when they bump up against the ceilings on women's aspirations. They'll find out that we were right.

As for me, I find little pleasure in anticipating the day of disillusionment when "they'll find out." I find less comfort in the generation gap I observe.

If I worry about the young, I also worry about my peers. At times we sound like parents who worked hard to make life easier for their children and now criticize these children because they've had it too easy. We wanted them to carry on our lives and are angry with them for living their own.

I suppose feminists think of yuppies the way the suffragists must have thought of the flappers. The suffragists fought for rights. The flappers came along and acted them out in speakeasies and flirtations. The suffragists had planned a series of next steps; the flappers turned them into the

Charleston. Today—if you will forgive my generalizations—the feminists who believed in sisterhood are followed by the yuppies who believe in personal success. One generation marched for progress; the next marks progress on a Nautilus chart.

But there is something else the midlife feminists of the 1980s have in common with the suffragists of the 1920s: aging. I think it is hard for any group of people to feel themselves bumped into middle age. It may be particularly hard when those who call themselves progressive find their deepest ideals wear-dated by those who are younger, as if ideals were pop music or hoop skirts. But it's also hard for the young when their elders don't listen and do judge.

I am enough of a creature of my times to share the alarm of friends and peers about the young. I think that social change is fragile. While the young aren't paying attention, women can drift back. But no generation can write the script for the next. Those who try only lose. Lose contact.

Once, another older generation asked of us: "What has happened to the younger generation?" I remember our response to their distance and dismay. We stopped paying attention.

MARCH 1985

Part 8

TAKING LIBERTY

CENSORING STUDS

BOSTON—In early February 1982, Studs Terkel went down to Girard, Pennsylvania, to defend his book against the banners. His performance in the school and at the open meeting was, I am told, vintage Terkel: intimate, winning, honest.

Those who know this man from Chicago could imagine the itch he felt to turn on his own tape recorder and capture the voices and the feelings of the people who had accused him of writing a dirty book.

Terkel is, after all, a professional listener. He has listened to Americans who survived the Depression and listened to Americans who make it through life one working day at a time in a factory or a restaurant. He has a passion for words as they are really spoken—expletives not deleted. The folk of Girard, even those who challenged the school's right to assign *Working* to the students, are much like the people between the pages of his book. As Terkel put it, "The exquisite irony is that they are the heroes and heroines of this book."

What was unusual about this scene was that Terkel came and even conquered.

But without Terkel's star performance, it would have been another version of a stock play that has run in hundreds of other places with names as unfamiliar as Girard. Warsaw, Indiana, St. Anthony, Idaho, Gardner, Kansas, Drake, North

Dakota, are only a few entries on the huge roll call of towns that have staged a censorship show.

The list of books that have been challenged or banned from school curricula and libraries in the last few years reads like a Who's Who of American authors. The words of challengers read sometimes like a parody. It is tempting to repeat the lines of the parent from Richford, Vermont, who criticized the school use of *Grapes of Wrath*, saying, "You would never find a book like that in the *Reader's Digest*."

But the censorship incidents are real and growing. The American Library Association's Office for Intellectual Freedom, which keeps track of these things, tells us that in 1981, reported challenges tripled nationally from 300 to 900. These come sometimes from the left and mostly from the right. But they almost always come from people who want limits: limits on what the libraries can hold, limits on what the schools can assign, limits on what the students can read.

If Robert Doyle, the ALA's assistant to the president, had to pick the hottest issues for censoring they would be "language," sexual references, agnostic and atheistic viewpoints, and secular humanism. Not far behind would be protests against books without a strong moral viewpoint, in which good is not always rewarded and evil not always punished.

When you listen, censorship controversy is not really between liberal and conservative, left and right. It's between those who think that the business of books is to expand our vision and those who only want to read what they believe. It's between those who think the business of schools is to describe the world as it is, warts and all, and those who worry that the warts will spread unless they are removed from the pages, the shelves, the schools.

Maybe the library, even the school library, seems like an

odd place for such a noisy conflict. Doyle says that, in fact, libraries try to maintain some political neutrality by "promoting the widest viewpoint." But in an era when the major intellectual struggle is against those who want to ensure a narrow viewpoint, this belief isn't neutral anymore.

The schools in particular are increasingly a focus for conflicting ideas, our investment in the future. All the regular procedures to approve textbooks, to define appropriate reading, have become more complex and more controversial. But there is a difference between an orderly review process and the lynch-mob censorship by which books are hung one by one.

Most of the time, as Doyle says, a book doesn't even get a day in court. Only 15 percent of the censorship challenges even make news. Most of the rest are handled quietly. In about half the cases, the ALA tells us, some form of censorship is imposed almost immediately. Sometimes this censorship is as informal as a Magic Marker in the hand of a teacher in Idaho who blacks out every damn and hell in the book.

Terkel did get his "day in court," a public court. He defended his work against people who hunt for words instead of meanings. He defended the real world, the wide lands. He left Girard with a farewell that should, with any luck, stave off the censors of one more book for one more day: "I hope you have a long, decent life, work hard, and READ."

FEBRUARY 1982

A SCIENCE TEST

BOSTON—The Scopes II trial in Little Rock [1981] goes on and on. One team of witnesses for the defense of evolution is followed by another team on the offense for creationism. One battery of definitions of science and religion is countered by another.

In Arkansas, they are playing according to secular rules and both sides have set out to prove they are more scientific than Thou. Over the issue of whether creationism has the right to equal time in science class with evolution, the creationists even swear (on the Bible) that God is not necessarily a religious concept.

With opposing lists of "experts," it all begins to sound like a custody battle for the children of Arkansas. And maybe it is.

In an interview, the Arkansas attorney general Steven Clark said that a big part of the conflict is symbolic, largely "a conflict between philosophical views" rather than scientific views.

The "friends of evolutionists" are more concerned with the value of proof. The "friends of creationists" are more secure with the value of believing. Proevolutionists think that it is good for children to be taught the truth. Procreationists think about what's good for children to be taught *is* true.

Proevolutionists talk about what is. Procreationists talk about what is right and what is wrong.

The question is whether the schools will be a forum for this debate.

For some time, the religious right has maintained that the real struggle in this country is between what they describe as secular humanism and fundamentalist religion. Anything that does not overtly support their set of religious values is undermining those values.

They regard the attempt of the civil libertarians to keep religion out of the schools as a secret attempt to keep "godless" humanism in the schools.

In curious ways, this argument has run through a number of the most hotly contested school issues, from science to social studies, from sex to school prayer. In the eyes of many on the right, banning prayer from the schools is promoting antiprayer. They ask for voluntary prayer the way creationists ask for equal time.

In sex education, even the apparently neutral teaching of reproduction—the biological "plumbing" course—is suspect. Not to teach morals, they say, is to teach immorality. In social studies, the exploration of cultures and human behavior, without value judgments, is another source of outrage. The teacher who isn't judging right and wrong is, some feel, teaching that there is no right and wrong.

It is no wonder that science comes in for the same test. Some scientists, like Darwin himself, have been religious, some not. But science itself is neutral. It may be overwhelmingly opposed to the notion that the world was created in one act six to ten thousand years ago, but it is neutral on the question of the existence of a Creator.

To the religious right, the very idea of being neutral on the question of God is heresy. They see little difference between amoral and immoral, between neutral and hostile.

You are either with 'em or agin 'em. By that definition, science is agin 'em.

Some of the arguments of the right are seductive ones. We are all more skeptical today of "objectivity," whether it is in science or journalism. We are all more concerned about the relationship between information and values.

But the battle between these two "philosophical viewpoints" is ultimately about the nature of knowledge. Is learning a matter of quest and questioning, where doubts are valued along with answers? Or is it elaborate justification created to support a single religious text?

Science begins with questions and pursues answers—testing, proving, disproving. It is this process of reasoning that underpins all of modern science. Creationism begins with answers and pursues doubts only to erase them. It is fundamentally hostile to science.

If creationists win their equal time, it will not be an easily shared custody. There is a deep and irreconcilable difference between the idea that learning is open-ended and the belief that knowledge is a closed Book.

DECEMBER 1981

REWRITING HISTORY

BOSTON—It isn't often that a school textbook triggers an international incident. It would never have happened if the subject were math or Spanish. Facts are facts: One plus one equals two; "yes" equals "sí."

But the catalyst for this event was history, and history isn't as cool as math and doesn't translate as easily as a foreign language. Beyond the data and datelines, its facts are often as complex as a billion biographies, as objective as memory, as important as truth, and as hot as politics.

So the news that the Japanese are literally rewriting history was enough to prompt bomb threats in Korea and official protests in China.

It appears that the Japanese Education Ministry ordered changes in the new books for the fall term: changes in emphasis, changes in wording, changes in the way they tell their youngsters about World War II.

As of this fall, the Japanese will have no longer launched "invasions" in China, Southeast Asia, and the Pacific. They will have "advanced." In the rape of Nanking, they will have no longer "killed and assaulted" 200,000 Chinese willfully but rather "in the midst of the confusion. . . ."

To understand the impulse of the Japanese Education Ministry, just imagine the difficulty of teaching young children about the brutality, the aggression, the wrong committed by the country they are also expected to love.

To understand the effect of these rewritings on Asians (an estimated eighteen million of whom died in World War II), just imagine how we would respond if the Japanese began to teach their children that on December 7, 1941, the Imperial Air Force "advanced" on Pearl Harbor.

The entire incident is in many ways a textbook case. It's a textbook case on the complicated role that history plays in our lives, our understanding of our world, country, families. It's a textbook case on the manipulation of history in the service of politics.

What happened in Japan is not all that unusual. In some way or other, every culture—every country—struggles with its past. To this day there are even heated arguments in this country about whether our early history should be taught as national heroics, led by profiles in courage, or with a more earthy ambiguity.

The more uneasy we are about that past, the more tarnished it seems to us, the more trouble we have telling it to our children. The Japanese have subtly muted their own blame. The official Egyptian guide who led a group of friends to the Pyramids three years ago described how they were built by "volunteer labor." For generations we have had extraordinary difficulty teaching children about the realities of slavery or the myths of cowboys and Indians.

As for our present history, I don't envy those publishers who will update the books to include Vietnam. The war is still being fought. The battle that raged over a monument in Washington was not about architecture, but about the place of the Vietnam War in American history.

The teaching of the past can be an explanation, a judgment, a justification. History can tell sides or take sides. In Argentina and Great Britain, a conflict that grew in part from two sets of history books will be written (I guarantee it) in two separate versions as well as languages. It happens all the time.

But the national autobiography of aggression and guilt is subject to the most peculiar revisions. Germany doesn't rest any more easily on its recent past than Japan. It took until 1962 for German schools to teach children about the death camps. Today there are new "historians" who assault those dead with grotesque rewrites of Nazi reality, calling the Holocaust a hoax.

It is as hard for nations, as it is for parents, to talk about their wrongs. They want respect from the young, and want to instill self-respect in the young. But we can't teach false pride. When we expunge guilt, pretend that it didn't happen, we are tainted by it, committing the ultimate assault on the victims.

Our friendship with our old enemy is due in measure to the way the Japanese acknowledged their aggression as well as their defeat. They told us they were wrong. They told their children they were wrong.

There is a statute of limitations to national guilt. On the whole, few blame the Japan of 1982 for the Japan of 1941. The next generation does not inherit the sins of its parents or grandparents. But it must know those sins. These are the only lasting reparations.

AUGUST 1982

WHEN PORNOGRAPHY AND FREE SPEECH COLLIDE

BOSTON—Just a couple of months before the pool-table gang rape in New Bedford, Massachusetts, *Hustler* magazine printed a photo feature that reads like a blueprint for the actual crime. There were just two differences between *Hustler* and real life. In *Hustler*, the woman enjoyed it. In real life, the woman charged rape.

There is no evidence that the four men charged with this crime had actually read the magazine. Nor is there evidence that the spectators who yelled encouragement for two hours had held previous ringside seats at pornographic events.

But there is a growing sense that the violent pornography being peddled in this country helps to create an atmosphere in which such events occur. As recently as last month, a study done by two University of Wisconsin researchers suggested that even "normal" men, prescreened college students, were changed by their exposure to violent pornography.

After just ten hours of viewing, reported researcher Edward Donnerstein, "the men were less likely to convict in a rape trial, less likely to see injury to a victim, more likely to see the victim as responsible." Pornography may not cause rape directly, he said, "but it maintains a lot of very callous attitudes. It justifies aggression. It even says you are doing a favor to the victim."

If we can prove that pornography is harmful, then shouldn't the victims have legal rights? This, in any case, is the theory behind a city ordinance that recently passed the Minneapolis City Council. Vetoed by the mayor last week, it is likely to be back at the council for an overriding vote, likely to appear in other cities, other towns.

What is unique about the Minneapolis approach is that for the first time it attacks pornography, not because of nudity or sexual explicitness, but because it degrades and harms women. It opposes pornography on the basis of sex discrimination.

University of Minnesota law professor Catharine MacKinnon, who coauthored the ordinance with feminist writer Andrea Dworkin, says that they chose this tactic because they believe that pornography is central to "creating and maintaining the inequality of the sexes. . . . Just being a woman means you are injured by pornography."

They defined pornography carefully as, "the sexually explicit subordination of women, graphically depicted, whether in pictures or in words." To fit their legal definition it must also include one of nine conditions that show this subordination, like presenting women who "experience sexual pleasure in being raped or . . . mutilated. . . ."

Under this law, it would be possible for a pool-table rape

victim to sue *Hustler*. It would be possible for a woman to sue if she were forced to act in a pornographic movie. Indeed, since the law describes pornography as oppressive to all women, it would be possible for any woman to sue those who traffic in the stuff for violating her civil rights.

In many ways, the Minneapolis ordinance is an appealing attack on an appalling problem. The authors have tried to resolve a long and bubbling conflict among those who have both a deep aversion to pornography and a deep loyalty to the value of free speech.

"To date," says Professor MacKinnon, "people have identified the pornographer's freedom with everybody's freedom. But we're saying that the freedom of the pornographer is the subordination of women. It means one has to take a side."

But the sides are not quite as clear as Professor MacKinnon describes them. Nor is the ordinance.

Even if we accept the argument that pornography is harmful to women—and I do—then we must also recognize that anti-Semitic literature is harmful to Jews and racist literature is harmful to blacks. For that matter, Marxist literature may be harmful to government policy.

It isn't just women versus pornographers. If women win the right to sue publishers and producers, then so could Jews, blacks, a long list of people who may be able to prove they have been harmed by books, movies, speeches, or even records. The Manson murders, you may recall, were reportedly inspired by the Beatles.

We might prefer a library or bookstore or lecture hall without *Mein Kampf* or the Grand Whoever of the Ku Klux Klan. But a growing list of harmful expressions would inevitably strangle freedom of speech.

This ordinance was carefully written to avoid problems of banning and prior restraint, but the right of any woman to claim damages from pornography is just too broad. It seems destined to lead to censorship.

What the Minneapolis City Council has before it is a very attractive theory. What MacKinnon and Dworkin have written is a very persuasive and useful definition of pornography. But they haven't yet resolved the conflict between the harm of pornography and the value of free speech. In its present form, this is still a shaky piece of law.

JANUARY 1984

THE GOETZ REACTION

EASTON—It is deceptively easy these early days of 1985 to be a radio talk-show host. All you have to do is utter the magic words—Bernhard Goetz—and the call-board lights up like a marquee. The story of the subway shoot-up has "legs," as they say in the news biz—staying power. And in this marathon, nearly all the public opinion has run in Goetz's direction.

Though we still don't know exactly what happened on that New York subway, each new tidbit of information seems to add supporters to the Goetz cause. It appears now that Goetz had a previous run-in with a mugger, compounded by a frustrating encounter with the law. The four young men he shot all had criminal records. Three of them were carrying filed-down screwdrivers. There were ten bench warrants for their arrests.

It doesn't take a fancy theorist to analyze why Goetz has

become a fantasy figure, an actor in the drama of the urban psyche. Even the mother of the nineteen-year-old man paralyzed by Goetz "understands": "A lot of people have been victims and have boiled up to the boiling point." Ironically, her own husband, the father of this young man, was killed in 1973 trying to stop a thief from taking his taxi.

Among the Goetz fans are many who are angry and many who are racists. But more pointedly, they are men and women who have studied quite the opposite lesson of urban survival than the one Goetz illustrated. They have learned not to fight back.

In or out of the city, every one of us as children absorbs a survival lesson called "how to avoid trouble." We learn to walk home another way, to circumnavigate a certain corner or store. We learn when not to stare back and when to run. We learn to give up turf. But at the same time, our instincts and school-yard mythology tell us to stand up and fight.

It's difficult to act according to a double message. It's hard for any of us, adult or child, to know when to avoid trouble and when to confront it. The line between courage and foolhardiness wavers so much that it's hard to decipher a portrait of our own best behavior.

Increasingly in the face of urban danger, the sentiment is that "it's not worth fighting over" a purse or a piece of jewelry or even a car. We are told to trade off our possessions for our safety, to instantly compute and to reduce risks by passive nonresistance. But sometimes we forget to calculate the emotional cost of accepting this passive posture.

In Grace Hechinger's book, *How to Raise a Street Smart Child*, the author tells what happened when an older and bigger boy asked to "borrow" her son's skateboard. "John wisely gave it to him and watched the boy speed downhill and disappear around a corner. He knew he would never see either boy or skateboard again. He also knew he had done the 'right' thing to give up his possession. But his sensible action was a far cry from his fantasies of what he would have wanted to do."

Caroline Isenberg, on the other hand, fought the would-be thief and rapist on the roof of her Manhattan apartment building in December 1984 and died at twenty-two from knife wounds. Her last words were, "All this for twelve dollars. I should have given him the money. I should have let him do it. I should have given in."

It becomes harder and harder to know when fighting back is foolhardy and when it is brave, when you can save your property or pride and when you can lose your life. The tragedy is when we even give up the power that we do have: the power of collective action.

Goetz, for example, was not alone on that subway car. There were other passengers. Yet, if the story is accurate, the existence of bystanders didn't at all inhibit the four men from hassling Goetz for money. Perhaps the four assumed that all subway riders had wised up and learned not to get involved.

In the course of any week, but especially those moments spent in danger zones, we repress a certain amount of everyday rage. It is not just those who have been mugged who feel this, but those who have felt "menaced." And those who have been bystanders.

Bernhard Goetz was not a profile in courage. He had a gun against pocketed screwdrivers. It was lucky that no bystander got hurt. He did more than brandish that gun.

But he struck a nerve in people who are angry with troublemakers and angry at their hard-learned lessons in avoiding trouble. A nerve in people who are angry at giving up the bicycles and the public domain. In the long term, the cure is building communities in the troubled turf that these young men called home and on the transient turf of a subway. But today, Goetz is a surrogate. By this under-ground explosion, he released the buried feelings of people struggling with fear and courage.

JANUARY 1985

PRIME TIME CAPITAL PUNISHMENT

BOSTON—The descriptions of his death were graphic enough. James David Autry, murderer, was strapped to a gurney in a Texas death chamber. From behind a wall lethal chemicals were injected into tubes that led to his body. As the drugs took effect, Autry began twitching; his knees jerked up. He grunted a bit and sighed. His stomach began to expand. He winced. His eyes looked cloudy. Then he was dead.

If Autry had his way, we would have been able to see all this on television. Indeed, if others have their way, we may yet tune in on death, Live at Five. We may enter the death chamber through the living room. Once again we may become spectators at executions.

It's been almost fifty years since the public could watch an execution in the United States. One of the last public hangings occurred at dawn, August 14, 1936, when a man named Rainey Bethea was hung before a raucous crowd of 10,000 in Owensboro, Kentucky. We are told, in a vivid account by *Time* magazine, that the spectators had spent the night before Bethea's death drinking and attending hanging parties. Through the early hours of that day, "Hawkers squeezed their way through the crowd selling popcorn and hot dogs. Telephone poles and trees were festooned with spectators."

By five o'clock, "the crowd grew impatient, began to yip, 'Let's go, bring him out.' At 5:20 A.M. Bethea, his stomach bulging with chicken, pork chops and watermelon, was pushed through the crowd to the base of the platform. At 5:28 there was a swish, a snap." Soon the spectators crowded in and "eager hands clawed at the black death hood. ... The lucky ones stuffed the bits of black cloth in their pockets."

It was spectacles such as this one which drove executions behind prison walls. But today television has the capacity to break through those walls again. As we resume the march of state-approved murders, it seems likely that television reporters will soon be allowed to bring the tools of their trade—cameras—into the death chamber, the way print reporters bring pencils.

In the face of this, an odd coalition has formed to support the notion that we should broadcast executions. Some who favor capital punishment as a deterrent to crime are convinced that watching an execution would scare criminals straight. Some who oppose capital punishment believe that the sight would enrage the public.

But there is no proof that witnessing an execution has a sobering effect on either the public or the crime rate. Indeed as Charles Dickens wrote in nineteenth-century England, "I have stated my belief that the study of such scenes leads to the disregard of human life and to murder." The evidence is on Dickens' side.

Watt Espy, a historian of capital punishment at the University of Alabama Law Center, has collected tales of the violence begat by violence. On May 9, 1879, following the hanging of two men in Attling, Georgia, a bunch of spectators got into a brawl and one man was killed. This was not unique.

When James Autry asked to have his death televised, he hoped that the audience would be moved to protest state-approved murder. But I suspect that the net effect would be numbness and tacit acceptance of violence. Today there are almost 1300 on death rows, 1300 bodies to be added to the sum total of television brutality. We are already too immune to human pain. We can barely differentiate between the grisliest true stories and the commercial tragedy of irregularity.

If anything, TV executions would be part of the trivializing process. As Hugo Bedau, a philosophy professor at Tufts University who has studied capital punishment, says: "Television manages to make us relatively insensitive with regard to human horror and violence. It arouses interest, gratifies curiosity, and utterly destroys our judgment. There's mom and dad and 2.7 children watching television and on the 6 o'clock news, there's a replay of the execution. Ho hum."

There's no scientific way to prove in advance the effect of televised executions on crime. Perhaps some psychopath would literally kill for twenty minutes of air time. But we do know something about the effect on the "audience." We do know something about spectators from the old days. As Will Rogers wrote in 1925, "Anybody whose pleasure is watching somebody else die is about as little use to humanity as the person being electrocuted."

MARCH 1984

HOW OLD IS OLD ENOUGH?

BOSTON—At some point in the late 1960s, when thousands of young men were being drafted to fight in Vietnam, the country became embarrassed about the checkerboard of laws that ruled the lives of eighteen-, nineteen-, and twenty-year-olds. A young man was old enough to die for his country, but not old enough to vote in it. A Marine could return from the Mekong Delta and then get carded at his hometown bar.

In that climate, support grew for a uniform age of responsibility. In 1971, the voting age was lowered to eighteen and in the next few years many states lowered the drinking age to eighteen.

In retrospect, it seems odd that we simply accepted the draft as the baseline, the duly designated point of adulthood. Instead or raising the military age, we lowered everything else to match it. We were embarrassed about the wrong thing.

Nevertheless, we allowed eighteen-year-olds to drink legally and openly. Soon, the lethal combination of alcohol and gasoline, drinking and driving, inflamed the fatality statistics. In New Jersey, for example, when the drinking age was lowered in 1973 from twenty-one to eighteen, the number of highway deaths of people under twenty-one tripled. On the average, teenagers have been two and a half times as likely as the average driver to be in an accident involved with alcohol.

Gradually, now, states have been raising the drinking age again and watching the accident rates go down. Today only four states still allow eighteen-year-olds to buy all kinds of alcohol. In eleven states the legal drinking age is nineteen, in six states it is twenty, and in the rest it's twenty-one.

But there are still a number of different laws coexisting side by side, border by border. This patchwork, as the President's Commission on Drunk Driving pointed out, becomes an absolute incentive to drink and drive. In Spokane, Washington, for example, nineteen-year-olds have to drive if they want to drink. They have to drive to the strip of waiting bars over the border in Idaho. And then they have to drive home.

Now there are two bills wending their way through Congress which would establish a national drinking age of twenty-one. The bill sponsored by Representative James Florio (D-N.J.) passed the House committee. Some have opposed this legislation as an example of federal intrusion. But surely the border traffic in search of a six-pack is a kind of interstate commerce.

The need for uniformity seems obvious. But there is a legitimate controversy about raising the age barrier again. For openers, there is nothing magical about the number twenty-one. If we were concerned solely with safety, we could reasonably ban the sale of booze to anyone under twenty-two or twenty-five. On the other hand, we could forget about drinking and raise the driving age to twenty-one—an idea which appeals to me enormously as the parent of a fifteen-year-old.

More importantly, there is the notion of a single age of responsibility. Isn't it rather insulting to tell a bona fide voter that he or she isn't old enugh to belly up to the bar?

I see the contradiction. Yet despite all the talk about a single age of adulthood, there are all sorts of uneven laws regulating the uneven process of maturity. Today, in many states, you can become "emancipated" from your parents by becoming a parent, even at fifteen. In most states you can get married with parental consent before you can vote. On the other hand, you cannot become a member of the House of Representatives until you are twenty-five or a U.S. senator until you are thirty.

In this case, the dangers warrant raising the drinking age. The number twenty-one is no more or less than a familiar compromise figure. Even the eighteen-, nineteen-, and twenty-year-olds seem to accept it. In the recent Gallup Poll, they favored a federal drinking age of twenty-one, by 58 to 38 percent.

I have no illusions that we'll stop young people from drinking entirely. Nor will we stop them from lying about their age—although perhaps we can raise the lying threshold from sixteen to nineteen. Yet it's been estimated that we can save 1250 lives each year with a new minimum age for legal drinking, and that's worth a try.

What then of the person convinced that any eighteen-year-old who can die for his country ought to be able to drink in it? Tell him that eighteen is much, much too young to die for the country.

FEBRUARY 1984

IF SHE SAYS NO

BOSTON—There are a few times when, if you watch closely, you can actually see a change of public mind. This is one of those times.

For as long as I can remember, a conviction for rape depended as much on the character of the woman involved as on the action of the man. Most often, the job of the defense lawyer was to prove that the woman had provoked or consented to the act, to prove that it was sex, not assault.

In the normal course of events, the smallest blemish, misjudgment, misstep by the woman—Did she wear a tight sweater? Was she a "loose" woman? Was she in the wrong part of town at the wrong hour?—became proof that she had invited the man's attentions. A woman could waive her right to say no in an astonishing number of ways.

But recently, in Massachusetts, three cases of multiple rape have come into court and three sets of convictions have come out of juries. These verdicts point to a sea change in attitudes. A simple definition seems to have seeped into the public consciousness. If she says no, it's rape.

The most famous of these cases is the New Bedford barroom rape. There, in two separate trials, juries cut through complicated testimony to decide the central issue within hours. Had the woman been drinking? Had she lied about that in testimony? Had she kissed one of the men? In the end, none of these points was relevant. What mattered to the juries that found four of these six men guilty was that they had forced her. If she said no, it was rape.

The second of these cases involved a young woman soldier from Fort Devens who accepted a ride with members of a local rock band, The Grand Slamm. She was raped in the bus and left in a field hours later. Had she flirted with the band members? Had she told a friend that she intended to seduce one of the men? Had she gone on the bus willingly? The judge sentencing three of the men to jail said, "No longer will society accept the fact that a woman, even if she may initially act in a seductive or compromising manner, has waived her right to say no at any further time." If she said no, it was rape.

The third of these cases was in some ways the most notable. An Abington, Massachusetts woman was driven from a bar to a parking lot where she was raped by four men, scratched by a knife, had her hair singed by a cigarette lighter, and then left half naked in the snow. The testimony at the trial showed that the woman had previously had sex with three of the men, and with two of them in a group setting. Still, the jury was able to agree with the district attorney: "Sexual consent between a woman and a man on one occasion does not mean the man has access to her whenever it strikes his fancy." If she said no, it was rape.

Not every community, courtroom, or jury today accepts this simple standard of justice. But ten years ago, five years ago, even three years ago, these women might not have even dared press charges.

It was the change of climate which enabled, even encouraged, the women to come forward. It was the change of attitude which framed the arguments in the courtroom. It was the change of consciousness that infiltrated the jury chambers.

The question now is whether that change of consciousness has become part of our own day-to-day lives. In some ways rape is the brutal, repugnant extension of an ancient ritual of pursuit and capture. It isn't just rapists who refuse to take no for an answer. It isn't just rapists who believe that a woman says one thing and means another.

In the confusion of adolescence, in the chase of young adulthood, the sexes were often set up to persist and to resist. Many young men were taught that "no" means "try again." Many young women were allowed to excuse their sexuality only when they were "swept away," overwhelmed.

The confused messages, the yes-no-maybes, the over-powered heroines and overwhelming heroes, are still common to supermarket Gothic novels and *Hustler* magazine. It isn't just X-rated movies that star a resistant woman who falls in love with her sexual aggressor. It isn't just porno-graphic cable TV that features the woman who really "wanted it." In as sprightly a sitcom as "Cheers," Sam blithely locked a coyly ambivalent Diane into his apartment.

I know how many steps it is from that hint of sexual pressure to the brutality of rape. I know how far it is from lessons of sexual power plays to the violence of rape. But it's time the verdict of those juries was fully transmitted to the culture from which violence emerges. If she says no, it means no.

MARCH 1984

THE SAGA OF KID-VID

BOSTON—To those who have been following the saga of the kid-vid world, the latest drama may sound like something out of an old vaudeville routine:

Onstage, a man encounters a woman just back from a week in the Catskills. "How was the food?" he asks.

"Just terrible," she answers, "and so little of it."

In the same spirit, the advocates of children's television have spent years decrying the quality of programming, and now they are lamenting the decline in quantity. If it's so terrible, why should we care that there's less and less of it?

Well, it turns out that there is a reason. In the past year of rapid kid-vid big chance, it's the better programs and, above all, the promises that have been cut.

The star of the disappearing act is "Captain Kangaroo," the only daily network program for children. This old favorite was sliced from an hour to a half hour, to make room for an expanded "CBS Morning News," and then canceled.

In several cities, programs like the highly acclaimed "The Great Space Coasters" and "Romper Room" have begun fading from five times a week to once a week.

What it adds up to is simply this: At this moment, over 50 percent of the nation's television stations have no, repeat no, kids' programming between 2 and 6 P.M. weekdays. There is also, no, repeat no, commercial network programming regularly scheduled for kids in the weekday afternoons.

Children's programming, which was tiptoeing into the daily world and planning a leap or two, has been pushed back to the kid-vid ghetto of the Saturday-morning cartoon clones.

Even there, the backsliding signals are being beamed loud and clear: NBC, which added health and sports features to its lineup last year, has subtracted them this year. ABC, which promised proudly to subtract two minutes of ads from each kid hour, has already added back thirty seconds.

Something happened or, to be more precise, someone happened. In May 1981, a former rock-radio disc jockey named Mark Fowler was appointed head of the Federal Communications Commission. Fowler is only one of the assorted foxes to be put in charge of the regulatory roosts by Reagan.

While the others call themselves deregulators, Fowler one-ups them by referring to himself as an "un-regulator."

Past commissioners have used their post to remind broadcasters of their responsibility to the smallest, most impressionable viewers. But Fowler has used his post to bawl out broadcasters for ever allowing themselves to be regulated.

In his maiden speech to the International Radio and Television Society last September, he set himself up as a kind of Jim Jones of the FCC. "As regulators," he said, "we must be ready to self-destruct. . . . I know our staff is ready to meet this challenge. . . ."

Fowler then offered his own theory of un-regulation: ". . . The commission should so far as possible defer to the broadcasters' judgment about how best to compete for viewers and listeners because this serves the viewers' interests."

Peggy Charren of Action for Children's Television refers to this as the Trickle Down Theory of Communications.

"What's good for CBS is good for the audience. What's good for Hanna-Barbera [the cartoonists] is good for migrant children."

Until now, the FCC has been the Damocles sword held over the head of broadcasters. Stations have had to fulfill certain public interest guidelines or risk their licenses. But not anymore. The broadcasters got the essential message. They could stop worrying about expanding children's programming.

When the marketplace prevails, kids' TV generally fails. Kids don't buy enough beer, deodorant, or soap powder. With insufficient headaches and hemorrhoids, they end up plugged into Saturday morning or lumped into the pre-Christmas specials between toy commercials.

As John Claster, the producer of the "The Great Space Coaster," laments, "In fairness to stations, the children's area isn't the most lucrative. And the younger age group isn't very good at defending itself."

One thing has remained the same. Kids under twelve are still watching an average of twenty-seven hours of TV a week, most of it adult fare, much of it inappropriate and indigestible.

In this vaudeville act, it may be terrible fare, but the portions are enormous.

DECEMBER 1981

A DECADE OF DEBATE

BOSTON—I don't know what you give a legal decision for its tenth anniversary. I don't know the proper etiquette. But it's been a decade now since January 22, 1973, when a young woman who had been raped and impregnated in Texas won the right for any woman to have an abortion in the United States. Surely some notice is due.

I suppose that those who regard *Roe v. Wade* as a tombstone would like to offer funeral wreaths. Others who regard it as a landmark would weave and wave banners. But maybe we ought to produce something more functional for this anniversary: a new vocabulary.

It seems that we've been stuck for a decade in a verbal war of attrition. Two groups have settled into bunkers labeled "right to life" and "right to choice." They have lobbed names and accusations at each other across the public terrain in an endless debate through courts and legislatures. The public argument has been cast permanently into a series of confrontations, one side against another, one set of rights against another.

The reasons for this deadlocked debate are understandable enough. In court we are only allowed to argue in the restricted language of the Constitution. The complex moral dilemmas of abortion end up straitjacketed by Constitution-speak. In the end, we can only talk about individual rights, right to life, and rights to privacy.

The irony is that the argument that goes on in the legal system is so removed from the argument that goes on in the mind of a woman faced with an unwanted pregnancy. The private struggle is less over rights than over responsibilities. It is less about conflicts with others than connections to them. It has less to do with the ablity to carry a pregnancy for nine months than to care for a child for eighteen years.

Carol Gilligan, whose work on women's development, *A Different Voice*, was based in part on her research with pregnant women facing this decision, never found one who fit the callous stereotype implied by the phrase "abortion on demand." Her women did not boast about exercising their "right" to an abortion.

They asked themselves, rather, questions about caretaking and responsibility: "Am I prepared to take care of this life? Is it irresponsible to have a child I cannot take care of?" She heard these questions from teenagers who initially wanted a baby "because I'm lonely," and she heard it from older women trying to imagine the impact of a new baby on families that were barely holding together. "Labeling abortion as a selfish choice," she says, "didn't always hold up."

At the same time, these women did not engage in metaphysical arguments about "life." In the courts and Congress, we hear one group insist that the fetus is a life and abortion is murder. We hear another group counter with philosophical and biological arguments: What is a human life? But in private, in the lives of women, the crucial fact is not the existence of life in the womb but in the world.

As Gilligan describes it, "It's because they know it's a life they're talking about that the issues of choice and responsibility are so key. Women are trying to say that to bring a life into the world means to take care of it."

I suspect that we intrinsically understand that this is not an argument about abstract principles but about human responsibilities. In poll after poll, most of us want to leave this decision up to the pregnant woman. We know instinctively that unless we're willing to take care of every unwanted child from birth to adulthood, we have to leave the decision to the woman. We have to give the right to one who carries the responsibilities.

But it is unsettling that there is, literally, no way to come into the legal system discussing this complex moral view. The language of law has few words in common with the language of personal decisions.

In court, we speak in the strident words of individual rights, insisting that one is more important than the other. Out of court, we speak about the interlocking web of responsibilities for each other.

I wish there were a new vocabulary to offer up for this anniversary, but I cannot find one that can be understood in both places. We are stuck now as we were on the day in January 1973, when the story of a woman's life was first translated into a matter of rights.

JANUARY 1983

333

Part 9

A FAMILY ALBUM

MESSAGES FROM MIDDLETOWN

BOSTON—I am glad I wasn't born in Muncie, Indiana. Ever since Robert and Helen Lynd chose that city as a specimen of America in the 1920s, and dubbed it Middletown, the people of Muncie have had all the privacy of a community of laboratory rats.

At least three generations have spent their lives being observed, quantified, stashed away into some statistical pattern. Studies have been Muncie's most important product.

Now [1982] they are into a multimedia spring. They are being profiled individually in a public television series, "Middletown," and profiled collectively in a book called *Middletown Families*.

Once again, the Muncie-Americans are bearing a message about our nation. A double message about the strength of our family life and the strength of our belief in its weakness.

On television I saw a portrait of the Snider family, headed by Howie Snider, ex-Marine, banjo-playing pizza-parlor owner, one step ahead of his creditors. It was a tale full of the passionate intensity of family members.

Then in the book, I read a portrait of the whole city. After conducting thirteen studies in the late seventies, an invasionary force of professors concluded that family life continues and in some ways is stronger than it was in the 1920s.

As sociologist Ted Caplow summarized, "We discovered increased family solidarity, a smaller generation gap, closer marital communication, more religion and less mobility."

The facts from Muncie were not shocking to those who have read other recent studies about American families. One after the other, researchers have checked in with news about the tenacity of family life. One after another, they have met head-on with the conviction, even in Muncie, that families are falling apart.

How do we explain this stark contrast between reality and attitude? Is it because we confuse change with collapse? Is it because we see a half-empty glass?

There must be a slew of theories. In a recent piece, "Middletown," author Caplow even suggested that "the myth of the declining family" has some value for its believers. "When Middletown people compare their own families," he wrote, "with the 'average' or the 'typical' family, nearly all of them discover with pleasure that their own families are better than other people's."

But I don't agree that this myth developed as a subtle way to applaud our own superiority. I suspect that it has deeper, more complex roots.

I think that we all carry around inside us some primal scene of a family Eden, an ideal of family life. Among the strongest yearnings we take out of childhood is the desire to create this perfect family.

We share a longing to have or to be a perfect parent, perfect mate. We share a youthful certainty that we will be able to give and take perfect love. We will experience the closeness, the union, the oneness of our Eden. We will never be impatient, never yell at our children. They will never be distant or rude.

But each generation inevitably falls short of its own ideals about family life, and our personal disappointments harden into a national myth. I suspect that we date our belief in the decline of families from our eventual descent into reality. The vague sense that something is missing in our family becomes a general notion that something is missing in the family.

In Anne Tyler's moving novel *Dinner at the Homesick Restaurant*, the elderly mother, Pearl, suddenly chokes up with a desire for the family life:

"Often, like a child peering over the fence at somebody else's party, she gazes wistfully at other families and wonders what their secret is. They seem so close. Is it that they're more religious? Or stricter, or more lenient? Could it be the fact that they participate in sports? Read books together? Have some common hobby? Recently she overheard a neighbor woman discussing her plans for Independence Day. Her family was having a picnic. Every member—child or grownup—was cooking his or her specialty. Those who were too little to cook were in charge of the paper plates.

"Pearl felt such a wave of longing that her knees went weak." She could be any one of us.

In real life there were, of course, ants at the picnic, and tears and tantrums. In real life, the neighbor occasionally also grew weak at the knees with her own longing for a perfect family.

So too in real life, our families fail our fantasies. We know that. But they aren't failures. At best, like the Sniders, they are complex, powerful, imperfect. And their strength is too easy to forget.

APRIL 1982

THE FAMILY THAT STRETCHES (TOGETHER)

CASCO BAY, Maine—The girl is spending the summer with her extended family. She doesn't put it this way. But as we talk on the beach, the ten-year-old lists the people who are sharing the same house this month with the careful attention of a genealogist.

First of all there is her father—visitation rights awarded him the month of August. Second of all there is her father's second wife and two children by her first marriage. All that seems perfectly clear. A stepmother and two stepbrothers.

Then there are the others, she slowly explains. There is her stepmother's sister for example. The girl isn't entirely sure whether this makes the woman a stepaunt, or whether her baby is a stepcousin. Beyond that, the real puzzle is whether her stepaunt's husband's children by his first marriage have any sort of official relationship to her at all. It does, we both agree, seem a bit fuzzy.

Nevertheless, she concludes, with a certainty that can only be mustered by the sort of a ten-year-old who keeps track of her own Frequent Flier coupons, "We are in the same family." With that she closes the subject and focuses instead on her peanut butter and jelly.

I am left to my thoughts. My companion, in her own unselfconscious way, is a fine researcher. She grasps the wide new family configurations that are neglected by census data takers and social scientists.

340

After all, those of us who grew up in traditional settings remember families which extended into elaborate circles of aunts, uncles, and cousins. There were sides to this family, names and titles to be memorized. But they fit together in a biological pattern.

Now, as my young friend can attest, we have fewer children and more divorces. We know that as many as 50 percent of recent marriages may end. About 75 percent of divorced women and 83 percent of divorced men then remarry. Of those remarriages, 59 percent include a child from a former marriage.

So, or families often extend along lines that are determined by decrees, rather than genes. If the nucleus is broken, there are still links forged in different directions.

The son of a friend was asked to produce a family tree for his sixth-grade class. But he was dissatisfied with his oak. There was no room on it for his stepgrandfather, though the man had married his widowed grandmother years ago.

More to the point, the boy had to create an offshoot for his new baby half-brother that seemed too distant. He couldn't find a proper place for the uncle—the ex-uncle to be precise—whom he visited last summer with his cousin.

A family tree just doesn't work, he complained. He would have preferred to draw family bushes.

The reality is that divorce has created kinship ties that rival the most complex tribe. These are not always easy relationships. The children and even the adults whose family lives have been disrupted by divorce and remarriage learn that people they love do not necessarily love each other. This extended family does not gather for reunions and Thanksgivings.

But when it works, it can provide a support system of sorts. I have seen the nieces, nephews—even the dogs—of one marriage welcomed as guests into another. There are all sorts of relationships that survive the marital ones, though there are no names for these kinfolk, no nomenclature for this extending family.

Not long ago, when living together first became a common pattern, people couldn't figure out what to call each other. It was impossible to introduce the man you lived with as a "spouse equivalent." It was harder to refer to the woman your son lived with as his lover, mistress, housemate.

It's equally difficult to describe the peculiar membership of this new lineage. Does your first husband's mother become a mother-out-law? Is the woman no longer married to your uncle an ex-aunt? We have nieces and nephews left dangling like participles from other lives and stepfamilies entirely off the family tree.

Our reality is more flexible and our relationships more supportive than our language. But for the moment, my ten-year-old researcher is right. However accidentally, however uneasily, "We are in the same family."

AUGUST 1983

WOMBS FOR RENT

BOSTON—Admittedly [early in 1983], the economy is in bad shape, but somehow I never expected to see a new breed of entrepreneurs arrive on the scene hanging out shingles that offer Wombs for Rent.

Remember when the real-estate moguls of the 1970s dealt in houses? It appears that their 1980s counterparts are dealing with uteri. While they aren't doing a land-office business quite yet, surrogate motherhood is an expanding market.

At the moment the star of the surrogates is Judy Stiver of Lansing, Michigan, who was set up by a lawyer in her own cottage industry. According to Judy's testimony, surrogate motherhood, pregnancy, and delivery were a little bit like taking in a boarder. She was promised $10,000 to give womb and board to a fetus for nine months and then deliver the baby to its reputed biological father, Alexander Malahoff of Queens, New York.

When asked why she decided to take this moonlighting job, Judy explained that she and her husband wanted some money to take a vacation and maybe fix up the house a bit ... that sort of thing.

Would I buy an egg from a lady like that? Frankly, I wouldn't even buy a pair of genes form her.

But that was just the beginning, or the conception, of this tale. The baby was born with microcephaly, a head smaller than normal, which usually means he will be retarded. Suddenly, this most wanted child was a pariah. Baby Doe was put in a foster home. The Stivers claimed he wasn't theirs. Malahoff claimed he wasn't his.

Pretty soon there were blood tests and lawsuits all around and a climactic scene on a Phil Donahue Show that looked like a parody of a Phil Donahue Show. Live and in color from Chicago—Whose baby is Baby Doe? Will the real father stand up please?—we learned the results of the blood test. Hang onto your seats: Malahoff was not the father, Judy's husband Ray Stiver was.

By any standards, this was a thriller with more identity crises than *H.M.S. Pinafore*. The fate of the baby was resolved right there on camera as the Stivers promised to bring him up just as if he were one of their own. So much for their vacation.

But for all its freakishness, I don't want to dismiss the story as just another human sideshow. This one was a long time in the making.

I don't know a soul who can't sympathize with the feelings and desires of an infertile couple. Over the past several years we have grown used to reading about dramatic help for couples. By now artificial insemination seems routine and in vitro fertilizations have been eased off the front page. We applaud their births as happy endings.

We have been, I think, numbed into regarding motherhood-for-hire as just another option. There are now at least eight and perhaps as many as twenty surrogate parenting services in the country. Anywhere from forty to a hundred children have been borne by surrogate mothers paid between $5000 and $15,000 in states where payment is legal. At least one entrepreneur aims to become "the Coca-Cola of the surrogate-parenting industry."

The tale out of Michigan was a jarring reminder that surrogate mothering is something qualitatively different, with hazards that we are just beginning to imagine.

Being a surrogate mother is not, as has been suggested, the flip side of artificial insemination. The infertile couple has contracted for more from a woman than an infusion of sperm. The pregnant woman has a stronger relationship with a fetus than a man has with a vial. The law governing this business, governing this web of parenting, is far murkier.

If the Stiver Story has a bizarre twist, there are other and equally mind-boggling risks. What if the biological mother decides, as at least two have, to keep the baby herself? Would a court of law hold that the contract was more sacred than the mother's rights?

What impact is there on a couple when the man seeks another woman to bear his child? The Malahoffs, it should be noted, separated when the child he believed was his was conceived.

344

What do you tell a child when he or she asks, "Where did I come from?" And what if the baby isn't perfect? Who holds the final responsibility for a child conceived through a contract?

In the Stivers' home, the boarder is now a son. They've learned something about chance.

We've learned something about a business and an idea that encourages people to regard parents as customers rather than caretakers. We've learned something about people who look upon a motherhood as biological work on a reproduction line. We've learned to be wary of people who regard babies as just another product for an eager and vulnerable market.

FEBRUARY 1983

A RELUCTANT FATHER

BOSTON—I don't think I'd like to spend a while lot of time with either of the leading characters in this [fall 1981] courtroom drama about a father's unwanted child.

Frank Serpico, the man who blew the whistle on police corruption in New York and lived to see the movie rights, doesn't come across as my idea of Mr. Right. Now a reluctant father, he describes himself as the victim of a woman who first used him as "a sperm bank" and now wants to use him as a money bank.

Nor does Pamela P. fit my qualifications for Heroine of the Year. According to the court ruling, this female lead told Serpico she was using birth control when she was planning parenthood. Then, after giving birth to a baby boy, she sued the father for child support.

In some perverse way, Frank and Pamela probably deserve each other. They could do time together in the swingles world of people users. But instead they are pushing at the frontiers of family law.

You see, theirs was a case just waiting to happen.

In the past decade and a half, in one case after another, the courts have declared that the state has no right to interfere in private decisions about childbearing. Most of these private decisions have been made by women.

For a host of medical, legal, and social reasons, the balance of power in procreation, the right to choose whether or not to become a parent, shifted toward and onto women. It has been possible, at least in theory, for a woman to use or refuse birth control, to seek or reject abortion, to give up the child for adoption or retain custody of it, even to sue or not to sue the father for child support.

In this climate, it was only a matter of time before someone claimed that men too should have the constitutional right to decide whether they want to be parents.

Serpico bitterly announced what some men have sworn since the first paternity suit and the first shotgun marriage: He was tricked into fatherhood. But what made this case different is that he proved it to the satisfaction of the family law court judge in Manhattan. A former lover of Pamela's testified that she planned to deliberately deceive Serpico.

In her decision, Judge Nanette Dembitz walked a fine line. She ruled that Pamela couldn't transfer the financial burden "for the child she alone chose to bear." Serpico could be required to pay minimal support for his son, but only if the mother were unable.

Later, this couple was back in court fighting about dollars and cents. But it's the larger question that remains most important.

346

We now have a precedent-setting case which suggests that a man too has a constitutional right to choice about parenthood. It even suggests that a man whose right to decision making is denied may be free of the responsibility for the results.

I think Judge Dembitz made the right call, a tough one, a close one. Serpico wasn't entirely "innocent," but he was the victim of a biological con game. He didn't ask to be a father. Nor did the baby, as they say, ask to be born, and the judge tried to factor in the baby's needs as well.

Still this decision opens some tricky issues. Since the original trial, one of Serpico's lawyers, Alan Levine, has heard from half a dozen men, all claiming to be similar victims—misused "sperm banks" of the world, united. One even claimed that he was tricked into sex.

Few cases like this one could stand up in court. In most, a man would be held equally responsible for birth control or for the unplanned result of sex.

But the same precedent could now be used in an abortion case. If a man wants an abortion and a woman refuses, is he still liable for child support? Or could this now be considered an infringement of a man's constitutional right of choice?

In the final sense, the Serpico case is a vivid example of the split growing between the world of the wanted and unwanted child, the planned and unplanned parent. Those who volunteer for parenting seem to share and value that commitment more, while those who are drafted have become increasingly sophisticated and angry resisters.

As for the children, there's a small boy in Manhattan right now with the dubious distinction of being a test case for a con artist mother and an unwanting father. Good luck to him.

NOVEMBER 1981

A TWELVE-YEAR-OLD MOTHER

BOSTON—It was a simple story, only three paragraphs long, and the grotesque news was flattened by restrained wire service prose.

From Kalamazoo, Michigan, came the report that the county prosecutor's office had brought charges of neglect against a mother. But this was not just another miserable entry into the log of everyday life. The baby, the alleged victim of emotional neglect, was four months old. The mother, the alleged perpetrator of emotional neglect, was twelve years old.

Now does this begin to ring a bell, strike a chord? If not, let me—straightforwardly, I promise—refresh your memory.

In May of 1981, this little girl was eleven and pregnant. She had been raped repeatedly by the man who lived with her, her mother, and sister. She didn't tell anyone about the pregnancy (perhaps she didn't know) until the end of July.

Finally she called the police and told a detective there that she didn't want to have a baby. She was after all, just going into fifth grade—too young to be hired as a baby-sitter.

The girl's mother—who would herself soon be charged with, of course, emotional neglect—did not approve of abortion. The girl's father, an ex-convict who lost a custody battle for his daughters, wanted her to have an abortion. The pregnant girl reportedly vacillated between parents and principles. At eleven, she was unable to make a mature decision about her body, life, future, fetus.

So the case went to court, to the court of Judge Donald Halstead. This is the judge who had signed a full-page Mother's Day ad in the newspaper written by an antiabortion group.

These are, as I promised, the facts:

It took Halstead three weeks to make the girl a ward of court. It took him another month to rule that he wouldn't rule. He said that he didn't have the authority to order an abortion.

By now, if you are counting, it was late September. The girl was over four months pregnant. No abortions are performed in Michigan beyond twenty-four weeks. But the case went next to a circuit court and finally to a federal court. It was the federal judge who, in late October, ordered Halstead to decide. So he did.

The girl was now twenty-three weeks pregnant. The man who had delayed judgment proclaimed that she was too far along to have an abortion: "The medical risks attendant to an abortion pose serious medical concerns offsetting the wisdom of allowing the minor child to have the baby."

Did I deliver these facts coolly enough?

Of course, there were opinions, too. Barb Listing, the president of Right to Life of Michigan, told the press back in the fall, "This ruling spares the young mother from the psychological trauma which would result from an abortion."

It has not been reported where this Ms. Listing was during the delivery on February 6, 1982.

We don't know much about what happened to these people next. We know that the rapist is in jail. We know that the young mother and her infant were in foster care together until April. We know that they are now in separate foster homes.

And now we know that this girl is going back to court. There is "probable cause" for emotional neglect proceedings against her. Within the next month there will be a hearing to decide whether to permanently remove the baby from the custody of the mother.

Will the twelve-year-old be found guilty of emotional neglect? Can a twelve-year-old be guilty of not mothering? And can a twelve-year-old mother? Am I getting too emotional? After all, this is the story of the girl who was "saved from the psychological trauma of abortion."

I have told this story not because I think it will change anyone's mind. I have heard all the rejoinders of the anti-abortion advocates: the sad saga of an eleven-year-old doesn't justify the killing of the unborn; the baby may grow up to be Beethoven.

I have told it rather because recently a group of anti-abortion zealots tracked down another eleven-year-old who had a scheduled abortion. They hounded the girl and her mother, yelling from balconies near their apartments and picketing the path to the hospital.

I have told it because some of the "right-to-lifers" consider the Kalamazoo story a victory. They consider the case closed, over, finished, when it has just been born.

I have told it finally because they have a right to know. Wait. Scratch that careful wording. They have the obligation to know.

JUNE 1982

350

FOR THE SAKE OF THE CHILDREN

DETROIT—At the moment [November 1983], Henry and Dianne Mistele are staying together for the sake of the children. Not that they planned it that way. The couple were divorced in April 1983, or at least sort of divorced.

The judge, David Vokes, a seventy-eight-year-old circuit court judge, ended their legal marriage—but with a hitch. He ordered the Misteles to continue living together until their fourteen-year-old sons turn eighteen.

Under the terms of this unique decision, Henry Mistele is responsible for maintenance and grocery money and $400 a month alimony. Dianne Mistele is responsible for cooking, housekeeping, and shopping. Henry sleeps in the bedroom and Dianne sleeps in the living room. Neither is allowed to bring dates home. If one leaves for an extended time, the other will get custody of the children and the one to leave will probably lose the right to return to the house.

To the amateur ear, this all sounds a bit freakish. We've gotten used to joint-custody rulings, to children who commute between parents and apartments. We've even gotten used to "birds-nesting," where the children stay put and the parents commute. But the average couple doesn't split in order to live together. The average judge doesn't rule that ex-husband and ex-wife share the same roof.

Nevertheless, to hear Judge Vokes talk in his office in

downtown Detroit, it seems almost sensible. Vokes is a man who married about 10,000 couples in his twenty-six years as a common pleas judge and lived to see more divorces than nuptials.

He expresses a kindly distress at this modern reality: "I see a lot of marriages where with just a little giving, they could keep going. Boom! Somebody stepped on somebody's toe and that's the end of the marriage."

It is clear that Judge Vokes, a mild man with a soft voice and a gray wiffle-cut, regretted the breakdown of the Mistele marriage. "Both the plaintiff and defendant are fine people, very high-class people, concerned with their families, both churchgoers. They had this lovely home out there," he remembers. But however wistful he was, under Michigan law, indeed under no-fault divorce law in forty-eight states, he no longer had the right to deny a divorce.

What this judge did have the right to do, indeed the legal obligation to do, was to make a custody decision "in the best interests of the children." So Vokes went out to the Mistele home, interviewed their three sons—one is sixteen and the twins are fourteen—and discovered, not surprisingly, that the children wanted to stay in their own home with both their parents.

Judge Vokes knew there would not be enough money for two households to live in the posh Gross Pointe Woods style to which one had become accustomed. Henry might find himself on the ropes. Dianne, for her part, hadn't worked since the children were born. Living together would be better for the family bank account.

All things considered, Judge Vokes decided to keep the family together until the children were grown. In return for "a little bit of inconvenience," he says. "I am certain they'll both be better off financially by the time the arrangement is over." As for the children, "I figure every month I bought is a bonus for the kids."

I can't dispute the judge's motives or even question his sincerity. Most of us, at one time or another, have shared an urge to patch up a disintegrating family, to reorder lives. But is the court the best navigator for the emotional and economic wrecks of divorce?

The reality is that few divorces are in the best interests of the children. Few children would give initial approval to the separation of their parents. Few families are better off. Is it for a court to decide whether or not a couple can afford to be divorced? Isn't that the decision, wise or foolish, of two adults?

The judge in this case came powerfully close to giving children an absolute veto on divorce. This ruling goes full circle back to the days before no-fault when judges could give or withhold divorce according to their own prejudices.

As David Chambers, a family law professor at the University of Michigan, says, "I just find this an absolutely unjustified level of intrusion on people living their lives. To take it to it hideous extreme, you can imagine the judge saying you must give each other a kiss in the morning, you must be sweet to each other, you must pretend to love each other. They could justify it all in the best interest of the child."

The current extreme is hideous enough. The Misteles aren't talking to the press, nor to each other apparently. Dianne Mistele has filed a petition that should be heard after Thanksgiving. Henry Mistele, for his part, questions whether what they've won is an actual divorce: "Isn't that why you get a divorce, so you don't have to live with each other?"

Judge Vokes may have set up a new category for the Census Bureau: Divorced but Living Together by Order of the Court.

NOVEMBER 1983

WHERE DID THE HINCKLEYS GO WRONG?

BOSTON—It is a painful, intimate trial, more psychodrama than courtroom drama, more about the mind of a man than the assassination attempt of a president.

If the Von Bulow case was a family tragedy caricatured into a public soap opera, the John Hinckley, Jr., case is a public drama refined into a family tragedy. This time the question isn't whether the defendant did it. The question is why he did it.

In the courtroom, they will argue the legal definition of sanity. The prosecution must portray him as an irresponsible spoiled brat who "felt ordinary work was beneath him." The defense must portray him as a man obsessed with delusions, unable to control his own behavior.

But in a larger world, we know that something went wrong with John Hinckley, Jr. We want to know what it was, how it happened. What goes wrong with people? What distorts the thing we call the human personality?

Before the trial, it was easy to speculate. We knew about the "country club" parents, about their oil money and their move from Dallas to Denver. We knew about an older brother and sister who seemed to do everything right.

We could note the physical similarities between Jodie Foster and Hinckley's mother as a young woman, draw the character similarities between Ronald Reagan and Hinckley's father, talk about the younger son who just couldn't make it in an achieving family. We could form a glib psychohistory, wrap up a perverse human story in reasons, and stash it in some distant corner, far away from us, from our families, our children.

But then, one after another—as if in some sad procession of the dearly beloved and bereaved—mother, sister, and brother took the stand. Instead of clearing the psychological path that led to the Washington Hilton, they made it seem more subtle and elusive and true.

They checked in with their own memories. They bore witness to John's tragedy and their own helplessness. They, too, tried to track how the son who had made his father laugh at ten, the brother who had been home-room president at twelve, faded into the loner who "managed to removed myself from the world."

In the most poignant moment of the whole trial, the mother, JoAnn Hinckley, explained, "John just seemed to be going downhill, downhill, downhill, downhill, and becoming more withdrawn and more antisocial . . . and so down on himself. . . . We were just terribly worried about him, we didn't know what was wrong, but we knew something wasn't right."

In desperation, she finally followed the "plan" of a psychiatrist who had seen Hinckley only a dozen or so times, and against all her instincts drove the son—"who looked so bad and so sad and so absolutely in total despair"—to the airport for a final good-bye.

By the end of the testimony, she seemed so much like any parent, devastated by a child's disintegration, shaken by self-doubt, still trying to understand. Did they give the boy too much or too little, hug him too close or push him away? Did they seek a psychiatrist too late, or accept his opinions too easily? What if they had not moved to Denver?

What if they had not put him on that plane? What if? What if?

Bertrand Russell once wrote, "Psychoanalysis has terrified educated parents with the fear of the harm they may unwittingly do their children." You could hear that fear in the courtroom.

The trial hasn't explained her son's distorted life. It has intensified the mystery. It hasn't answered the questions; it has increased them.

But in a particular way, the very confusion of this psychodrama became a reality. It offered all of us a refresher course on how inexact our understanding of a human life really is.

Like all peoples, we devise myths to help know ourselves and our world: myths of religion and psychiatry, of chemistry and culture. There is truth in them. Yet none finally, fully, explains how a person becomes.

None solves the mystery of how a single person with his or her own uniqueness engages in a family, an environment, to become a self. None finally solves the mystery of why one child grows up and another breaks down.

In the courtroom finally there will be a decision about guilt and innocence. But in real life there is only the pathetic echo of JoAnn Hinckley's simple wish: "We wanted John to be self-supporting, to be a happy child, to stand on his own feet."

MAY 1982

RONBOY ON THE DOLE

BOSTON—The portrait was not designed to warm the hearts of the American people: Ronald Prescott Reagan, twenty-four, standing in line for unemployment benefits.

Ronboy is not, after all, a typical laid-off automobile worker nor a card-carrying member of the truly needy. He is, rather, a dancer with the Joffrey Ballet on a regularly scheduled furlough.

Rondad, on the other hand, has long expressed his opinion that families should take care of their own, instead of leaping, or arabesquing if you will, right into the government's arms.

On one occasion, Rondad said we should all look to the Mormons as our model. On another occasion, he said, "I made a point to count the pages of help-wanted ads in this time of great unemployment. There were twenty-four full pages of classified ads of employers looking for employees." It does not appear, however, that his son pounded the pavements in his ballet shoes before he headed for the unemployment lines.

But the point of all this isn't to snicker at family inconsistencies. As deputy press secretary Larry Speakes said, "The Reagans talked to Ron about being helpful and he expressed a desire to be independent and they respect that desire." He is not the first son of a famous father to try and make his own way in the world. The Reagans are no more in control of their son than the Windsors are of young Prince Andrew.

What is most notable about this modest family rebellion is the course that Ronboy has taken. He has refused help from Rondad and accepted it from the government.

The president sincerely extols the virtue of American families taking care of their own nuclear and extended troubles. He also and equally sincerely believes in the virtues of individualism. But he often ignores the contradiction which runs through a great deal of our recent social history.

When you look through the figures carefully, the real "breakdown of the American family" has been a break for independence. The greatest statistical changes have come as the old and the young choose to live on their own. And choose they do.

A running theme throughout the life of the elderly is that they "don't want to be a burden." A running theme throughout the life of the young is that they "want their own freedom." The more financially comfortable older people are, the more likely they are to maintain a separate household. The same is true with younger people.

But our kind of independence often depends on the existence of government programs. Ronboy is on his own this month with unemployment compensation (and a working wife). Millions of senior citizens are independent with the help of Social Security.

I don't mean to imply that Social Security and unemployment compensation are government handouts. We have done everything to differentiate these programs from welfare or charity. We pay in and we take out. We describe them as "entitlement programs," which is to say that we are "entitled" to them.

But if the government has replaced families in some times of need and trouble, it's partially because many families were unable to perform all these functions and partially because many of them prefer the impersonality of government assistance. In our concern about the government interference that comes with money, we often forget about the family interference that comes with money.

Whatever nostalgia we have about a mythical and real past, in which people took care of their own in times of trouble, we have elaborate and expensive entitlement programs partially because millions of us would rather go to a bureaucracy than a brother-in-law.

The elderly would rather receive a check from the government than from the children. Reagan the Son finds it easier to take $125 a week from the government than from Reagan the Father.

For better and for worse, our independence often depends on the same government programs which the president has threatened. Rondad might think about that as he watches Ronboy "making it on his own."

OCTOBER 1982

THE RIGHT TIME FOR MOTHERING

BOSTON—There they are, the harbingers of Mother's Day, 1982:

An article in the paper warning about the problems of teenage mothers. An ad for a television program warning about the problems of older mothers. A magazine piece warning about the problems of mothers in their twenties who try to raise a baby and a career together.

359

Sifting through these charming seasonal gifts of media mothering, I decided that the only years left uncovered by dire warners were the magical years between one and ten, and the wonder years between sixty and ninety. But I also understood, finally, why the most common question about mother these days is not "why" or "whether" but "when."

Not long ago, young women on college campuses would stop visitors from the real world with an anxious inquiry: Can you balance career and family? Today the same people with the same anxiety are asking, What is the best time to have a baby?

The old issue, "juggling," has a new twist, "timing." The balance of work and children now hinges on the sequence.

There is a notion that if a woman can pinpoint and plan the "best time" to become a mother, then everything else will fall into place. If the key words in real estate are location, location, location, now the key words in mothering are timing, timing, timing.

Frankly, I have always been intrigued with the age gaps between mothers and children. Of my two closest friends, one is five years older than I and the other is five years younger. But among us, we have children who range from twenty-five years to four weeks old. The oldest girl has her own apartment, the youngest her own crib.

We are a walking sample of decisions. One of us had children first and career second. The next nurtured both from infancy, like twins. The youngest established her career first and had her children second.

There is no doubt in my mind that the planning and nonplanning, the spacing and timing of our children, made enormous differences in our lives. We were and are and will be different ages at our children's different ages.

So, the three of us share certain experiences in the time-study business. We know with certainty that a girl of fifteen or eighteen needs to have a mother and not be one. Beyond that we know about trade-offs. A new mother at twenty-five has more energy and less self-confidence. A new mother at thirty-five has a stronger identity and a weaker back. A mother who gives birth at twenty-seven has more freedom at forty-five; a mother who gives birth at thirty-five had it at twenty-seven.

But if asked to arrive at a consensus in the planning-motherhood business we would all offer the practical, safe advice of the 1980s: Start a career first, a family second.

Yet at the approach of this Mother's Day, I confess to certain qualms. Not about whether the advice is good, but about why it's good. I wonder if too many women are trying to "fit" children into their lives at a convenient moment. Convenient for the work force, convenient for the status quo.

I admire their determination to follow a sensible life plan. Yet I wonder if this determination doesn't prevent them from rewriting the plan.

It makes sense for a woman in business to become a manager before she becomes a mother. It makes sense for a woman who is training to be a doctor to postpone a family until she finishes residency. It makes sense to become established before you become pregnant. Yet maybe this sense is a setup.

In the ongoing tension between family and work, we are constantly devising private solutions instead of revising the public ones. We work within the requirements of a make-it-or-break-it marketplace, instead of challenging them. Too often we end up forced to fit our families in and around the pieces set in place by work.

Does our adjustment now begin at conception? Is this a sign of our flexibility or the working world's rigidity? Is it our free choice or their choices? Is it our family planning or theirs?

I don't, I'm sorry to say, have a perfect alternative maternal schedule to propose for this Mother's Day. There are solid reasons to plan around the workalogical clock. Yet once a year, those of us who are already mothers should tip our hats to the truth. Ultimately, children don't fit into a schedule. They expand it, complicate it, enrich it.

In the motherhood business, time is still more crucial than timing, timing, timing.

MAY 1982

SQUEALING ON TEENAGERS

BOSTON—Maybe there isn't anything unique about this generation of parents and adolescents. Teenagers have always demanded independence on one day and longed for limits on another. They have always lurched unpredictably between maturity and irresponsibility.

Parents, for our part, have often stalled as we try to shift gears at these mixed signals. We have our own desire to protect our kids while encouraging them to grow up.

Still, this is a time when childhood has shrunk and adolescence has stretched, and the problems in this space have increased.

There is a pervasive unease among parents now: a feeling that our kids have won a host of dubious freedoms. A feeling that we as parents have lost authority while retaining responsibility and concern. At times our parenting role is reduced to picking up the pieces.

I think that some of this concern, at least about teenage sexuality, was reflected in late 1981 when family-planning programs were refunded under Title X. In that bill, Congress required family planning projects "to the extent possible . . . [to] encourage family participation."

It was a sensible piece of congressional advice. The best of the family-planning people are aware that it isn't enough to provide adolescents with contraceptives. The counselors have begun to deal with families, not just teenage "patients." Previously parents felt locked out of this medical and emotional counseling.

But something happened to this positive legislation on the way from the Capitol to the Department of Health and Human Services. The specific instruction by Congress to "encourage" the involvement of parents was twisted into the order of the administration to "mandate" parental involvement.

Now [early in 1982], if the draft of regulations making their way around Washington is finalized, HHS will be able to force any clinic to send a notice to the parents of a minor seeking prescription birth control. The Administration of the Great De-Regulator proposes a single federal rule to affect all our families.

As University of Pennsylvania's Frank Furstenberg, sociologist and author of *Unplanned Parenthood*, put it: "To have a blanket policy that prescribes the same solution for all teens in all circumstances is ludicrous."

So is the "solution" itself. In effect, parents would be getting a report informing them that their children are sexually active. Furstenberg calls it "the pink slip approach. It's more or less the way truancy is handled. We don't know

363

how to deal with it, so we send a notice to the home. But that doesn't deal with the issue."

Of course, not every parent of a sexually active teenager will get the news on a pink slip. According to family-planning studies, half of the parents of teenagers who come into clinics already know. Furthermore, these rules only cover girls, because only girls use prescription drugs or devices.

Those teenagers who don't want to tell their parents, for right or wrong reasons, can use drugstore birth control or, of course, no birth control at all. Even now, the typical teenager who comes into a clinic has been sexually active and unprotected for an average of six months.

It comes down to this: Would the result of these regulations lead to greater parental involvement? Would that lead to sexual restraint on the part of teenagers? Or would the threat of clinic-as-informer result in more teenage pregnancies? What are the risks and benefits of this federal program?

No one has yet figured out how to help those families where communication over the issue of sexuality has simply broken down. Family planners are experimenting with mixed results.

We do know that teenagers who don't talk with their parents can either avoid the clinic or lie about their identity. It is unlikely that they will stop having sex.

So, as Jeannie Rosoff, president of the Alan Guttmacher Institute, puts it: "We have a choice. Parents are anxious but sane. They would prefer that kids not have sex that early, but they want to be more sure that they don't get pregnant. They will have to decide which is the lesser of two evils and come down."

In poll after poll, we parents have said that we want family-planning clinics available for teenagers, and we also want to be advised. We want just what the Congress ordered, a variety of programs geared to "encourage" parental involvement.

But we don't need this hoax. Whatever our anxieties, the federal government cannot mandate family communication.

JANUARY 1982

FAMILY SECRETS

BOSTON—My friends are at the age when we begin to talk less about child care and more about parental care. The subject of our lunchtime conversations has shifted. Once they leaned heavily toward pediatrics, now they include geriatrics. Our long-distance telephone checkups on each other's lives also run down a longer list. Once they accounted for sons and daughters. Now they include mothers and fathers.

In middle age, most of us are flanked by adolescent children and aging parents. We are the fulcrum of this family seesaw, expected to keep the balance. As one set of burdens is lifted gradually by independence, another is descending, sometimes slowly, sometimes abruptly, pulled by the gravity of old age or illness.

In the past year, a neighbor of mine has helped her son choose a college and her mother choose a retirement home. A friend who has just stopped accompanying her children to their doctor's appointments has begun driving her father to his. A colleague who filled her thirties with guilt about being a working mother is entering her fifties with guilt about being a working daughter. It's her parents who need her now.

It was to be expected, I suppose. After all, it is nothing more than the reality of the life cycle. But in fact it wasn't expected. Not really.

Like most Americans, my friends were raised to believe that independence was the norm. We learned to value it, nurture it, respect it, and demand it of ourselves and others. Today we "stand on our own two feet." It was hard for some of us to have that independence challenged by the helplessness of our children. It is much harder to see our parents become needful.

Some of this difficulty is familiar and Freudian. The child in us always wants our parents to be stronger, to be caretakers rather than caretaken. When we mother and father our mothers and fathers, we feel a bit like orphans.

But this stage of life, of mid-life, is also hard because many of our parents lied to us, just as we in turn lie to our children. Perhaps *lie* is too harsh a word, but let me explain.

In America today it is considered neurotic, or at least unhealthy, to teach children that they owe us for their orthodontia, their college tuition, their very life. We do not have children "to take care of us in our old age" anymore; at least we don't say that. The model of a sacrificial parent waiting for a return on her investment has become a satire. Raising them is supposed to be an act of free love.

So we tell the young that we need nothing in return. We free up their emotional inheritance so they can spend it on the next generation. At the same time we prepare for our own old age—buffer our lives against "needing"—with IRAs and Social Security, with medical insurance and Medicare.

But Social Security doesn't make telephone calls, and Medicare doesn't visit the hospital, and while independence extends longer and wider into the late decades now, only rare people leave this life without becoming somewhat dependent on others, especially their children.

The lie—that parents will remain independent—is not a malicious one. It's not even deliberate. It is believed when told by thirty-year-old fathers to eight-year-old sons, by forty-year-old mothers to twelve-year-old daughters. It is handed down in good faith by generations of parents when we are in our prime.

We believe our own lie because we cannot imagine—even those taking care of our own mothers and fathers—that it will happen to us. It is virtually impossible for a forty-five-year-old to know what he will be like at seventy-five, what he will want, what he will need, what he will resent. Yet by forty-five, he has seeded the ground for his own child's middle-aged shock.

Our terror of losing this prized American possession—independence—is what makes us define a good death as a sudden death. We choose to believe that we can avoid becoming a burden on our children. Our shame about aging prevents us from knowing and telling our children the dirty little secret of our human existence: When we too are old we may need them, need to lean on them.

Here, in the middle of life, we are just learning the truth from one generation, still hiding it from the next.

MAY 1985

THE DOUBLE SAFETY STANDARD

BOSTON—The two girls are inside. It is ten o'clock and dark. They are thirteen. The mother is not being unreasonable when she tells them that visiting hours are over. She doesn't want them on the street late at night. They *know* that.

Instead, their friends will walk over here for ice cream and cookies and conversation. That's different. The friends are boys, and boys are allowed out on the street late at night.

The mother, scooping the ice cream out of the container for all of them, thinks to herself: It has begun—the slow separation between what boys can do and girls cannot.

Not long ago, the freedom of all four was curtailed by the joint fact of their childhood. They were equally small, young, weak, protected. Now they are growing out of the vulnerability of their youth. But the girls acquire a new vulnerability: their sex.

She has known these boys most of their lives. Their independence, mobility, physical freedom are growing exponentially. The freedom of the girls is growing, too, but carefully, within certain fences and fears, prearranged routes and routines.

Are the parents of daughters overprotective? the mother asks herself. Do we stunt their growth with our caution? What else can we do in the face of the reality of their greater risk?

There is one statistical fact that slams down like an iron door against their freedom of movement. The fact of assault.

Just recently, a woman was raped in the neighborhood. At that time, there was hardly a neighborhood in which a woman was not raped. That is the painful truth that divides the lives of growing boys and girls.

If parents are congenitally concerned with safety for all their children, we still worry differently about daughters. We don't want to, but we have to.

Years ago, during a wave of crimes against women in Israel, a council of men asked Golda Meir to put a nighttime curfew on females. Meir said no. If men were the problem, she answered, let the council enforce a curfew against men.

Now, a mother who had cheered Meir puts a curfew on her daughter. Like generations of parents before her, she chooses safety over growth for her child, protection over risk. It's what parents usually do, and she is, for better and worse, no exception.

The son of a friend has just returned from California. At twenty, he traveled back and forth by thumb. His father worried, but he also accepted this as a rite of passage, an adventure of adulthood. The risk was worth the returns of self-confidence, experience, independence.

But if the young man had been a young woman, the balance of payments for this adventure could have been quite different: the real risks greater, the anxiety greater.

In Simone de Beauvoir's book, *The Prime of Life*, she describes a year during her life when she took leaps, deliberate physical challenges. Among other things, the writer hitchhiked regularly and alone.

As a woman, the mother understands De Beauvoir's deliberate rebellion, her need to act as if she were completely free. De Beauvoir forced herself to unlearn fear, to learn independence.

But as a mother, she thinks such behavior is foolhardy.

As a mother she teaches her daughter the lessons that she may someday have to unlearn. She watches other parents teach these same lessons. She sees older girls not allowed to walk home from movies alone, older girls who learn that they need a man to be safe from men.

It is eleven o'clock now and the thirteen-year-old boys have to be home. Today, only an hour separates their freedoms. But that gap will grow.

The mother will do what she can. She will, at some point, buy lessons in self-defense. She will encourage other, safer, kinds of growth and risk. She will struggle against her maternal anxiety.

And she will also rage. Rage in sorrow against the violence that forces parents, of all people, to become the agents of their daughters' suppression.

JUNE 1981

SHAMPOO ABUSE

BOSTON—I am all for the crusade against teenage drugs. I have given my blessing as Nancy Reagan launched each new campaign against the hard stuff. I even praised the antidrug comic characters, The New Teen Titans, that were introduced last week at the White House.

But as the parent of a teenager, I am afraid that we are still overlooking one of the most widespread drug problems among our adolescent population. I am talking, of course, about shampoo.

370

Too many parents are still unaware of the rising addiction of our children to shampoo. We have enormous trouble even calling it "addiction." After all (let's be frank about this), most adults are social users.

In all likelihood, we were the ones who originally brought the product into our children's lives. In the beginning, we may have been pleased to see them adopt such a wholesome clean activity.

When our friends asked, "It's ten o'clock at night. Do you know where your children are?" we said smugly that they were just in the shower. Just in the shower! I blush at our naiveté.

But slowly some of us realized that our children were in the shower before school and after school and three times on weekends. The fact of the matter is that they were always in there, lathering up.

When, finally suspicious, we checked their supplies, what did we find? Shelves lined with an assortment of plastic bottles, a panoply of hair paraphernalia. We had to face the truth: The bathroom had been turned into a head shop.

If there are parents of teenagers out there who still refuse to face this desperate situation, pay heed. Ask yourself the four warning signs of shampoo addiction:

Is your son using more than six fluid ounces a week on his scalp?

Is your daughter saving up her allowance to buy yet another ultrarich formula to change her hair behavior?

Do your children NEED clean hair to feel that life is worth living?

Do their moods vary with the conditions of their roots?

If you answered yes to any of the previous questions, I submit to you that your young ones, too, have developed a chemical dependency on lauramide dea, dihydroxyethyl, methylcellulose, and perhaps even sarconsinate. Check the labels.

I don't want to be too hard on the teenagers. After all, they are at a young and vulnerable age. It's the pushers who are everywhere, even on television. They are not just hustling shampoo, but even (I hesitate to say the word) conditioners.

What do you suppose the advertisers mean when they tell our children: "Sometimes you need a little Finesse, sometimes you need a lot." What sort of escape is really being offered by the pushers with their hallucinogenic notion: "Hair so clean it will set you free." Free from the greasies? Be serious.

What merchant of Madison Avenue has snuck a subliminal message along with the tom-tom heartbeat that promises their shampoo will "Enhance, En-hance" these innocent souls?

Every evening our children see lives transformed in sixty seconds by a single dose. People turn silky and sexy. They bounce on trampolines and point hair-dryer guns at their heads and are beloved. Is it any wonder that the kids want some, too?

In fairness, the government tried to tell us about this potential epidemic. They went so far as to label the bottles with a warning: "Keep out of the reach of children." But most of us were too worried about what was being drilled into their heads to think about what was being massaged into their scalps.

Now our children are awash in Suave and Preference, full of Pert and Silkience. Some, the hard core, have even lost their allowances to Pantene, the cocaine of the shampoo world.

But not all is lost. If the New Teen Titans won't clean out the head shop, it's up to the tough love of parents. Sweep the house clean of lauryl sulfate. Check the shower for traces of suds. Smell your children's heads before they go off to school.

And if you think you're getting paranoid, remember this: Shampoo spelled backward is oopmahs.

MAY 1983

A FAMILY LOVE TRIANGLE

BOSTON—The man on the telephone is writing a Father's Day article on dads and daughters. It is to be a piece, he says, for the New Fathers, the ones who have graduated from Lamaze, done consumer research on Pampers, and are now memorizing songs from "Sesame Street."

For these men, the meaning of the word fathering has evolved from siring to nurturing. What he would like to give them as a greeting, as a present, are some pointers on raising daughters to be, you know, strong, healthy, achieving.

I am afraid that I fail my caller. I have no recipe to share with him for the psychic Wonder Bread that promises to build self-esteem in Ten Ways. I am doubtful of all the double-blind crossover studies of parenting techniques that list causes and effects.

After floundering awhile, I hang up and a familiar image of my own father flickers out of my memory. In the still photo of my mind he is there, smiling on me. That is what I should have told the reporter. The secret ingredient of fatherhood is approval.

But maybe that isn't trendy enough, or specific enough. I think about young women that I know, women whose

373

ambitions and conflicts were forged in that first relationship with a man. If we are starting all over again, reinventing fatherhood as if it were a cultural product, new and improved, what would make it easier?

I suspect that what I would market for the next generation of girls is more than a "new" father. The best thing I could give them would be a renovated husband for their mothers.

It seems to me that many of the daughters I know grew up in a love triangle, although not quite the one imagined by Freud. Their fathers incorporated some of the liberated messages of the past decade and a half.

These men were not like the earlier generations of fathers who bought education for sons, and husbands for daughters. Their father pride swelled with the achievement of girls as well: report cards, degrees, titles. They encouraged daughters to do and be their best.

Poll their opinions today and you would turn up a well of resentment against barriers that would keep their own from having a shot at the top, even the boardroom. As one, a man who fought for his daughter's right to equal time on the public hockey rink, put it, "The fastest way to become a feminist is to become a father of a girl who wants something."

But these fathers have not felt such easy, unconflicted support for their wives' ambitions. The men who struggle for equal time on the hockey rink may resist their wives' demands for shared housework. The men who want their daughters to chair the board may be uneasy if their wives earn more money. The men who reward achievement in their daughters may worry about it in their wives.

I've heard replays of these double messages all the time from young women who grew up in these triangular households. They grew up listening to stereophonic ideas about women. Be a strong and achieving woman who conquers the world. Be a caretaking, semitraditional wife.

374

For these young women struggling now to make their own lives, the models of daughter and wife collide. In their first love affair they experienced an updated version of the old conflict between love and work.

It was even harder when these messages reverberated in families split by divorce, especially when the success of a woman was enmeshed with the failure of a marriage. The daughters of divorce were often left to wonder, What does a man want?

So what message should I have given my telephone caller to relay to the "new" fathers for Fathers of Daughters' Day? That children absorb what they see more deeply than what they're told. That if you want to build self-esteem in your daughter, support it in your wife. If you want children to believe your ideas, live them. Be the father you wish you had and the husband who's good enough for your daughter.

And don't forget the approval. A daughter can carry that with her forever.

JUNE 1984

THE POINT OF GROWING UP

BOSTON—In some ways this was a classic scene. Two females side by side on the streetcar, one sharing her troubles—a late alimony check, a demanding boss, unpaid bills—and the other listening. Two females, one upset, the other comforting.

But these two females were not friends: They were mother

and daughter. Moreover, the one seeking understanding was the adult, and the one extending it was the child, no more than ten or eleven years old.

As a fellow traveler, I followed their conversation out of the city until I had to leave them on their way to a more distant suburb. But the dialogue stayed with me as I walked from streetcar stop to doorstop. It seemed to crystallize something that I have seen more than once, more than a dozen times in current life and culture: a type of emotional role reversal.

I remember when the first studies were done of teenage mothers. Sociologists clucked at the sad comments of these girl/mothers who kept their babies because, they said, they wanted someone to love them. It was all hopelessly backwards, inside out, upside down. Parents were supposed to fill needs, children to supply them.

Now that dynamic seems common, almost endemic to contemporary parents and children. Not by coincidence do movies such as *E.T.* or *Firstborn* routinely portray helpless parents. Not by coincidence have television shows such as "Diff'rent Strokes" and comic strips such as "Sally Forth" featured precocious children. Bill Cosby's new entry to prime-time television is unique precisely because it stars a set of stable parents who seem to know more than their children— indeed, to know best.

The plot of a movie, *Irreconcilable Differences*, reflects the upside-down world of parent-child relationships as well as anything I've seen. The dialogue in that movie is only a slight exaggeration of what I heard on the streetcar. The mother, whose marriage has just fallen apart, turns to her child and says, "What am I supposed to do now? . . . Who's going to take care of us?" The child uncomfortably tries to reassure her mother that "most parents get divorced." This ten-year-old finally sues for the right to divorce her wildly immature parents. The theme seems to be that a child has to force parents to grow up.

Psychologist David Elkind has chronicled the phenomenon of the child hurried into adulthood: the "adultified child." These are the same children who are now expected to be "understanding" of their elders. A group of such adultified children at Fayerweather Street School in Cambridge, Massachusetts, offered a remarkable passage in their book, *The Kids' Book about Parents*:

"We have noticed," they wrote, "that there are many times when our parents are sad, angry, depressed, irritable, disappointed, hostile, or plain 'in a bad mood.' As we get older, we find better ways of dealing with them when they're in these moods." The children are now expected to "deal" with us.

I don't know precisely why many of us rush our children into role reversal or premature friendship. I suspect it is a combination of stress, isolation, and the ethic of openness. An enormous number of children experience the fallout of the most common stress of adulthood—divorce. When the nuclear family is broken down into its parts the remains are, for better and for worse, more egalitarian. Parents' weaknesses and failures are more obvious, their needs more raw. In urban isolation, parents may have no one else to turn to.

But it's not just the result of divorce. Our children are much more likely to know about the entire range of family troubles, economic stress, health, than we were at their age. How many parents today knew their own parents' income or of their grandparents' illnesses? How many saw their parents cry?

My generation of parents doesn't believe as much in secrets. We believe in sharing. We don't believe in hiding our feelings. We believe in openness. But how many times do we unburden ourselves by burdening our children? How many times do we push them into adulthood because we are weary or feel unable to handle their dependence? Have we become the subjects of some *New Yorker* cartoon of parents complaining, "My children don't understand me"?

I am not a fan of rigidity or of distant, authoritarian parenting. But I see a great many pseudosophisticated children who need parents and not tall pals. They need to believe that grown-ups can solve their own problems, that adults are helpers, that parents are emotionally stronger. That is the point, after all, of growing up.

NOVEMBER 1984

Part 10

ELLEN GOODMAN: IN TOUCH

LIVING OFF THE LAND

CASCO BAY, Maine—I leave the cottage on my foraging trip in full gear. A pot, a scarf, a long-sleeved shirt, pants, a layer of insect repellent. I am going hunting again for berries.

This is excess season here. For just a week or two, the late blueberries, the middle-aged raspberries, the early blackberries, all overlap and overwhelm this environment. They draw me into the edible world as lollipops on a Disney tree would lure a rural child.

I consider the buffet before me. The blueberries exact a price in time and stooping. The raspberries will disintegrate in my hands en route to my pot. The bushes of blackberries, the most aggressive fruit in this country, will attack the nearest poacher with an arsenal of thorns.

Today, muffins on my mind, I go for the blues. Like a volunteer in the ecological chain, a missing link, I squat here, eating berries, being eaten by mosquitoes.

I don't know exactly why it is peaceful kneeling in some berry patch, the knees of my jeans stained with purple, working the territory side by side with the bees. I am not a country woman. Not since ten have I ventured outside an eight-hour radius of indoor plumbing.

But summer after summer, like others, I come to the country to visit nature the way some tourists visit monuments. In the city, we must keep off the grass; in the country, we walk on the land. In the city, we control environments, even weather; in the country, we accommodate.

Our ancestors probably took delight in the rarity of cultivated gardens; we take delight in the rarity of wildflowers. Our ancestors tried to escape from a hand-to-mouth existence; now many of us escape into it.

I know how absurd this must sound to a country native, but many members of the urban world of displaced persons never get over the notion of free food. I have a continual sense of wonder that here I can walk out our door and collect food. I can dig for clams, cast for mackerel, lift the seaweed for mussels, and collect these blue eight-millimeter pearls that now roll into my pot.

In the city, people work all week for money in order to trade it for food. We buy food from people who have bought food from people who have bought food from people who may actually have planted it and picked it.

Is it any wonder that we treat our home-grown tomatoes like prima donnas, offering them to neighbors in return for praise of "our" achievements?

My own work is as indirect as any. I put food on the table with words. It's an odd barter, but perhaps no odder than that of people who make policy or laws or Rubik's Cubes or the thousand other oddities that come with this civilization.

In our time, work is often and peculiarly disconnected from the fundamentals of food and shelter. We are as distant from reality as the children who think that money comes from the machine at the bank.

But today, I make my "living" in the bushes. Hand to mouth.

I am hardly living off the land. Nor will I draw pretty pictures of farm labor. One of life's ironies is that the people who harvest food earn the least. The berries in my pot, an hour's labor, might be worth a dollar. How many of our grandparents or great-grandparents who worked with their hands longed to escape such drudgery?

But for just a little while, it's worth remembering that we all do live off the land. For just a little while, I am not a tourist in another world, buying souvenirs at the supermarket. Creeping carefully along this ground, harvesting my small wild crop, I have a sense of place. This place, my place.

I walk home from the bushes with my pot of pearls, scratching my mosquito bites, nibbling my catch, as proud as any other hunter. Today I walk like a native on this earth.

AUGUST 1982

OF OLD HOUSES AND NEW MARRIAGES

BOSTON—Slowly, it is becoming our house. With each new coat of paint, each box unpacked, each tile set into place, we begin to feel our presence in its past.

The house is old and built of solid mid-nineteenth-century stock. It doesn't make way easily to its latest inhabitants. Nor do we lay claim as if it were virgin territory, and we were land-rushing pioneers.

We treat the house, the house which is slowly becoming ours, with some respect. We, after all, have moved into it. It may be our new house, but we are its new comers.

From the beginning we paid homage to its prior life. This

is what we chose, the old brick, the fireplaces, the woods that become warm and worn with time. Newcomers, we didn't create this building, but we accept its patches and imperfections.

At the same time, we do not regard ourselves as curators in a museum. This is not Sturbridge Village. Yes, other families have settled here, other lives have been played out here. But now it is our time. We renovate, renew this structure, make changes. Slowly it is becoming ours.

I stand in the middle of the living room, empty except for a plant and a piano, and think of how different this is from moving into a brand-new house. Here we seek some balance between its history and our future.

It is like this, I think, with second marriages or perhaps just midlife marriages. In a few days, before the last box is unpacked, the last faucet in working order, we will be married. It has not been what our families call a whirlwind courtship. We are among the lucky people who were friends first and didn't lose the friendship in love.

Our first marriages, like most, followed a predictable outline. Each of us married, lived together, bore children, bought houses. This time, as if to break the jinx, we have run the reel in reverse.

Young people, first-timers if you will, take on marriage as if it were a plot of land. With luck, they build something new and welcoming. With luck, they always feel at home with each other.

But second-timers are natural renovators. We know the structure of marriage enough to be wary of the ways the foundation weakens. We know it enough to seek comfort again in its shelter and support.

More than that, we have learned something about balancing a respect for each other's past with a need to create something that will be ours.

Like many second-timers, we come to this marriage with

two sets of china and children. Like most people in midlife we come equally well-equipped with experiences. Over decades, all of us acquire friendships, careers, habits, ideas, ideals, the stuff that sticks together and becomes the self.

Renovators, remarriers learn to tip a hat to that self, the life we move into, the one we have chosen. We are more hesitant about knocking down supporting walls, relationships, egos. We are more conscious of the energy that went into their creation.

Newcomers to a second marriage, we know the cracks, the flaws in each other's lives. We take note of all the vulnerable places where partial repairs have been made of the past damage.

Yet we also acknowledge a desire, a right, to make changes, to build something out of these pasts that we can live with comfortably. We make careful plans, respectful renovations, changes.

This home that I am standing in is still in process. There is a box of table linen somewhere. A sink is missing between the manufacturer and the plumber. But slowly this is becoming our house. Slowly, too, this will become our marriage.

NOVEMBER 1982

CONFESSIONS OF A TAPE-DECK OWNER

BOSTON—Let me begin this tale of urban crime with a small piece of family lore. My father was a man so intent on believing in an honest world that he wouldn't, on principle, lock the car. I don't mean the doors to the car. I mean the ignition.

For this particular principle he was well rewarded, or should I say targeted. During one brief period in the early sixties, our car was driven off no less than three times.

I, however, have always considered myself relatively (to him) street-smart, somewhere between savvy and paranoid. Nevertheless, last week I got ripped off and it was, everyone seems to agree, my own fault.

Where did I go wrong? you ask. I blush to confess this, but I was foolish enough to actually be the owner of an automobile radio with tape deck.

But first, the story. We had not one but two visitations from our local tape-deck removal service. On a Saturday night, he smashed the vent window and took nothing. On a Monday night, returning to the scene of the crime with better tools, he wrenched off a chunk of dashboard and made off with the audio system.

According to experts in criminal time-study management, this probably took no more than forty-six to fifty-three seconds. The hit-and-run music lover did not even deign to pick up the seventy-five cents I left in the little toll box or the yellow sweater in the back seat. He was, clearly, a specialist.

In any case, I awoke Tuesday morning to find a deep dark cavity decorated with dangling wires in the very spot where Mozart once reigned. How did people respond to this pathetic turn of events in my life? The repairman who heard it replied that, "Well, sure, right, they take tape decks."

The first friend I encountered simply shook his head: "You mean, you actually had a tape deck? In the city? A German tape deck?" He then laughed. At me.

The second friend went through a brief, utterly matter-of-fact personal history that included the removal of four tape decks, one of them in broad daylight in a restaurant parking lot. He showed me his Sony Walkman.

Even my husband seemed less upset with the intent of thievery than the technique. He would have accepted a neater piece of work with equanimity. He was angry that the crook had no social conscience. Sure he took the deck; that was understandable. But couldn't he have left the dashboard? Wouldn't a decent crook clean up after himself? (With a dustpan, perhaps?)

By the very end of the day, I have been convinced by an entirely unsympathetic group of listeners that anyone who owns one of these things has to expect robbery. Indeed, one colleague suggested that having a tape deck in a car was in and of itself a form of entrapment.

I, a tape victim, had been asking for it.

Not that these people weren't kind and helpful. In the forty-eight hours since my experience in the most mundane of crimes, I have received assorted strategies on how to cope.

First, there is the Unilateral Disarmament Strategy. You will never have a car stripped down by others, I have been informed, if you do it yourself. This suggestion came from a man who traded in his 1980 BMW with everything for a 1974 Ford Mustang with rust.

A more pitiful version of this strategy, The Pacifist Plea, was suggested by a sign on a battered Toyota window in the city. This owner, throwing himself on the mercy of the criminal world, wrote: "This car has no stereo, no tape, no money. There is nothing in the glove compartment. Please don't break the window. The door is unlocked."

On the other hand, there is the Escalation Strategy, a bigger-and-better defense for every criminal offense. The current recommendation from the protectors is a $550 alarm system, the MX of burglar alarms, that would at worst puncture the eardrums and at best puncture the motivation of the thief.

With all this advice, I now sit faced with two alternatives. I can chuck the music and the illusion that someday I will spend my commuting hours learning French. Or I can spend $550 for the protection of my right to hear a $5.95 tape.

Of course, I have another thought, that I don't even say out loud: Maybe the thief will be caught and the audio system returned. I guess that's the sort of fantasy you'd expect from someone who'd put a tape deck in a city car.

FEBRUARY 1983

WHEN YOUR BACK GETS SORE AT YOU

BOSTON—I am writing this column lying down in the corner of the city room with a keyboard on my stomach. This is not an ordinary everyday event in my life or in the life of this city room.

It is, in fact, an admission of defeat: the defeat of mind by matter, will by body. I have been betrayed by anatomy, laid low and laid up.

In short, my back is wrecked.

How did this happen to a normally upright citizen? you may ask. The long answer is that, once upon a time, our primitive ancestors decided to do something for which they were not equipped. They decided to stand on two feet.

The short answer, however, is: squash. The game, not the vegetable.

For the past half-dozen years, in the effort to keep fit, I have voluntarily entered a small white room several times a week.

I have gone there, armed only with a racquet and a small green ball, to battle age, infirmity, and the bulge. There, with the aid of a partner, I usually hit the ball, occasionally hit the partner, and from time to time hit the wall. Hitting the wall in squash, I hasten to tell you, is not like hitting the wall in jogging.

One day I lunged to the right. This particular lunge was

different from all other lunges for only one reason. This time my back refused to follow me.

Until that moment, I had always made the decisions for both of us. It was an authoritarian relationship, I grant you, but one which I had never questioned.

What I didn't know, of course, was that my back had been repressing rage, anger, and stress for decades at the arbitrary way I had called the shots.

This time it simply refused to follow my lead. It deserted me.

During this painful period of our separation, I have discovered my own dependence. I have spent the better part of several weeks on my back, staring at the ceiling, obsessively going over the course of our relationship.

I remember now with a grimace how I once callously got up and down, how I bent over with abandon, slumped without a second thought. I am now ashamed at the way I had taken my back for granted.

I know I am not the only one who mistreated and lived to regret it. I have come into contact with the entire underground of fellow back sufferers. I have met dozens of other people whose lives have been ruptured, whose relationships have slipped, who have been temporarily divorced from their daily lives.

They were not all repentant. One simply refused to accept any fault. All he had done was reach over to pick up a pencil and his disc had dropped out. Another kept shifting the blame to the chair she sat in. A third predictably blamed everything on his mother's genes. And a fourth refuses, just refuses, to even admit that anything is wrong and give in to this back blackmail.

But I have decided to accept my 50 percent. With the aid of assorted therapists, my back and I are trying to learn how to communicate, to live in harmony and interdependence.

After admitting to decades of neglect, I finally understand why it was forced to take this extreme action before I would pay attention.

I am also learning to listen when it is trying to tell me something. To tune in early and often, long before it screams in pain.

My back in turn is learning that it must develop a much wider support system. The discs and I can't do it alone in this world. We must lean on other things around us.

No, it's not easy making the transition to a partnership of brain and muscle, sense and sinew, decisions and discs. There are occasions when I long for the old days when I was the boss.

But this has got to be better than having your back sore at you all the time.

NOVEMBER 1981

BAD RISK BOWWOW

BOSTON—In February 1981, our dog bit a man. This was an occasion for a good deal of hand wringing, not to mention column writing.

It was also an occasion for an insurance claim of something less than $100, for the cost of a doctor visit and a pair of blue jeans.

That was that. When the last form was signed and the last line written, I closed the case on the non-news story of the year.

How was I to know that the insurance company was just beginning?

In June, I received what was to be the first of a series of letters from my insurance agency informing me that my dog was now a bad risk.

Oh, they would be thrilled to continue covering me as a happy homeowner (at those prices who wouldn't be thrilled?), but I must waive forever the right to make a claim if the doggie did it again.

Enclosed, for my convenience was a dog-bite exclusion form.

What was going on here? you ask. Well, it appears that the average insurance company, short of Lloyd's of London, is perfectly willing to cover anyone for dog bites as long as (1) they do not have a dog or (2) the dog doesn't bite anyone. Once the dog actually bites someone, they immediately strip him of his right to insurance and wipe him off the books.

I grant you that it's hard to fathom the mind of an insurance-policy maker. But this was the limit. Insuring dogs until they bite is like selling health coverage as long as you are healthy and fire coverage as long as you are fireproof.

My opinion on this subject was presented calmly enough to the insurance agent. This poor beleaguered soul, given the job of interpreting policy to the world, offered the following information. In the actuarial world—as opposed to the actual world—all dogs are divided into two categories: biters and nonbiters. Once a biter, always a biter.

What, no second chances? I asked. My dog after all was a first-time offender.

No, she answered, the only loophole to this law was if I could prove that it wasn't the dog's fault.

Ah, I said, fault is in the eyeteeth of the beholder. It

depends on your point of view. The bitee, the electrician, believed that it was within his rights to go to the room with the fuse box. The biter, however, had no way to know that the bitee was an electrician and not a burglar. Could Zachary be tried before a jury of his peers?

On that fine legal point the insurance agent referred me to the insurance company.

There I reached Margie. Margie, bless her soul, has a dog named Dusty that also would have bitten under similar circumstances. But the insurance company, we commiserated, doesn't care about that sort of thing. The only way the company would have forgiven Zachary is if he had bitten a real, honest-to-god burglar.

However, as Margie noted, the burglar probably would not have made a claim against me in the first place. "I don't think the average burglar would have come looking for the medical claim. But these days, you never know."

What about a second chance? I asked Margie. Could we put Zachary on parole? No, she answered. It appeared that the insurance companies of America do not believe in canine reform.

At that point I began to feel somewhat hurt. The dog they regard as an offender, I regard as a defender. As one of the few in my neighborhood who have never been robbed, it occurred to me that the insurance agency ought to encourage dogs.

If they were going to eliminate my dog-bite insurance, they ought to at least give me a discount on my burglary insurance. After all, they give a break for the mechanical burglar alarm, why not for a four-legged system complete with teeth?

You will not be surprised to learn that this utterly reasonable approach also failed. Policy, explained the sympathetic Margie, owner of Dusty, is policy.

At this moment, then, we are now the owners of a one-time loser, a dog with a record, blackballed from the insurance racket, condemned without a trial.

JULY 1981

WHEN POLITICS IS A FAMILY BUSINESS

BOSTON—I never get through the political season entirely untouched. To this day I cannot walk past the poll workers, watch the returns, see the candidates' families on television, or read the morning afters without thinking of my father.

You see, I come from a political family. I still have the campaign brochures to prove it. I am the daughter on the left in the smiling photograph of the candidate's family. I also have a few buttons and leftover bumper stickers. My father would be amused. He used to call them my inheritance.

My father ran for Congress when I was a teenager. It would be foolish to pretend that I can write objectively about him or his campaign, but it had a touch of the crusade. You could see it in the newspaper clippings of 1956. A liberal Democrat had taken on the incumbent in a conservative Republican district, and almost made it. Almost.

If you have not been in politics, it is difficult to explain the psychology of a campaign, a race, what we in Boston call a "fight." There is some kind of irrational energy, some natural amphetamine rush to the finish. There is often a passion about running for office, a focus as narrow and intense as ambition, a desire as great and yawning as a love affair.

My father wanted it. To this day I can recite lines from his speech at the dozens of coffee hours and meetings along the way to Election Day. "I want to be your congressman." I can also remember his spirit, his irrepressible humor, the times when he went for the joke and lost the vote. I remember his ego and the way he kept it in check with generosity, with a touch of irony and a core of privacy.

But most of all I remember what I learned, watching my father, the candidate.

It is popular now, I know, to feel sorry for political families, to think of them as long-suffering and neglected. It didn't feel that way to me. Licking stamps, taking the day off from school to work the polls, staying up late for the returns, hearing the issues and the strategy in the living room, I knew that we were in a family business. Together.

My father was a lawyer in real life and I never saw him at work. But for six months at a time, I had a chance that few children have: to view their parents in public, in performance, in controversy, and in complexity.

I heard my father make people laugh and think, but I also heard him, bone-tired, tell the same joke twice in one speech. I heard people come up to him in adulation, but I also heard the man who threw the campaign literature back at me: "I wouldn't vote for him if he was the last man on earth." I saw him elated and exhausted. I also saw him in defeat.

In 1956, before there were exit polls and television, my sister and I were able to read precincts and do our own projections as quickly as any computer. We knew early in the evening that my father would ride Adlai Stevenson's coattails to a loss. But we hung in there together at the "victory celebration" that ran way past midnight.

The next morning, defeated and deeply in debt, my father put on his suit and his tie and his optimism and went to the office.

It was this last gesture that was imprinted on my psyche more than perhaps any other. I learned from my father, the candidate, that this is what you do, this is what a grown-up does. When life disappoints you, when the world takes a whack at you, you still get up, get dressed, and go back to work.

I wonder sometimes if my father knew how much more I learned from observing him than from listening to him. He was a man of great warmth and energy and control. I am not sure anymore that the control was all good. He never allowed himself much time to mourn, much time to run through the directory of emotions: anger, disappointment, depression.

Ten years later, at fifty-seven, when cancer infiltrated his life, he was unwilling to talk about death. At the end, malignancy struck at the words of this most articulate man, and he was unable to speak at all. But at hard moments in my own life, I still hear, "Get up, get dressed, go back to work."

I think of my father most during his peak season of politics, because this is when I got to know him in a hundred ways. We were a political family, yes, but put the emphasis on "family."

NOVEMBER 1982

NOTES FROM AN ANTILAWN SNOB

BOSTON—My lawn is turning brown. It does this un-American thing because of my benign neglect and with my complete approval. Actually, I feel a sort of perverse, vaguely self-righteous pride about its decrepit state.

I lately have taken to sneering at lawns, those plush, thick, emerald stretches of natural Astroturf that look as if they were taken in to be done every week. I have an urge to go about like some Carry Nation with a shovel, turning over the soil, making designs in the edging, planting crabgrass wherever I go.

My pleasure is of the miserly judgmental sort shared by runners and anorexics. It's the pride that comes from staying on your diet while all about you are eating Cheez-its, or from staying sober while all your friends are putting lampshades on their heads.

The fact is that I hate lawns. Something about them strikes me as theater of the absurd. I suspect it is the absolute fundamental wastefulness of all these little green things sticking out across the landscape. I cannot believe that people devote hours of labor, gallons of water, fertilizer, and attention to the care and maintenance of something as fundamentally parasitic as a lawn.

As far as I am concerned, there are two kinds of people in the backyard world: people who grow grass and people who grow vegetables.

The grass growers do it all for show. Unless they happen to own a cow, the lawn doesn't give them food. It doesn't give them shade. It doesn't give them anything. On the contrary, it makes demands.

Grass is a perfect case study of the natural leech, the power of the powerless. The better you take care of it, the more it demands. Give it water and it will demand mowing; fertilize it and it will require edging. It will hide its demanding nature by letting you walk all over it.

I didn't always feel this way. Once upon a time I, too, was an active grass grower. When I first got my home, complete with God's little quarter-acre, I assumed the care of all the dependents that came with it.

I felt responsible for the upkeep of the small square of grass in the front yard and the rectangle in the back.

I seeded it and weeded it, sowed and mowed it, hedged and edged it. I bought it hoses, fertilizers, and machinery. The damn thing simply sponged off me.

Slowly I began to feel alienated from this water-guzzling, England-aping, space-wasting, time-gobbling, spendthrift show-off. I began to realize that lawns are the bound feet of our culture, proof that we are so well off that we can support indolence.

This is what we do: We "develop" farmland into suburbia, pave paradise with grass. The grass, in turn, supports an industry of turf builders, fertilizer salesmen, and a class of professional gardeners who rake it all in at a basic annual cost of two cents a square foot or $870 an acre.

If that weren't bad enough, grass requires some eighteen to twenty inches of water a year, whether you live in Portland, Oregon, or Tucson, Arizona. Watering a lawn in Arizona is like raising Medflies in San Jose.

My own rebellion against the green flats of suburbia was to join the other people, the vegetable growers.

Today, half of my original lawn is now vegetating. Vegetables, you see, have a social conscience. Offer them a bit of precious water and, like shmoos, they will roll over and beg to be eaten.

Tomatoes, for their part, feel a moral obligation to return your efforts with a salad. Eggplant never demands MORE, MORE MORE. It altruistically contributes its life to the community ratatouille. And while it is harder to walk on zucchini than grass, one never has to mow it. One simply has to force friends to eat it.

If I were not such a craven social creature, I would have thumbed my nose at lawn mowers long ago, and turned over the last bit of greenery in front of my house.

Instead I simply cut off its supply of water and food. At this moment, the lawn is on its own and losing. And I'm forever dreaming of a cabbage patch.

AUGUST 1981

THE SUSPECTED SHOPPER

BOSTON—It is Saturday, Shopping Saturday, as it's called by the merchants who spread their wares like plush welcome mats across the pages of my newspaper.

But the real market I discover is a different, less eager place than the one I read about. On this Shopping Saturday I don't find welcomes, I find warnings and wariness.

At the first store, a bold sign of the times confronts me: SHOPLIFTERS WILL BE PROSECUTED TO THE FULL EXTENT OF THE LAW.

At the second store, instead of a greeter, I find a door-keeper. It is his job, his duty, to bar my entrance. To pass, I must give up the shopping bag on my arm. I check it in and check it out.

At the third store, I venture as far as the dressing room. Here I meet another worker paid to protect the merchandise rather than to sell it. The guard of this dressing room counts the number of items I carry in and will count the number of items I carry out.

In the mirror, a long, white, plastic security tag juts out from the blouse tucked into the skirt. I try futilely to pat it down along my left hip, try futilely to zip the skirt.

Finally, during these strange gyrations, a thought seeps through years of dulled consciousness, layers of denial. Something has happened to the relationship between shops and shoppers. I no longer feel like a woman in search of a shirt. I feel like an enemy at Checkpoint Charlie.

I finally, belatedly, realize that I am treated less like a customer these days and more like a criminal. And I hate it. This change happened gradually, and understandably. Security rose in tandem with theft. The defenses of the shopkeepers went up, step by step, with the offenses of the thieves.

But now as the weapons escalate, it's the average consumer, the innocent bystander, who is hit by friendly fire.

I don't remember the first time an errant security tag buzzed at the doorway, the first time I saw a camera eye in a dress department. I accepted it as part of the price of living in a tight honesty market.

In the supermarket, they began to insist on a mug shot before they would cash my check. I tried not to take it personally. At the drugstore, the cashier began to staple my bags closed. And I tried not to take it personally.

Now, these experiences have accumulated until I feel routinely treated like a suspect. At the jewelry store, the door is unlocked only for those who pass judgment. In the junior department, the suede pants are permanently attached to the hangers. In the gift shop, the cases are only opened with a key.

I am not surprised anymore, but I am finally aware of just how unpleasant it is to be dealt with as guilty until we prove our innocence. Anyplace we are not known, we are not trusted. The old slogan, "Let the Consumer Beware," has been replaced with a new slogan: "Beware of the Consumer."

It is no fun to be Belgium in the war between sales and security. Thievery has changed the atmosphere of the marketplace. Merchant distrust has spread through the ventilation system of a whole business, a whole city, and it infects all of us.

At the cashier counter today, with my shirt in hand, I the Accused stand quietly while the saleswoman takes my credit card. I watch her round up the usual suspicions. In front of my face, without a hint of embarrassment, she checks my charge number against the list of stolen credit vehicles. While I stand there, she calls the clearinghouse of bad debtors.

Having passed both tests, I am instructed to add my name, address, serial number to the bottom of the charge. She checks one signature against another, the picture against the person. Only then does she release the shirt into my custody.

And so this Shopping Saturday I take home six ounces of silk and a load of resentment.

NOVEMBER 1981

SLUM DRIVER

BOSTON—I am moving into a new car this week.

I have poured the last can of oil into the insatiable beast and taken the last nostalgic trip through the neighborhood. As soon as I finish packing the last box, I shall be ready for moving day.

But why, you ask, would a person need packing boxes to move out of a car? A car after all is not a house, despite the fact that it costs as much as a decent down payment.

The truth of the matter is that I, an otherwise neat person who keeps her clothes and her copy clean, have a secret mobile life.

I am the shopping-bag lady of the auto world. I belong to a subcategory of Americans who are not closet slobs, but rather car slobs.

We are the sort of people you don't want to have move into the parking space next to you. Believe me. Sooner or later, we turn every car into a slum.

I am not alone in this. Although there is no particular support group for my fellow slum drivers in this car-obsessed world, I can spot the others at any red light or parking garage.

There are the telltale gypsy moth droppings on the roof, the venerable ice-cream cones next to the baby seat, the tattered bumper sticker of days gone by: DON'T BLAME ME,

I'M FROM MASSACHUSETTS. That sort of thing.

Slum drivers are people who know not the wonders of hot wax, who have their car washed only when the seventh grade is fund-raising. If confronted, some of us deny it. One insists that she is merely saving dust samples for her geology class. Another swears that he is growing cultures out of his son's cookie crumbs.

But, like other sinners, we recognize each other for the terrible things we do in our cars. I'm not talking about sex in the back seat. I'm talking about coffee all over the front seat.

On moving day I will excavate the items currently living in my motor vehicle. This task requires a certain archaeological skill.

To begin with, there is the hatchback of many wonders. If you dig through the goodies destined lo these many months for the Salvation Army, you come across a snow scraper. This is a particularly handy item in July.

To the left of it is the ubiquitous umbrella. This is the only umbrella I have never lost, since in four years it has never left its cozy spot over the spare tire.

Below these two items, on the floor of the hatchback, are assorted newspapers. These are part of an experiment I am conducting to determine how quickly a newspaper yellows. For your edification, the one dated October 18, 1977, has a fine brittle quality to it that is rarely reproduced outside of Egyptian museums.

Moving forward, into the back seat, I also find the sneakers which I bought for jogging in 1978. These have logged some 30,000 miles . . . in the car. Add to these intriguing artifacts two barrettes, one earring, a sweater I took off in November of 1980 and a squash ball, and you have your everyday items for shopping-bag car ladies.

Now, on to the front seat. Aside from two-dozen normal

magazines being transported between home and office, we find here two vintage $15 parking violation notices awaiting summonses, and a raft that sprang a leak in the summer of '79.

Stuffed between the clutch and the passenger seat we see a dozen ordinary credit-card receipts and parking stubs and a ball-point pen that leaks ink. This is so I will be ready if I am audited while driving past the Internal Revenue Service. There are also several candy wrappers, but I have no idea where they came from. I suspect some pervert left them there to cast aspersions on my willpower.

Once I pack all these scraps of my past, the best thing to do would be to throw them out. I could have a clean slate, new resolve. But it occurs to me that I shall have to start all over again, creating that unique sense of history, of warmth, of the messiness that is me-ness.

Perhaps I will simply move them with me. I think that the peach pit on the dash could lend a real homey touch.

JULY 1981

OUT OF TIME, INTO PLACE

BOSTON—My vacation, like a mood, passed. For weeks, I lived, at a distance from my everyday life, on an island. Islands are, I am told, prime locations for vacations. Surely ours was.

We were removed from mainland and mainstream. The

world lapped in and out of our cove with no more urgency or emergency than the tide.

Even the newspapers arrived at our mailbox late. With their vintage datelines, we didn't read them dutifully, but randomly, leisurely. By the time they arrived, the stories had already fallen into the space between news and history.

I had a sense, those weeks, of what it must have been like in the days before instant communication, when people received "news" across oceans. They learned about opening volleys in battles that were already won or lost. They were a chapter behind, hearing about things after they had happened. By contrast, we are usually up-to-date people, with news on the hour every hour.

I for one am by nature and profession a news junkie. For most of the year, I stay hooked to a twenty-four-hour cycle, following names and faces from the front to the back pages and into obscurity.

Yet I didn't find my news lag unsettling. I wondered instead whether the daily alarm was mellowed among our ancestors by the time it took news to travel. I wondered how much of their perspective was formed by that distance.

I know the news that entered our cottage had been altered as it aged. The things that seemed important, no, Important, changed. It was as if I had dropped out of a soap opera audience, and lost track and interest in the cast of characters, the governments, the wars, the trends and bills.

In those weeks, the story that stuck with me most in one of my old papers was not about worldly events but about the distant event of another world. In the vastness of space, scientists are observing a new solar system being born.

I might have ignored this astronomical discovery in my own pressing workaday life, in the confusion of breaking news. But here it stuck with me. I thought about it walking on country roads and lying in the hammock. I had the space to wonder about something cosmic, a vast time frame.

The only other bulletin that made the front page of my vacation mind every day was the weather. The state of the skies, like the condition of my tennis backhand, and the status of the clam flats seemed to make a legitimate claim for attention.

By contrast, the belated stories of munchkins, the tales of national politics, the war bulletins, rattled around in some space I had already emptied. The transience of daily events became more apparent at days' length across the bay. At times I even heard bizarre echoes of the old Tom Lehrer song: "They're rioting in Africa, tra, la, la."

Because the papers that came to our cottage were no longer news and not yet history, I asked different questions of them. Would Aquino's death be an isolated murder or the beginning of the end for Marcos? Would Barbara Honegger be seen as some minor Joan of Arc or a crazy lady who heard voices? Would it all be Important?

I wonder if our ancestors, less bombarded by daily bulletins, removed by time and space, were more able to weigh Importance. Were they also more able to live in the near and far ground of their lives? While we live in daily cycles, were they more focused on both the minutes and the aeons, minutiae and fundamentals, weather and solar systems?

I know only that my return here was as abrupt and startling as the crash of a Korean airliner. Immediately I am back to news that comes in bulletins, up-to-the-minute events. Again, I stay tuned.

Perhaps there is no leisure in our world of instant communications. While our ancestors carried letters on frigates from one capital to another, the leaders of nations are now pressured to respond as quickly as questions and answers can be formed, telephone lines joined, computers alerted.

I suppose that it is inevitable. Communication has kept

pace with potential catastrophe. Distance, disengagement, is now a luxury for islands and vacations.

Mine is over. Still, somewhere in the cosmos, a solar system is being born.

SEPTEMBER 1983

ABOUT THE AUTHOR

ELLEN GOODMAN writes a column for the *Boston Globe* that is syndicated by the *Washington Post* Writers Group and appears in nearly 400 newspapers across the country. She was awarded a Pulitzer Prize for her columns in 1980. A frequent television and radio commentator, Goodman is the author of *Turning Points*, *Close to Home* and *At Large*. She lives with her husband, Bob Levey, and her daughter, Katie.